Crisis of Conscience

STUDIES IN CANADIAN MILITARY HISTORY
Series Editor: Dean F. Oliver, Canadian War Museum

The Canadian War Museum, Canada's national museum of military history, has a threefold mandate: to remember, to preserve, and to educate. Studies in Canadian Military History, published by UBC Press in association with the Museum, extends this mandate by presenting the best of contemporary scholarship to provide new insights into all aspects of Canadian military history, from earliest times to recent events. The work of a new generation of scholars is especially encouraged and the books employ a variety of approaches – cultural, social, intellectual, economic, political, and comparative – to investigate gaps in the existing historiography. The books in the series feed immediately into future exhibitions, programs, and outreach efforts by the Canadian War Museum.

John Griffith Armstrong, *The Halifax Explosion and the Royal Canadian Navy: Inquiry and Intrigue*

Andrew Richter, *Avoiding Armageddon: Canadian Military Strategy and Nuclear Weapons, 1950-63*

William Johnston, *A War of Patrols: Canadian Army Operations in Korea*

Julian Gwyn, *Frigates and Foremasts: The North American Squadron in Nova Scotia Waters, 1745-1815*

Jeffrey A. Keshen, *Saints, Sinners, and Soldiers: Canada's Second World War*

Desmond Morton, *Fight or Pay: Soldiers' Families in the Great War*

Douglas E. Delaney, *The Soldiers' General: Bert Hoffmeister at War*

Michael Whitby, ed., *Commanding Canadians: The Second World War Diaries of A.F.C. Layard*

Martin Auger, *Prisoners of the Home Front: German POWs and "Enemy Aliens" in Southern Quebec, 1940-46*

Tim Cook, *Clio's Warriors: Canadian Historians and the Writing of the World Wars*

Serge Marc Durflinger, *Fighting from Home: The Second World War in Verdun, Quebec*

Richard O. Mayne, *Betrayed: Scandal, Politics, and Canadian Naval Leadership*

P. Whitney Lackenbauer, *Battle Grounds: The Canadian Military and Aboriginal Lands*

Cynthia Toman, *An Officer and a Lady: Canadian Military Nursing and the Second World War*

Crisis of Conscience:
Conscientious Objection in Canada
during the First World War

Amy J. Shaw

UBCPress · Vancouver · Toronto

20 19 18 17 16 15 14 13 12 11 10 09   5 4 3 2 1

Printed in Canada with vegetable-based inks on ancient-forest-free paper (100% post-consumer recycled) that is processed chlorine- and acid-free.

Library and Archives Canada Cataloguing in Publication

Shaw, Amy J. (Amy Jeannette), 1972-
    Crisis of conscience: conscientious objection in Canada during the First World War / Amy J. Shaw.

(Studies in Canadian military history; 1499-6251)
Includes bibliographical references and index.
ISBN 978-0-7748-1593-2 (bound)
ISBN 978-0-7748-1594-9 (pbk.)
ISBN 978-0-7748-1595-6 (e-book)

    1. World War, 1914-1918 – Conscientious objectors – Canada. 2. Conscientious objection – Canada – History – 20th century. 3. Conscientious objection – Canada – Public opinion – History – 20th century. 4. Draft – Canada – History. I. Title. II. Series.

UB342.C2S53 2008   355.2'24097109041   C2008-903479-1

Canadä

UBC Press gratefully acknowledges the financial support for our publishing program of the Government of Canada through the Book Publishing Industry Development Program (BPIDP), and of the Canada Council for the Arts, and the British Columbia Arts Council.

This book has been published with the help of a grant from the Canadian Federation for the Humanities and Social Sciences, through the Aid to Scholarly Publications Programme, using funds provided by the Social Sciences and Humanities Research Council of Canada.

Publication of this book has been financially supported by the Canadian War Museum.

UBC Press
The University of British Columbia
2029 West Mall
Vancouver, BC V6T 1Z2
604-822-5959 / Fax: 604-822-6083
www.ubcpress.ca

Contents

Acknowledgments

I AM INDEBTED to Jonathan Vance who guided my work and whose generosity in terms of his time and experience helped me find my own voice (except when it included too many sub-clauses). I am also grateful to Richard Rempel, whose passion for his work was part of what inspired me to look at conscientious objection in the first place.

I also owe a debt to several archivists. Among them, special thanks go to James Craig of the Pentecostal Assemblies of Canada, Jane Zavitz Bond of the Society of Friends Archives, Gordon Heath and Mark Steinacher of the Baptist Archives at McMaster University, Sharon Larade of the United Church and Victoria Archives, Joan Links in the microtext room at Robarts Library of the University of Toronto, and the many who assisted me at Library and Archives Canada.

I am obliged to Emily Andrew and Holly Keller at UBC Press who guided me gracefully through the submission and revision processes. Thanks go to colleagues who commented on portions of this work at conferences, and to the three anonymous readers whose suggestions improved the work markedly. I would also like to thank Eileen Hsu for her thoughtful suggests about the cover, and Deborah Kerr, whose diligent copy-editing added very much to the clarity of the final product.

My colleagues at the University of Lethbridge deserve recognition as well for setting an exceedingly high standard for collegiality and academic community. Especial thanks go to Lynn Kennedy who, from the beginning, has provided support for the book on a host of levels, ranging from its organization to its title (including her helpful suggestions for alliteration). Her staunch friendship has been much valued over the years.

And of course I would like to thank my family for their support. I owe a debt also to Bert and Sherry Van de Graaf who allowed their home to be invaded, to Rodena and Sue for their help with childcare, and to Blake for wide-ranging patience and understanding. Thanks also go to Howard for valuing the role of the historian so highly, and to my son Damon to whom, with a great deal of love, this book is dedicated.

Crisis of Conscience

Introduction

To MANY CANADIANS, the First World War seemed a great opportunity. Participation in the war seemed to signify Canada's coming of age: the country would be fighting on an equal basis with the mature European nations. And the cause seemed fine – the rescue of small nations, the defence of democratic values. The war offered not only a chance to promote the young nation's greatness, but also a rare and coveted opportunity for personal heroism. Furthermore, it seemed to bring a sense of accord and common purpose to the country. The formation of the Union Government, the backing of the major churches, and the support of the suffragists all offered a unity that, it was hoped, would live on after the war.

The national myth created around this interpretation of the war is persistent. The rift that the war in general and conscription in particular exacerbated between French and English Canada is, of course, acknowledged, but the sense remains that, excepting that conflict and the discontent of a few radicals, the picture of unity was basically accurate. However, one quiet and disorganized minority of young men found themselves particularly at odds with the conscription legislation. They were conscientious objectors: men who refused military service when conscripted because of religious or ethical beliefs that forbade killing or, often, joining the military in any capacity. Their experience is a useful lens, offering insight into the developing relationship between Canadians and their government, expectations of appropriate masculine behaviour, religious freedom and identity, and questions of voluntarism and obligation in a democratic society.

The Borden administration's Military Service Act (MSA) of 1917, which introduced conscription, included a clause offering limited exemption on the grounds that the conscript "conscientiously objects to the undertaking of combatant service and is prohibited from so doing by the tenets and articles of faith, in effect on the sixth day of July, 1917, of any organized religious denomination existing and well recognized in Canada, at such date, and to which he in good faith belongs."[1]

Conscientious objectors, then, were members of an officially recognized category, but one with significant limitations. Although there were important differences in legislation, similar recognition existed in Britain, New Zealand,

and the United States. In Canada, conscientious objection was an option taken not only by members of the historic peace churches – the Mennonites, Doukhobors, Brethren in Christ (Tunkers), Hutterites, and Quakers (Society of Friends), for which the framers of the act made a certain allowance – but by smaller sects such as the International Bible Students Association (Jehovah's Witnesses), Plymouth Brethren, and Christadelphians, as well as by members of the mainstream Protestant and Catholic Churches. Just as the conscription of an individual's body was intensely personal, so too were the individual beliefs that led some Canadians to refuse compulsory military service.

The term "conscientious objector" covers a wide range of very different young men who, for an equally wide variety of reasons, "could not see [their] way to join the military."[2] Most of those whose objections were recorded used Christian and biblical arguments to support their stance. Becoming a soldier went against the commandment "thou shalt not kill" and did not harmonize with the New Testament doctrine of turning the other cheek in response to a blow. Members of several sects also believed that military service violated the biblical proscription against being "unequally yoked" with unbelievers. Some objected to being put in a position of having to obey military orders that might conflict with their religious and ethical scruples. The Christian discourse of the war, and the limitations the government put on acceptable objection, encouraged such biblical frames of reference.

The limited interpretation of bona fide conscientious objection meant that conscientious objectors (COs) in this period were predominantly religious, rather than espousing more general personal ethical objections. The restriction also meant that the position of another type of CO, one who disagreed with the aims or means of this war but not with all wars or potential conflicts, a response sometimes termed "selective conscientious objection," was not recognized.[3] Some men who defined themselves as conscientious objectors, or were labelled as such by the press, expressed their objection primarily in political or nationalist terms, although the tribunal system did not recognize such diversity. In Canada, although objectors also came from mainstream Catholic and Protestant Churches, or were individuals with no religious affiliation, only members of established churches with non-resistant principles had a chance of recognition for their objection.

Just as objection was based on a range of beliefs, the manner in which individuals responded to conscription legislation was far from homogeneous. Many conscientious objectors, by accepting non-combatant service, found a way of reconciling their personal moral obligations with the state's need for a collective response to the war. "Absolutists," in contrast, were those who remained committed to non-resistance and opposed to all forms of military service.

When they venture beyond this degree of diversity, studies of conscientious objectors invariably run into problems of definition. In terms of this study, what the Canadian government recognized as a legitimate conscientious objection could not be the sole criteria for inclusion; many young men spent time in jail and at least one died because they did not qualify for exemption on conscientious grounds. Furthermore, the Borden administration's definition of allowable objection, and its response to COs, evolved over the course of the war. Questions of legitimacy, as well, cannot be addressed here to any extent. I have not attempted to discover whether an objection was valid, or the extent to which it might be, as many tribunals supposed, a pose to mask fear or lack of patriotism. What this disparate group of young men had in common was simply their decision to identify themselves as objectors, thus taking a public stand for their beliefs, rather than opting to resist through various forms of draft evasion. Some of the men who took to the woods to avoid being drafted no doubt did so for conscientious reasons. But they cannot be counted, or their decision discussed here in any detail. Problems of records and the need for some degree of concision in an already nebulous category mean that only those who defined themselves publicly as COs, and defended their position as legitimate under the exemption clause of the Military Service Act, have been included here.

Conscientious objection in Canada has received relatively little scholarly attention. There is work on Second World War COs, as well as some valuable collections of memoirs, but almost nothing on their First World War counterparts.[4] This is a significant lacuna, partly because the First World War was the template in many ways for conscription in the second. Scholarship that has addressed conscription during the Great War has focused on the division it caused between French and English Canada, as in Elizabeth Armstrong's *The Crisis of Quebec* or Jean-Yves Gravel's *Le Québec et la guerre, 1914-1918.*[5] The implications of opposition from radical labour are ably examined in A. Ross McCormack's *Reformers, Rebels, and Revolutionaries.*[6] The larger pacifist religious denominations have included discussions of their experiences with conscription in their histories. Valuable here are Frank H. Epp's *Mennonites in Canada, 1786-1920: The History of a Separate People,* Arthur Dorland's *Quakers in Canada: A History,* and E. Morris Sider's *The Brethren in Christ in Canada.*[7] These, however, are broad surveys, and they do little more than touch on the experience of adherents who conflicted with the government and wider Canadian society over conscription. Scholarship that focuses on members of specific religious or political groups is also limited in that it can relay only their own experiences, with no means of assessing the degree to which those experiences parallelled by or differed from those of other objectors. Thomas Socknat's *Witness against War: Pacifism in Canada, 1900-1945* provides a much-needed survey of pacifism in Canada. Some biographical work has also been done on anti-war activists, such as Kenneth McNaught's study of J.S. Woodsworth, *A Prophet in Politics*. There is also some valuable work on women pacifists, especially Barbara Roberts' *"Why Do Women Do Nothing to End the War?" Canadian Feminist-Pacifists and the Great War*, and "Women against War, 1914-1918: Francis Beynon and Laura Hughes," but, even taking these studies into account, the field of Canadian peace history is clearly in its infancy.[8]

There are many broad but valuable theoretical and sociological studies of conscientious objection as a political and philosophical phenomenon.[9] In *Consent, Dissent, and Patriotism*, Margaret Levi discusses what makes citizens comply with or resist government demands such as conscription. The political and religious implications of such pacifist reaction are also debated in Charles Moskos and John Whiteclay Chambers' *The New Conscientious Objection: From Sacred to Secular Resistance*. Moskos and Chambers review the religious and philosophical evolution of conscientious objection, and James Childress, in his study *Moral Responsibility in Conflicts: Essays on Nonviolence, War, and Conscience*, discusses the bases of individual non-violent resistance. But the response of conscientious objection needs to be historicized. To the task of discovering who these self-marginalized figures were must be added that of placing their objection in its appropriate context. It is important to examine what elements in Canadian society affected the decision to object, the experience of objection, and how mainstream society viewed the COs. Contextualizing their response should also help provide an answer to the key question of why objectors in Canada were unable to organize or to mount any effective resistance to conscription.

The concept of obligation is a central theme in the discourse of the First World War. The Canadian government's main narrative was the successful prosecution of the war, seen in terms of the country's duty as well as its safety. Most citizens shared a similar view. But at the same time, a second, albeit less vocal, narrative of obligation existed – the duty of the Borden administration to respect both the promises made to the historic peace churches and the tradition of liberal individuality inherited from Britain. These competing responsibilities were not new. Moskos and Chambers describe the CO as a figure that goes back to the origins of the Western state and as durable a type as the citizen-soldier: "Conscientious objection is at the core of the individual's relationship to the state because it challenges what is generally seen as the most basic of civic obligations – the duty to defend one's country." At the same time, allowing refusal has become the hallmark of democratic society.[10] Balancing the fundamental tension between these two species of obligation lies at the heart of the Canadian government's treatment of, and allowances for, conscientious objection.

Canadian peace historian Thomas Socknat has argued that the First World War marked a transformation in pacifism, a move from the primarily religious pacifism of the nineteenth century to the primarily political dissent of the twentieth.[11] In terms of the history of anti-war protest, it is, then, a crucial time to examine. Socknat's discussion centres on liberal pacifism more than religious non-resistance. As the conscientious objectors in the present study were primarily religious pacifists who found it necessary to make a political expression of their non-resistant beliefs, an exploration of their experience offers a new angle from which to examine the politicization and radicalization of pacifist dissent.

Scrutinizing this kind of pacifist reaction to conscription is also important because the First World War was the first experience of large-scale overseas conscription in the Commonwealth countries and because it served as a model for conscription in the next war. Political scientist Margaret Levi, among others, has argued that the First World War marked a turning point in the relationship between the citizen and the state.[12] A discussion of the provision for, and reaction to, conscientious objection is central to understanding the evolution of this relationship.

The First World War is also a critical period in the context of war resistance because of the importance of this conflict in Canadian nation building. Conscientious objectors chose to stand outside the picture of solidarity and sacrifice that was such an integral part of the nation-building process. War typically intensifies the perceived need for a scapegoat and for an "other" to define oneself against; thus, a consideration of the reaction to the COs offers a fresh perspective on Canadian self-perception during the war.

Their study adds to the history of minority rights and religious freedom in Canada. It is important to remember that the experience of conscientious objectors in the First World War took place before the "rights revolution."[13] Their assertion of their right *not* to serve in the military was part of that transformation in the discourse of citizenship. Thus, a discussion of how and why these men challenged accepted ideas about obligation and the necessity of a unanimous response to the crisis is needed. That they were an unpopular, harassed, and often quite badly treated minority in wartime also makes them an important object of study in terms of the evolution of ideas about minority and individual rights in Canada.

As many objectors were deemed "foreign" – of German or Russian ethnic origin – an examination of conscientious objection should add to the study of several aspects of identity in Canada. The issue of ethnicity was certainly a significant aspect of their experience and the public stereotype of the CO. Indeed, for the Doukhobors and the Mennonites of Western Canada, ethnicity was the primary determinant in their status as exempt. The insularity of many conscientious objectors, along with the fact that some spoke the same language as the enemy, raised nativist hackles and made many Canadians suspicious of their loyalty and value as citizens. Public discussion of conscientious objection often focused on the need to educate people with such peculiar views in order to make them "better" Canadians. This attitude saw objection itself as foreign, something not done by "real Canadians."

Discovering the economic background of objectors will also add to the discussion of class relations and identity in this country. In his study of objection in Britain, John Rae asserts, "For the majority of politicians and public men involved, concern had been prompted by the imprisonment of one man – Stephen Hobhouse."[14] Hobhouse was an absolutist objector who came from a wealthy and politically prominent family. Historian Thomas Kennedy further maintains that "While it is obvious that the Government reacted positively to the complaints of prominent persons and organs of opinion, it is questionable whether, in the light of hostile public feelings, they were willing to respond to the suffering of unknown men without influence."[15] In Britain at least, a class bias existed; conscience was easier to recognize, and appease, in prominent persons. Another aim of this book is to assess the degree to which a similar situation existed in Canada, although it was complicated by an absence of conscientious objectors from among the elite.

A discussion of the response of conscientious objection, and of attitudes towards men who took on such a role, is also important in terms of gender and identity. Margaret Higonnet, among others, has shown that war throws aspects of gender identity into sharp relief.[16] Refusing to join the military left a man vulnerable to charges of cowardice and selfishness, at a time when being a "team player" constituted a significant characteristic of appropriate manliness. Going to war when called was also a prime aspect of the male responsibilities of citizenship. The decision of COs to give primacy to other duties challenged this idea and was a component of why and how they were maligned. Their refusal to perform the masculine duty of wartime soldiering resulted in the removal of the masculine prerogative of voting: they were disenfranchised under the Wartime Elections Act 1917. A closer examination of a group of men who were perceived as failing to fulfill their appropriate roles in this crisis contributes to the discussion of gender and masculinity in Canada.

Both Canadian and British COs were derided in language that criticized their masculinity. The rising popularity of imperialism and the influence of social Darwinism cultivated an ideal masculinity in which intellectualism was subordinated to physical robustness and a patriotic team spirit. British objectors in particular were prey to charges of unhealthy over-intellectualism. The idiosyncratic response of conscientious objection in both countries was suspicious at a time when comradeship was a strong component of manly virtue. By failing to join with their fellows, objectors were not simply being cowardly or lazy, but were privileging an individual, contemplative response over one of group loyalty and action.

The stereotypical Canadian objectors, however, had another, equally important characteristic. Their perceived refusal to listen to "reason" – to accept the war as just and therefore properly in accord with their religious principles – worked to brand Canadian COs as prohibitively stubborn and rather stupid. For a young man, the tribunal system set up to publicly judge the sincerity of his exemption claim was unfamiliar and frightening. Newspaper accounts of conscientious objectors' exemption tribunals often ridiculed the COs' inability to express their desire for exemption convincingly, or according to the terms laid out by the government. The Canadian vision of the objector as obstinate and uneducated was also connected to nativist attitudes against the Mennonite and Doukhobor Churches, with their foreign languages and separate schools. This vision of the oafish objector was sharpened by the fact that many of them relied on a literal interpretation of the Bible, although the tribunal judges generally responded in kind, using biblical references to show instead the propriety of war in the Christian tradition.

I am also curious as to why the tradition of conscientious objection made up a relatively small aspect of the contemporary discourse of the First World War and is not part of our collective memory of the conflict. True, objectors were few in number, but such was the case in other countries as well. In Britain, John Rae, acknowledging problems of definition, estimates that throughout the war there were only about 16,500 COs and that, "as a percentage of the total number of men recruited voluntarily and compulsorily during the war, 16,500 conscientious objectors represented 0.33 per cent."[17] In Britain, there were fewer than a thousand absolutist COs – those who could not reconcile themselves to any form of non-combatant or alternative service and were imprisoned and often badly mistreated. Objectors in Britain caused a shocking amount of trouble in relation to their numbers and received a great deal of attention in Parliament and the press.

One problem in making comparisons between Canada and Britain is that figures for conscientious objectors were not kept in Canada, and many of the records that might have been used to ascertain the number of men who fell into this category have been destroyed. However, because of the strict limitations the Borden government imposed on recognized objection, it is possible to make a rough estimate of how many Canadian men might have fallen into that category. The 1911 census reveals that approximately 15,077 men of military age belonged to sects that had protection under Orders-in-Council for their pacifist religious beliefs – the Society of Friends, Mennonites, Tunkers, and Doukhobors. A further 11,321 belonged to sects that appealed to the Central Appeal Tribunal that their adherents ought to receive exemption on the grounds of membership in a denomination with pacifist tenets – the Christadelphians, International Bible Students Association, Plymouth Brethren, Seventh-day Adventists, and Pentecostal Assemblies.[18] Attempts to offer an estimate, however, are complicated by problems with nomenclature. Several small sects, some with specific pacifist beliefs, some without, referred to their members as "Brethren." As a result, when such a term is applied to an objector, it is not always clear to which sect he belonged.[19] Furthermore, some members of pacifist churches went to war, and some members of mainstream churches objected. Some men, as well, objected but received exemption on other grounds. Still, it seems safe to argue that there were in the neighbourhood of twenty-six thousand potential conscientious objectors in Canada, some of whom would have accepted non-combatant service. Given that my focus is on how these men were perceived by the Canadian public, rather than a strict accounting of conscientious objection, I have not limited my study to absolutists. Since Canada had about a fifth of the population of Britain at the time, the fact that its numbers of conscientious objectors were probably similar to those of Britain makes their comparative silence, both during and after the war, significant and curious.

Drawing a picture of the Canadian CO can be aided by examining Canadian conscientious objection in a comparative context, using especially the British example but also those of the United States, Australia, and New Zealand. This is justifiable partly because Ottawa took the same comparative approach when trying to formulate its own CO policy, referring to the military service legislation enacted in New Zealand and the United Kingdom. It is also useful because the comparison brings out some interesting details that might otherwise have been overlooked. In Britain, conscientious objectors, despite their small numbers, received a great deal of attention in Parliament and the press. When I began my research, I expected to find something similar in this country. Canada was still very much a British colony at this point, with similar parliamentary and legal systems to those of the mother country. If increased immigration meant that the religious and ethnic background of its people was starting to diverge from Britain's, there was still enough similarity, it seemed, that the pacifist movement in Canada would probably not diverge sharply in its broad outlines from that in Britain. It did. My first hint of this was my discovery that almost no biographies treated the men who had been COs during the First

World War.[20] As well, newspaper articles on conscientious objectors were comparatively few and far between. Britain and the United States both have a much fuller literature, primary and secondary, on their experiences of objection.[21] In Canada, the conscientious objector to the First World War is, to some degree, remarkable by his comparative absence.

This is partly because, in Britain, opposition to the war was personified, to a certain extent, by the conscientious objector. There, the stereotype of the "slacker" and the CO were closely associated. The British image of the "conshie" was quite often a sort of artistic Bloomsbury figure, an idealistic pacifist with a rather suspect masculinity, an elevated opinion of his own importance, and a tendency to think too much. In Canada, by contrast, the figure of the "slacker" and anti-conscriptionist was associated quite strongly with Quebec, and the image of the pacifist objector to military service seems to have been buried under that province's political objection to participation in the war.

Another reason for the lack of visibility was that Canada produced no organized resistance to conscription such as the No-Conscription Fellowship (NCF) in Britain. Perhaps the Canadian objectors drew less attention than their British counterparts because, lacking organization, they constituted less of a threat. A main focus of this study has been to discover the reasons for this inability to come together. Canada's weaker radical liberal and socialist tradition played a part, as perhaps did the eager insecurity of a colony anxious to prove its maturity and imperial goodwill on the world stage. More importantly, however, the experience of conscientious objection in this country was shaped, predictably, by who was objecting. The presence of thousands of members of non-resistant churches, mostly of Anabaptist descent, was the defining factor in pacifist anti-conscription activity in Canada. Their pacifism was, to a great extent, passive, following the biblical directive to "resist not evil." This, combined with the tendency of many groups to live in isolation and avoid interaction with mainstream political society, worked against their ability to combine with other dissidents. For most religious objectors, obedience to authority, so long as it did not violate other aspects of their faith, was stressed. This made the discourse of their dissent distinctive and helped shape the larger experience of pacifist dissent in Canada.

Their presence also affected the wording of the Military Service Act (MSA), specifically the definition of a legitimate conscientious objector. Many of these groups had entered Canada under specific promises of exemption from military service. The exemption clause in the MSA was a means of keeping these promises, I would argue, rather than any real concession to the right of individual freedom of conscience. Thus, it was granted as a privilege to groups with specific characteristics rather than as a right available to any individual. The exemption clause, in limiting legitimate objection to those belonging to recognized churches with pacifist tenets, served as a wedge, dividing religious from secular objectors, and members of pacifist churches from adherents of churches that supported the war but who themselves opposed military service. This worked against the organization of pacifist anti-conscription dissent.

The particular nature of leadership in the non-resistant churches also affected the wider experience of conscientious objection in Canada. Some historians have argued that because Mennonite bishops were instructors rather than charismatic leaders, and were therefore most comfortable in an unassuming role, they experienced difficulty in dealing with government officials.[22] I have found no direct evidence that such was the case in this country: those Mennonites who took on the unaccustomed and exhausting roles of organizers and advocates for their people seem by all accounts to have done an able and commendable job. But this feature of Anabaptist doctrine, in which leadership roles are played down, did affect the larger pacifist movement in Canada. Bolstered by tradition, belief, and at least a measure of government recognition, some of these people might have taken on a role in coordinating and supporting an organized resistance to conscription. None were able to do so.

The lack of leadership, and the subsequent lack of support necessary for such an unpopular and public stand, was also due to the absence of prominent intellectuals and political figures, or objectors from influential backgrounds.[23] This also affected the comparative lack of publicity accorded COs in Canada. In Britain, the long imprisonment of Stephen Hobhouse, whose family had important political connections, caused a minor sensation.[24] Similarly, the two presidents of the No-Conscription Fellowship, Clifford Allen and Fenner Brockway, went on to active political careers. The NCF also had support from prominent intellectuals, such as Bertrand Russell, and members of the Independent Labour Party, such as future prime minister Ramsay MacDonald. For various reasons, Canada did not attract objectors, or supporters for objection, from among the country's political and intellectual elite.

Another difference is that, though both Britain and Canada provided an exemption clause for members of historic peace churches, the countries were dealing with rather different groups. Whereas many of the religious pacifists in Britain belonged to the Society of Friends, in Canada, the greatest number of COs came from the separational pacifist churches, such as the Mennonites or Doukhobors. Mennonites and Quakers had begun entering Canada in the eighteenth century, and their pacifist beliefs were recognized in subsequent militia acts and immigration guarantees. Later amendments included recognition of the non-resistant principles of the Hutterites, Tunkers, and Doukhobors.

These five are considered the "historic peace churches" in Canada. The government had actively recruited many of these groups to settle, especially in the West. Mennonites placed particular emphasis on an 1877 speech by the governor general, Lord Dufferin, in which he promised that "the battle to which we invite you is the battle against the wilderness ... you will not be required to shed human blood."[25] Ottawa was most concerned with meeting its obligation to the historic peace churches when conscription was introduced, and the limited exemption clause reflected that limited sense of obligation.

Canada had a smaller percentage of Quakers than did Britain, and this coloured the experience of its pacifists. Quakers tended to be members of the ethnic majority; they were also often wealthier and more politically active than other pacifists and more integrated into mainstream society than were members of the other peace churches. In Canada after the Boer War, Quakers had been making efforts to bridge religious and liberal political pacifism, being the instigators for the first peace society in Canada, the Peace and Arbitration Society, and they carried on that trend after the First World War. Historians Peter Brock and Malcolm Saunders have linked the relative weakness of pacifism in Australia during the First World War with the small number of Quakers in that country.[26] It seems fair to argue that the small number of Quakers in Canada also shaped objection in this country. A man claiming conscientious objection in Canada was more likely to belong to a branch of the Anabaptists, whose religious beliefs advocated varying degrees of separation from secular society, than to the Quakers. This had an effect on the prominence of the movement at the time and on its absence in Canada's memory of the First World War. A Mennonite objector was more likely to return to his farm with an increased assurance of the iniquity of involvement with the state than to publish about his experiences or take on an activist role.

The clause in the Military Service Act providing exemption on conscientious grounds was restricted to members of well-recognized religious denominations with clear proscriptions against military service. In Canada, then, what carried most weight was not an individual's personal objection but that of the church to which he belonged; respect was accorded to the dictates of his recognized, established denomination rather than his own conscience. An individual belonging to a mainstream church, or to no recognized church at all, was not entitled to exemption on pacifist grounds. This limitation had important significance. It reduced the provision for conscientious objection in this country from an individual right to a privilege accorded certain groups. The limitation on grounds of exemption is important because it followed a wider trend in the tendency of the Canadian government to treat its people in terms of their corporate rather than individual identity. Given that conscientious objection is one of the few forms of dissent that does not require the mobilization of a group, it is interesting that this most individual protest was acknowledged only if it was not made individually at all. The use of the collective conscience of the church as a proxy for the individual conscience of the soldier left the political fortune of the individual dependent on the political stance of his church. Canada's constitutional principles of the value of "peace, order, and good government," with their connotations of collective stability, contrasted with Britain's more liberal attitude. The individual basis of the conscience clause in the British act seems to have been partly based on this difference. An examination of provision for, and reaction to, conscientious objection to military service, then, is a useful lens through which to examine the varying values of these countries.

I am also interested in the experience of the COs themselves. The objector was not in a comfortable position. Even before conscription, there was a great deal of pressure on individuals to conform to the goals and attitudes of wartime Canada. The memoirs of the British conscientious objectors show that the obloquy they faced from their friends and neighbours was often intense. Those most successful at standing apart from the atmosphere of national chauvinism in Canada were the members of the pacifist religious sects. They had doctrinal support, backing from their community, and less interaction with unsympathetic mainstream attitudes. To make matters easier, their pacifism, at least in the beginning, was generally respected. Their stance, at least in its basic outline, was familiar to mainstream Canadians, and they were not perceived as potential subversives like the socialist objectors or the International Bible Students' Association. Of course, attitudes towards the objectors were not uniform or static throughout the war, and that is another aspect of the experience of conscientious objection examined here. This book traces the evolving definition of who could be classified as a legitimate conscientious objector, follows the attempts made by various denominations to have their stance protected, and makes the argument that gaining exemption was closely connected to perceptions of a denomination's respectability.

Why, then, has such an important group not been the subject of previous scholarly attention in Canada? The apparent reluctance of COs to publicize their own experiences has certainly played a role here, but perhaps the primary reason for the lack of attention to First World War conscientious objectors in Canada is the dearth of records. It is not that the COs did not generate paperwork. As a precursor to conscription, Canadians filled out registration cards, and conscientious objectors were urged to identify themselves as such. There were also local exemption and appellate tribunals, whose records would have offered clearer evidence of who actually was objecting. Tribunal records would also have helped to indicate public attitudes regarding these men, especially because local tribunal judges were generally chosen from members of the community rather than the judiciary. These records, however, are no longer extant.

David Ricardo Williams' biography of Chief Justice Lyman P. Duff, *Duff: A Life in the Law,* explains their absence. Duff, judge of the Central Appeal Tribunal, personally retained the tribunal records when the office of the appellate court closed in June 1919. "A few years later," and apparently after an illness, he burned them all. Duff justified his actions, which resulted in such a loss to historians, on the grounds of national interest: "The papers of the local tribunals and appeal bodies in Quebec were full of hatred and bitterness and would have been a living menace to national unity." Williams adds that, "whether by design or coincidence," E.L. Newcombe, Duff's colleague on the court, also burned records he had amassed as chairman of the Military Service Council.[27] The only explanation I have found for Newcombe's act turned up in his response to a 1921 letter asking whether the military service files had been destroyed. The correspondent was one of several people who had lost their naturalization certificates in this process, having included them in their applications for exemption. Newcombe replied that the records had indeed been destroyed: "These files, I may say, were very numerous and bulky and were thought to be of no further use after the conclusion of peace."[28]

The destruction of this material has caused me to rely more heavily upon contemporary newspapers, which recorded tribunal results. One problem with this is that only a few trials were discussed in any detail. Much of the time, the decisions of the judges, given as "exempted" or "not exempted," were simply accompanied by a list of names and addresses. The grounds for which exemption had been asked or granted were generally not included. Requests that were discussed in greater detail tended to be those in which an unusual element had caught the interest of the reporter. Objectors who said or did something shocking or romantic drew attention. Thus, the objector who said he could not even help the wounded if they were under military auspices merited a headline, as did the ones who sang hymns on their way to imprisonment after a general court martial.[29] The limitations of newspaper coverage were also evident in occasional, frustrating reports such as this one from the *Toronto Globe* on Christmas Eve 1917: "There was the usual conscientious objector, who got the usual refusal by the court."[30]

The lack of records compelled me to compile a provisional listing of conscientious objectors, using mainly newspaper accounts and the attestation papers in the Canadian Expeditionary Force (CEF) database (see Table 1 in the appendix).

Although I am more interested in how conscientious objectors were seen by mainstream Canadian society than in calculating how many men objected, some sort of groundwork needed to be done first. How could I examine perceptions of conscientious objectors if I did not know who was actually objecting? One interesting discovery in my search is the fact that the CEF database is composed predominantly of men who were *not* recognized as bona fide objectors at the time. Members of groups that Ottawa intended to be exempted, including Mennonites and Doukhobors *excepted* from the MSA, generated little newspaper or government attention as individuals. Thus, most of the conscientious objectors do not appear in the tables.

To the dearth of government documents is added possibly the most important problem in dealing with conscientious objection – that of definition. With some regret, I decided fairly early on that I could not discuss political objectors, or at least men who defined their own objection as purely political.[31] To try to treat political objection as well as religious would have rendered the scope of my study impossibly wide and taken it to ground already ably covered. One of the ironies of this focus is that I have found myself following, in some respects, the limited definition offered and accepted by the Canadian government. However, unlike the government, I recognize that the separation of political and religious objection was (and is), for many people, an artificial one. For many in the No-Conscription Fellowship (NCF) in Britain, political and ethical grounds against participation in the war were conflated.[32] In Canada, Ross McCormack's study of socialist dissidents has shown that their pacifism and anti-militarism were similarly complex and "grew out of Marxist integrationalism, Christian ethics, and the experiences of workers whose strikes had been broken by troops."[33]

Problems of definition are not limited to the sometimes nebulous boundary between political and religious objection. Although the Canadian government recognized only members of the historic peace churches as objectors, I have extended my definition to include anyone who claimed exemption on conscientious grounds in the exemption tribunals. But even that can be problematic. The *Montreal Gazette*, for example, mentioned the tribunal of Alpine Augustine Grant McGregor, a farmer from Port Arthur, Ontario, who was arrested for failure to register under the MSA and sentenced to two years' imprisonment. In an "impassioned address" to the court, McGregor declared that "the whole thing, including the MSA was illegal."[34] Although the headline reads "Objector Sentenced to Jail," it is not clear whether this man ought to be counted as a conscientious objector. On the face of it, his objection seems more political than conscientious. An examination of his file as a member of the Canadian

Expeditionary Force does not clarify matters. The file is incomplete, but Alpine McGregor must have reconciled himself to at least some form of military service because it did note that he was discharged as part of the general demobilization on 25 April 1919, rather than for misconduct, as unrecognized COs generally were.[35] Menno Gingrich was only seventeen years old and working as a shoe fitter when he joined the CEF on 21 February 1916. He disappeared shortly afterward, however, and, by 10 October 1916, was struck off strength as a deserter. A member of the United Brethren Church, he was named after a Mennonite founder. Did he develop a conscientious objection once he enlisted? Until and unless other evidence comes to light, Alpine McGregor and Menno Gingrich sit, along with several other men, in a file labelled "unclear," their objections a casualty of definition and record keeping.

The situation in which individuals sometimes offered multiple grounds for exemption, and received it in another, more easily proved, category such as occupation or being the sole financial support of family members, presents another possible problem. I have decided that the surest way is to let the man speak for himself. If he identified himself as a conscientious objector, even if he claimed exemption on other grounds as well, I have defined him as such. An individual's responses and principles are not static, and my examination of the CEF files of COs has shown that some rescinded their objection or modified it to accept non-combatant service. These men have also been included simply because they did make a conscientious objection and because the variety of the CO response is an important part both of their experience and of the way Canadians saw them.

THE BORDEN ADMINISTRATION chose to treat conscientious objection as a privilege accorded members of religious denominations meeting specific criteria. Although this is reductive nearly to the point of offering no right of exemption on conscientious grounds at all, it does have its uses as an organizing principle. The chapters of this book follow the experience of objection according to the different groups who claimed exemption. Chapter 1 examines the Canadian government's decision to implement compulsory military service, the terms and workings of the Military Service Act and its component tribunals, and public attitudes regarding questions of obligation and voluntarism.

The presence in Canada of non-resistant sects of Anabaptist origin has been an important factor shaping pacifism throughout this country's history. Chapter 2 looks at the groups generally referred to in Canada as the historic peace churches – Mennonites, Tunkers, Doukhobors, Hutterites, and Quakers. Since most of them had been induced to settle in this country under specific promises of exemption from military service, Ottawa had a visible obligation to these groups when compulsory military service became law. I examine the historic peace churches' distinctive discourse of dissent: their interaction with the government, each other, and the particular challenges they faced in reconciling their non-resistant beliefs with those stipulating obedience to authority.

Chapter 3 discusses other religious denominations that objected to enforced military service but did not have the protection of earlier Orders-in-Council. These groups were generally small, their doctrines unfamiliar to most Canadians. The Christadelphians, Plymouth Brethren, Pentecostals, Seventh-day Adventists, and the International Bible Students Association fall into this category. The variation in the ways that COs from these groups were viewed, and the reasons that two of them, the Christadelphians and the Seventh-day Adventists, eventually managed to gain limited recognition for their conscientious objection, is illuminating of contemporary ideas about freedom of religion and what constituted good citizenship.

The Borden government chose to stipulate membership in a well-recognized pacifist religious denomination for an exemption on conscientious grounds. Chapter 4 looks at those men who had an ethical objection to military service but who were not members of an organized denomination or who belonged to a church that officially supported the war. Although apparently not numerous, some Anglicans, Baptists, Methodists, Presbyterians, and Catholics did ask for exemption from military service on conscientious grounds. Lacking the protection of a group not only handicapped these men in their efforts to convince the tribunals of their beliefs, but also meant they were more exposed and vulnerable to negative public opinion.

Chapter 5 discusses contemporary Canadian attitudes regarding the conscientious objector. It examines perceived differences between objectors and the degree to which attitudes towards these men changed over the course of the war. This chapter attempts to gather together public discussion of conscientious objection to form a picture of the stereotypical Canadian CO and to examine the ways in which it corresponded to, and differed from, both the actual experience of COs discussed in the previous chapters and the stereotypical image of the British CO.

The Conclusion looks at how the experience of objection in the First World War shaped the ways in which both the government and the historic peace churches approached conscription in the Second World War. It then draws some conclusions about the phenomenon of conscientious objection in First World War Canada and advances some reasons for the lack of an organized anti-conscription movement in this country.

The emphasis on obedience to government authority and the specifically biblical terms of reference used by many conscientious objectors might seem to distance them from twenty-first-century realities, even among their co-religionists. The divide is not so wide as it might at first seem. Debates about obedience to authority and the place of dissent in political culture still have resonance today. The search for balance between the rights and obligations of individuals and minority groups against those of the democratic majority is an ongoing one. In spite of the ostensible cynicism of a violent and secular century, governments around the world still often speak of wars in religious terms and of pacifists and war resisters as lax in their civic and religious duties. In such a climate, the experiences of these otherwise model citizens, who disagreed with their government and mainstream society about a matter of conscience, remain as relevant as ever.

1

The Responsibilities of Citizenship:
Conscientious Objection and the Government

IT IS GENERALLY accepted that the First World War was a crucial moment of transition in the development of the Canadian state, as it was for the other countries involved. The changes brought about by the war, not the least of which was conscription itself, meant an expanded role for the state in everyday life and altered the social relationship between Canadians and the federal government. The provisions made for conscientious objection, and the treatment of objectors, are important in this context. An examination of government definitions of and allowances for conscientious objection is crucial in understanding this transformed role of the state in the lives of individual Canadians. This chapter briefly discusses the pressures that affected Ottawa's decision to enact conscription legislation and the administration of the Military Service Act as it was relevant to those considering conscientious objection. It also attempts to contextualize their decision to object, especially in ideas about duty and obligation. The concept of obligation is central to a discussion of the legal and political experience of the CO. Canadian society placed a premium on duty, and the exemption clauses in the Military Service Act were an admission that a man might have other duties that could justifiably prevent him from undertaking military service. A man claiming exemption from such service on conscientious grounds was making a claim that his spiritual or moral obligations outweighed his duty to the state, a difficult contention because of its intangibility and a wartime atmosphere that preferred sacrifice and loyalty to the group over individual goals.

CONSCRIPTION WAS NOT a novelty in Canada, although the Great War marked its first large-scale use and the first time that Canadians were drafted for overseas service. In *Broken Promises: A History of Conscription in Canada*, J.L. Granatstein and J.M. Hitsman show that conscription had been a policy, often a problematic one, since the country's beginnings. Militia service had a long tradition in Canada, stretching back to the eighteenth century, but the first Militia Act of the new Confederation received royal assent on 22 May 1868. To the regular volunteer militia, which drilled annually, the act added a reserve militia in which all physically fit males between the ages of eighteen and sixty were liable for service unless exempted or disqualified by law. Exemption from service in the militia extended to judges, clergymen, professors, staff of penitentiaries and lunatic asylums, and the only sons of widows.[1] Provision for conscientious objection had always been included in the laws surrounding compulsory militia service. The first Militia Act provided for exemption from personal military service and bearing arms for Quakers, Mennonites, and Tunkers. By 1899 this was amended to also include Doukhobors and Hutterites – together, these five groups constitute the historic peace churches in Canada. But, in spite of this long tradition of militia service, Canadians had little direct experience with military conscription. The volunteer militia had not been called out since the Northwest Rebellion of 1885, and the contingents sent to the South African War had been made up entirely of volunteers mainly paid for and commanded by Britain.[2] The lack of immediate experience with conscription was coupled, in many quarters, with a sense of conscription as "un-British" and a confidence in the efficacy of the voluntary system.

That confidence is implicit in the history of the Canadian Defence League, founded in 1909 as a "non-political association to urge the importance to Canada of universal physical and naval or military training in the belief that such training conduces to the industrial, physical, and moral elevation of the whole people."[3] The league advocated the compulsory peacetime military training of youths between fourteen and eighteen years of age. Granatstein and Hitsman minimize its influence, showing that only one major public meeting was ever held and that, by 1913, "the organization was in an advanced state of decay."[4]

For the first years of the Great War, support for voluntarism and pride in the country's "citizen-soldiers" was the dominant note. By late 1916, however, the tone began to change. Many individual Canadians held strong views about the necessity of conscription, as evidenced by numerous letters to the editors of newspapers, and the resolutions and delegations to the prime minister from various clubs, service groups, city councils, and churches.[5] As recruits became harder to find, many who had initially lauded the voluntary system joined those who had supported conscription since before the war. Throughout the summer of 1917, Canadian newspapers were full of cries for compulsion. Voices in the House of Commons, however, tended to be more circumspect. Joseph-Adélard Descarries, the Conservative MP for Jacques-Cartier, echoed a common theme when he argued that obligatory enlistment was not needed, because "the people of Canada have given noble proof of their loyalty."[6]

For those calling for conscription, a primary argument was its apparent military necessity. The commander of the Canadian Corps, Sir Arthur Currie, was sure that the draft was the best and only option. He charged bluntly that "The only solution of the problem of Canadian recruiting is conscription. My experiences in France have shown me, as a soldier, the necessity of conscription if we desire to maintain at full strength our fighting divisions to the end of the war."[7] J. Murray Clark wrote to the *Toronto Globe* that he had been in favour of conscription since the beginning of the war, "as this is the only equitable and democratic method of defending the safety of the State, which certainly is in jeopardy."[8] Frank Oliver, MP for Edmonton, voiced his "own individual opinion" that "with the world in arms and with the world having adopted the principle of universal military service, for a single nation to refuse to adopt, or fail to adopt that principle is to leave itself at a very serious disadvantage."[9]

Advocates of drafting soldiers often portrayed the war as being fought in Canada's own defence, overlooking the fact that Canada, as part of the British Empire, had come to the aid of the mother country. The *Toronto Globe* urged readers to remember, "For the Allied nations this is a war of defence – the defence of national independence against the immoral ambitions of Germany."[10] A pamphlet put out by a recruiting organization called the Military Service Council argued the same position: "We are in the war primarily to defend and maintain freedom and self-government in Canada."[11] To emphasize their argument that this was a defensive war, conscriptionists often painted dark pictures of the results of relying on the voluntary system: "We must bear in mind that if the Germans win there will be in Canada not only conscription of wealth and men, but a more horrible conscription of women."[12] Lieutenant-Colonel P.E. Blondin, at a speech in Joliette, Quebec, made a similar promise: "If Germany is victorious conscription will come, but it will come for the service of Germany."[13]

This argument sidestepped the negative aspects of enacting Canada's first draft for overseas service by reminding readers that the war was defensive in nature and that, if the changes brought about by conscription were upsetting, they ought to blame the enemy rather than the current administration.[14] But the focus in Canadian newspapers tended to be on conscription as a positive end in itself. An editorial in the *Toronto Globe* quoted the French socialist Jean Jaurés, who had declared that the effect of conscription would be "not to militarize the democracy but to democratize the military system." The editor extended this premise, seeing conscription as a means to "democratize citizenship." "The freedom of the individual is bound up with the defence of the nation. The small nations that seek freedom and independence and the untrammeled development of their civil life are forced to adopt a system of universal service. This is the case with Canada. In her search for honor and military strength and freedom she finds it only in compulsory national service."[15]

Conscription, therefore, was also widely advocated on democratic grounds, as a means to ensure the "equalization of sacrifice." A *Canadian Baptist* editorial contended that "the selective draft" was "the only equitable method between man and man. It puts rich and poor on an equality in the rank and file of the army." After the Military Service Act was promulgated, the *Ottawa Citizen* lauded it as "a democratic measure, calling the rich as well as the poor – indeed bearing more heavily upon the rich in that it is more difficult for a young man of means to claim exemption on the ground that his labour is needed at home for the support of his relatives." It also suggested that the MSA was equitable between provinces and "racial groupings."[16] The allusion was obviously to Quebec and the French Canadians, whose rates of voluntarism, for a variety of reasons, did not equal those of the rest of the country.[17] To force a rough parity of sacrifice on Quebec was a prime motivation for conscription in the minds of many of its proponents.

The broad association of conscription with equality and democracy placed conscientious objectors in a most unfavourable light. The draft promised a parity of sacrifice and a recognition of group goals that many Canadians hoped would continue after the war. Objectors had chosen to differentiate themselves from that picture of unity and to retain allegiance to different, individual goals. This left them open to charges of selfishness, along with the more predictable allegations of cowardice.

Linked to the supposed democratic advantages of conscription was the contention that to oppose it was to abandon the soldiers overseas. One letter to the *Toronto Globe* asked, "How will the men who are now wading through the depths of hell in defence of the Empire feel toward their fellow-Canadians who failed to stand by them in this crucial hour?"[18] The prime minister, in a speech introducing the conscription bill, praised those who had already volunteered and asked, "If what are left of 400,000 such men come back to Canada with fierce resentment and even rage in their hearts, conscious that they have been deserted and betrayed, how shall we meet them when they ask the reason?"[19] The Military Service Council warned that if conscription were not introduced, the "blood that was shed by valiant Canadians" would have been in vain: "If we falter we betray those who have 'borne the battle' for us. We cast the splendour of their sufferings and sacrifice in shadow forever."[20] Prefacing his remarks with a recitation of "In Flanders Fields," John Wesley Edwards, Conservative MP for Frontenac, Ontario, asserted his support for the Military Service Bill "because I believe it is the only means whereby we can do our duty to the men who have gone to the front and who are at present fighting in this great cause."[21]

Advocates of conscription also linked it to efficiency. The voluntary system, they argued, was a haphazard one. Allowing men to choose whether they would go to war meant that those needed to maintain key industries at home might go overseas, and those whose occupations were not so valuable might remain in Canada. Only conscription would redress these inefficiencies and alleviate the manpower problems the country was facing. The voluntary system had a further drawback in that many Canadians saw it as their duty to urge enlistment, often to the point of serious harassment, on all apparently eligible men. Robert Craig Brown and Ramsay Cook argue that compulsion was a political necessity in English Canada, especially in its urban areas, in large part because of the "frenzied atmosphere" created by the volunteer recruiting societies.[22] A *Toronto Globe* editorial maintained that conscription would end the "quasi-persecution" into which recruiting zeal in some places had been transformed. Selective service would mean that eligible men in mufti would no longer face such stigma; Canadians would know that those who remained at home did so because they were needed there or not needed at the front.[23] One man wrote to the *Toronto Globe* that, due to the frenzied atmosphere of the recruiting societies, he "could not go to a public meeting ... walk down a street ... go to Sunday school ... or Church ... without being told that I am a shirker."[24] A large delegation representing recruiting leagues across the country came to the prime minister on 14 April 1916 to protest such recruiting methods and to argue for compulsion. The voluntary system, it asserted, was not voluntary at all, given the intense moral suasion to enlist. Conscription would end the harassment of those who were not overseas, because everyone would understand that they had bona fide reasons for staying at home.

This line of reasoning extended itself to eugenics, promising racial efficiency. Chief Justice T.G. Mathers of Manitoba described voluntary service as "iniquitous" because it distributed the burden of sacrifice unequally and drained the country of "its best blood."[25] According to this argument, the "best" men volunteered first for the army. If they were lost, the sole remaining breeding stock would be the "inferior" men, usually of an "inferior" race, who selfishly and cravenly stayed home, sheltering behind the sacrifices of others. Mrs. C. Robertson wrote to Borden, "I know there will always be shirkers, but it's awfully hard to see our very best going, and so many of the others to stay behind and reap the benefit of their sacrifices." Clarenden Worrell, the Anglican bishop of Nova Scotia, protested more strongly: "Why men of infinite value to the community should be called upon to sacrifice themselves in order that a number of worthless and non-producing creatures may go on in their animal enjoyment is beyond comprehension."[26]

Not everyone who supported conscription was advocating the same thing. Demands for conscription of soldiers were often accompanied by calls for a corresponding conscription of labour, male and female, and for conscription of wealth. E. Beveridge wrote to the *Manitoba Free Press,* "It is surely elementary in a democratic land that personal rights should take precedence of property rights: that, as a corollary, conscription of property should at least go hand in hand with the draft of man-power." This was also the position of the Imperial

Order of the Daughters of the Empire (IODE), along with several other organizations, clubs, and labour unions.[27] The *Toronto Globe* stated its own position frankly: "Conscription? Conscription? Cram it with its ugliest, most inhuman significance and we stand for it, will enlist for it, will suffer for it. That first – the enlistment of every free citizen, of all his wealth, of all his power, of all his service, everywhere and always until this whole disproved and discredited and utterly pagan idol War, is smashed forever."[28]

Robert Borden's papers contain dozens of telegrams advocating conscription. Churches, city councils, unions, and all sorts of voluntary associations expressed their desire that their government enact compulsory measures for the equalization of sacrifice, not only in terms of fighting men, but also in terms of dollars and cents. "The conscription of fighting men," wrote the *Toronto Star,* "carries with it an obligation to conscript all the essential resources of the country and to place the nation on a war footing."[29]

Some Canadians did speak out against the draft. In spite of other editorial allusions to the Militia Acts, early negative responses to the calls for conscription often discussed the lack of historical precedent for such a move. Onésiphore Turgeon, long-standing Liberal MP for Gloucester, New Brunswick, found talk of conscription antithetical to the aims of the war. "We are engaged in this war," he argued, "for the very purpose of effacing, if we can, conscription from the face of the earth."[30] Fears about national unity also caused some to hesitate about conscription. A 1916 *Toronto Globe* editorial had argued that conscription was not practicable in a country "so mixed racially as Canada."[31] For some Canadians, the disruption promised by conscription, especially between French and English Canada, overwhelmed its possible benefits. The Liberal leader and former prime minister Wilfrid Laurier was the strongest proponent of this view, though he also argued that conscription would deal "a severe blow to our policy of immigration."[32]

Furthermore, the "citizen-soldier" was an important part of the myth of the war, and voluntary service was necessary to maintain that character of Canadian identity. Author and social reformer Nellie McClung linked conscription, at least rhetorically, to slavery.[33] But S.D. Chown, general superintendent of the Methodist Church, argued that resorting to conscription should have no negative effects on Canadian integrity: "It is probably no more detrimental to moral character than the voluntary system, inasmuch as since killing must be done, our men should feel that they are executing the stern and righteous will of the nation rather than performing a self-imposed task."[34] If some men felt they could not kill, conscription, in this light, could offer an abdication of personal responsibility: the country as a whole, not the individual, had decided on the necessity of fighting.

One letter to the *Toronto Globe*'s editor called for a plebiscite and for a conscription of wealth along with that of men. The author felt that most of the country opposed conscription but remained silent to avoid making trouble for the government in such an important time. It is interesting that voices against conscription also used democratic rhetoric to support their contentions. They focused, as well, on class issues. Many radical labour leaders opposed conscription, seeing it as a precursor to industrial conscription and vowing that workers would lay down their tools if Ottawa enacted such a policy.[35] Some labour leaders even argued that, though conscription might be necessary for the upper classes, the labouring classes were already sufficiently well represented at the front.[36]

Almost absent from this debate was any mention of pacifism. Pro-conscriptionists talked of efficiency and equality, whereas anti-conscriptionists countered with predictions of social division and labour strife. That some people might have a conscientious objection to conscription hardly registered. Given what was to come, this was not surprising.[37]

THE PRECURSOR TO CONSCRIPTION, although the Borden administration never admitted as much, was national registration. In the first week of January 1917, Canadian males between the ages of twenty and forty-five were asked to fill out cards with information on their age, parentage, nationality, physical condition, profession, and whether or not they were willing to perform national service by enlisting in the Canadian Expeditionary Force (CEF) or taking up special employment. The stated goal of national registration was the more efficient use of Canadian manpower, but it elicited some trepidation. Social reformer J.S. Woodsworth objected to registration because the people had not been consulted and because he believed that conscription of material possessions should rightly precede conscription of manpower.[38] Editorials and letters to the editor, however, were mainly supportive. The *Manitoba Free Press* argued that Canadians had a duty to comply with registration and tried to calm those who feared it as the vanguard of conscription: "The question as to the use to be made by the Government of the information supplied does not affect the duty of the citizen to reply to the question ... If no compulsion to service of any kind follows, no citizen will have cause for complaint. Should compulsion be proposed it can become effective only if assented to and supported by the majority of the people. And the question how far the majority is justified in imposing its will on the minority, especially in matters of conscience, will then have to be decided."[39]

The *Free Press* likened the registration to a simple census and advised against making trouble where it was unnecessary. There was some opposition to registration from organized labour, who feared conscription of labour, but very little on pacifist grounds.[40] Some members of the historic peace churches had qualms about filling out the cards. The Bergthaler Mennonite Church in Manitoba refused to participate in the registration process and instead submitted a list of its members. Apparently, this was deemed sufficient, as the government made no attempt to force the issue. The other historic peace churches, after reassurances from Ottawa, complied with the request.[41] Approximately 80 percent of Canadian men filled out the cards, and returns showed that the estimated pool of available men numbered 286,976.[42]

The results of national registration were not yet tabulated when Robert Borden left for England on 12 February 1917 to attend the Imperial War Conference, the War Cabinet, and to visit the front.[43] The British prime minister hoped to convince him that conscription was necessary. David Lloyd George, on opening the War Cabinet, was clear about what he needed from Borden and Canada: "the first thing we must get is this: we must get more men."[44] Borden also visited the four-division Canadian Corps and found the need for reinforcements to be "urgent, insistent and imperative." Keeping the corps up to strength would require seventy-five thousand men a year, but there were only ten thousand in England and eighteen thousand in Canada; fewer than five thousand had joined the Canadian Expeditionary Force in March, and almost none of these had joined the infantry.[45] What Borden saw at the front was apparently the key element in his decision: "What I saw and learned made me realize how much more critical is the situation of the Allies and how much more uncertain is the ultimate result of the great struggle."[46] Whatever had been in his mind before he left Canada, he returned home convinced of the necessity of conscription. Borden stressed that the decision to end the voluntary system was an independent one, effected by his meeting with the Canadian soldiers, and denied the suggestion that he was influenced by any request for conscription from the British prime minister.

Several letters to newspapers and to Borden had argued that conscription did not need to be the subject of an election, as it had always been law in Canada. However, the Borden administration chose to have Solicitor General Arthur Meighen draft a new act, because the old Militia Act raised men by lottery, which was deemed too inefficient for a time of total war, when selective service was needed to keep necessary industries going. But Borden emphasized that the Military Service Bill was not a novel measure: "The compulsory clauses in this Bill are precisely of the same character, and based upon the same principles, as those which have been in force in this country since 1868."[47]

By this time, the matter of conscientious objection had entered the discussion. W. Lambert wrote to offer his congratulations to the prime minister, calling the conscription bill "the best thing you ever did." He had some advice for Borden, however, about what grounds for exemption should be included: "But for Gods sake dont [sic] put in any conscientious objector's clause. I was in England when Mr. Asquith brought his bill with the conscientious objectors clause in. And that clause caused no end of worry and headache for the tribunals. It also caused a great deal of injustice."[48]

That same day, Borden received another letter offering contrary counsel. On behalf of the Christadelphian Church of Canada, Edwin Hill expressed concern that, "In their excusable anxiety in directing public affairs," His Majesty's government "may when drafting 'Public Conscription' for Military and National service overlook those of His Majesty's Royal subjects, whose religion forbids their being engaged in war, Military or Naval, and may not provide such provision for them as was done in Section 11 and 12 of the Militia Act II and VII, Chap III."[49]

Acknowledging Borden's busy schedule, Hill inquired politely whether a formal petition might best be made in person or by mail. Like Lambert, he cited the example of protection for conscientious objection in Britain and in the American Civil War; unlike Lambert, he urged that the Borden administration follow these precedents.[50]

The Military Service Bill was introduced in Parliament on 11 June 1917. Its debate centred largely on exemption for farmers. The conscientious exemption clause was discussed in the House only once, when Emmanuel Devlin, a Liberal MP representing Wright, Quebec, questioned Minister of Justice C.J. Doherty about which religious denominations would be exempt and whether a man "who declares before a tribunal that he cannot conscientiously take up arms for the killing of another human being" would be exempt. Doherty explained that an individual conscientious objection would need to be paired with membership in an organized and well-recognized religious denomination, and clarified the benefits of this: "Now the questions, what are the tenets and articles of faith, and what is an organized religious denomination well recognized in Canada, are all matters of fact susceptible of proof otherwise than by the mere statement of the applicant." In response, Devlin observed that "a man [would] have no right to decide according to his conscientious beliefs." So too did C.A. Wilson, MP for Laval and another Liberal, who argued for some further consideration, using the illustration of the courts' flexibility in allowing affirmations for those whose religious beliefs prohibited them from taking oaths. There was some discussion about the necessity of three levels of tribunals and some deliberation about which specific religious groups might properly be included in the act. Meighen, however, refused to specify denominations. He demonstrated the need for an exemption clause based on "question[s] of fact" (proof of church membership, rather than a statement of conscience) by describing the problems faced in Britain by the larger-than-expected number of men taking advantage of that country's conscientious objection clause.[51]

The Military Service Act was signed into law on 29 August 1917. It declared that all male British subjects between the ages of twenty and forty-five were liable for military service and grouped them into six classes according to age and marital status. When a man's class was called up, he was deemed to be an enlisted soldier subject to military law. The MSA contained a schedule of categories for exemption from service. These included workers in essential war occupations, certain specially qualified workers, those whose enrolment would result in serious hardship for their families due to financial or business obligations, and those suffering from ill-health or infirmity. The last ground for exemption from military service was that a conscript "conscientiously objects to the undertaking of combatant service and is prohibited from so doing by the tenets and articles of faith, in effect on the sixth day of July, 1917, of any organized religious denomination existing and well recognized in Canada, at such date, and to which he in good faith belongs."[52] This was a much narrower definition than in Britain, which, though it arguably had as its main focus the scruples of groups such as the Society of Friends, did not specifically require religious affiliation as grounds for conscientious exemption from compulsory military service. The British act simply offered as the fourth and last possible ground for exemption that a man have a "conscientious objection to undertaking combatant service."[53]

The framers of the MSA had followed the progress of conscription in Britain, and the limitations in the Canadian act seem in part a response to the difficulties raised by the rather more generous grounds for conscientious objection in the British act.[54] The Military Service Council explained the decision to restrict exemption to religious organizations simply by reminding Canadians that "the thought of man is not triable."[55] Religious affiliation, by contrast, was more easily verified. The exemption clause in the original British legislation had also led to problems with tribunals unsure about whether they could offer absolute exemption or exemption from combatant service only. The conscientious objection clause was eventually clarified: "Any certificate of exemption may be absolute, conditional, or temporary, as the authority by whom it was granted think best suited to the case, and *also* in the case of an application on conscientious grounds, may take the form of an exemption from combatant service only, or may be conditional on the applicant being engaged in some work, which, in the opinion of the tribunal dealing with the case, is of national importance."[56]

This was the most open conscientious objection clause of any country during the First World War. However, John Rae also describes the British act as having "the defect of its virtues ... The provisions of the other countries might have been narrow, but they were unambiguous; and they did not leave the crucial role to bodies of locally elected men."[57]

In drafting conscription legislation, Canadians had a further example in New Zealand, which had also had conscription since 1916. In New Zealand, a man could appeal against military service on the grounds "That he was on the fourth day of August, 1914, and has continuously been a member of a religious body the tenets and doctrines of which religious body declare the bearing of arms and the performance of any combatant service to be contrary to divine revelation, and also that according to his own conscientious religious belief the bearing of arms and the performance of any combatant service is unlawful by reason of being contrary to divine revelation."[58]

Like Canada, New Zealand provided exemption only to members of religious groups, not on individual grounds. The act in that country also provided that the Military Service Board – the judicial body to which all appeals were to be made – should not allow any appeals on the grounds of conscientious objection "unless the appellant shall signify in the prescribed manner his willingness to perform such non-combatant work or services, including service in the Medical Corps and the Army Service Corps, whether in or beyond New Zealand, as may be required of him at such rate of payment as may be prescribed."[59] Appellants, therefore, could not gain absolute exemption from military service on conscientious grounds.

The United States had also enacted conscription legislation soon after its late entry into the war. Its clause providing exemption on conscientious grounds developed and expanded over the course of the conflict but was relatively vague for the first part of the war.[60] The Selective Service Act of 18 May 1917 offered only the option of non-combatant service and only to members of recognized peace churches.[61] A December 1917 directive of the US Army adjutant general's office urged draft boards to treat those with "personal scruples against war" as conscientious objectors. On 20 March 1918, President Woodrow Wilson issued an executive order allowing secular and unchurched religious objectors to opt for non-combatant service.[62]

Australia was the only country to have a plebiscite directly on the subject of conscription, and Australians twice voted against the draft. The governor general blamed its defeat on "the Irish Catholics, the women's vote, and a large section of the agricultural population who, he claimed, objected to the land being denuded of labour."[63] Australia did have conscription for home service and, since 1903, had had compulsory military training, or "boy conscription," under the Commonwealth Defence Act. Exemption from combatant service alone was provided to "persons who satisfy the prescribed authority that their conscientious beliefs do not allow them to bear arms."[64] Hugh Smith posits that this wider basis for exemption existed because Australia did not have an established church: "In a country without an established religion the individual's religious beliefs were not to be the sole criterion for exemption."[65]

Canada had chosen a more clearly delineated definition of acceptable conscientious objection to military service than Britain and the United States, but even that was open to a degree of interpretation. A further limitation and development of Ottawa's definition of conscientious objection came when the central appeal judge ruled that only sects for which pacifism was integral, that is, for which acceptance of military service would mean expulsion for the individual concerned, would fall under the terms of the exemption clause. Since the religious groups qualifying for exemptions were not specifically named in the MSA, registrars depended on rulings by the central appeal judge to determine the legitimacy of certain claims. Central Appeal Judge Lyman Duff, who also sat on the Supreme Court of Canada, eventually ruled that Mennonites, Tunkers, Christadelphians, Seventh-day Adventists, and Quakers all qualified as bona fide pacifist sects eligible for exemption. Denominations such as the Plymouth Brethren and the Pentecostal Assemblies did not meet Duff's criterion of having pacifism as an integral doctrine. Significantly, individuals from the eligible denominations did not receive a blanket exemption but were required to prove both their membership in an exempted group and their own personal objections. In practice, this tended to apply less strictly to the Quakers and the Mennonites than to the other groups.

In addition to this, and rather confusingly, certain groups were *excepted* from the act, including "Those persons exempted from military service by Order-in-Council of August 13, 1873, and by Order-in-Council of December 1884."[66] This referred to the Doukhobors and Mennonites whose immigration to Canada had been based largely on explicit pledges of such exemption from military service. Borden explained this exception in an otherwise intentionally universal measure: "It is absolutely clear that the faith of a country thus pledged must be kept."[67] The framers of the MSA believed they had found a solution to the important and awkward problem of how to define conscientious objection. However, the definition was not fixed and would evolve during the war, as various religious groups made their cases for inclusion within the terms of the act and as these claims were accepted or rejected.

CONSCRIPTION BECAME LAW in Canada on 29 August 1917, but the new Military Service Act had no immediate effect upon the number of men sent to the front. To give legitimacy to such a potentially divisive law, the Borden administration decided it needed to form a coalition government. The Conservatives had already extended their mandate once, and although the British government offered to pass an amendment to the British North America Act to enable it to be extended a second time, Borden deemed this likely to undermine "the moral authority of the Government."[68] There had been calls for a Union Government, and an end to supposedly divisive and wasteful party politics, since early in the war. But, on 6 June 1917, Sir Wilfrid Laurier, the leader of the opposition, advised Borden that he could not accept conscription and would therefore not enter a coalition government that adopted such a policy. Many members of his Liberal Party, however, did support conscription and defected to Borden's new Union Party, formed on 12 October 1917.[69]

The election of the Union Government on 17 December 1917 gave Borden's Unionists a strong majority (outside of Quebec) and seemed to offer proof of the overwhelming preponderance of pro-conscription sentiment.[70] However, the true situation was less straightforward than this. Prior to the election, the Conservative government had passed the Wartime Elections Act, which enfranchised the mothers, wives, sisters, and daughters of soldiers. Under the act, naturalized immigrants from enemy countries who had arrived in Canada after 1902 lost the right to vote. Also disenfranchised were enemy aliens, conscientious objectors, Mennonites, and Doukhobors. Opponents saw these changes as egregious machinations whereby those who might be relied upon to vote with the government were enfranchised and those who might not, or who had earlier been Liberal supporters, had their right to vote removed. Wilfrid Laurier remonstrated that "this act is a blot upon every instinct of justice, honesty and fair play ... It takes the franchise from certain denominations whose members from ancient times in English history have been exempt from military service, and who in Great Britain never were, and are not now, denied the right of citizenship."[71] Also decried was a new Military Voters Act that allowed a soldier to vote simply for the government or the opposition and, if he could not specify his riding, permitted organizers to choose the constituency where his vote would be counted. Neither was the election campaign an exemplary one. Desmond Morton has called it "one of the ugliest in Canadian experience."[72] Because of the deliberate and spiteful portrayal of French Canadians as slackers at whom conscription was aimed, Granatstein and Hitsman refer to the campaign as "one of the few in Canadian history deliberately conducted on racist grounds."[73] Thomas T. Shields was merely representative of the general tone of the election when he wrote to the *Canadian Baptist* calling Henri Bourassa a traitor and asking, "Shall Quebec, which has done nothing to help win the war, dominate the rest of Canada?" For Shields, as apparently for many Canadians, a vote against the Union Government was a vote "for the Kaiser."[74]

Under the Wartime Elections Act, conscientious objectors were deprived not only of the right to vote, but also of the right to claim CO status if they did vote.

Few Canadians protested. Even the *Toronto Globe*, though in gentler language than most, agreed with the new ruling: "War service should be the basis of war franchise." The COs themselves, the paper believed, would probably share its viewpoint: "We find no fault with them for their beliefs. This is a free country and they have been welcomed to our shores, but they will, I am sure, deem it not unfair that those who are liable to do battle and to all the sacrifices of the war should constitute the democracy which controls the destiny of the country in the time of war."[75] Many of the disenfranchised, including the Mennonites, Doukhobors, Christadelphians, Plymouth Brethren, and the International Bible Students' Association, did see participation in politics as an interaction with the sinful secular world that should generally be avoided. The *Globe*'s contention, then, had at least some substance.

Conscientious objectors, to the many who agreed with their disenfranchisement, were deprived of the vote because they were not fulfilling the normal obligations of a citizen. In an article for the *North Atlantic Review*, British economist and social reformer Sidney Webb agreed, arguing that an individual, no matter what his conscience told him, was obliged to defer to whatever his government decided was right: "The individual citizen has committed the conduct of the nation's collective affairs to the Government, and whether the Government acts as he thinks unwisely, his obligation and duty as a citizen is, so far as action is concerned, to acquiesce in their judgement at any rate until the next Election Day comes round."[76] Webb's argument is eloquent, though based on the conception of a limited and obedient citizenship.

It is important to remember that voting was the prerogative of masculine, adult citizenship. Because of this, removal of the franchise was not just a punishment for the objectors' dissenting behaviour, but also a slur on their manhood. That the Wartime Elections Act enfranchised female relatives of soldiers made patent the sense that war service was the basis of citizenship and that, in these terms, conscientious objectors were beyond the pale.

Their disenfranchisement involved more than ideas about appropriate masculine behaviour. Although it is not explicitly stated, the CO separation from the unifying patriotism of the war was, arguably, seen as most serious in that it threatened the brave new world that Canadians hoped and believed would follow the Great War. This offers a partial explanation for why CO disenfranchisement sparked so little protest. At best, objectors were opting out of the bright future that lay ahead; at worst, they were sabotaging it. In diverse ways, various individuals and groups imagined the remade world that would arise from the sacrifices of the war. The focus was variously on church unification, political equality for women, social improvement for the poor, or Canada taking a leading role in the British Empire. Sacrifice improved character, and the sacrifices of the war, individual and national, *had* to mean a better post-bellum political, social, and religious environment. Conscientious objectors seemed to be shirking the sacrifices of the war and giving the lie to the optimistic picture of Canadian unity.

Some Canadians did protest the disenfranchisement, on the grounds that its limitation of individual freedom greatly resembled the "Prussianism" the Allies were avowedly fighting to destroy. Quoting Lord Hugh Cecil, speaking in the British Parliament against a similar disenfranchisement, A.W. Keeton reminded the *Christian Guardian* of the German chancellor's reputed quote of "Salus populi suprema lex" – the safety of the state is the highest law. He warned readers that if they accepted this disenfranchisement, they were becoming that which they wished to destroy.[77] James E. Lawrence asked,

> What manifestation of the true spirit of democracy can be expected from such political autocrats as they who, fearing an appeal to the electorate of the country as a whole on the merits of their past conduct and present policy, and, presumably upon a former, though expired, mandate from that same constitutionally enfranchised electorate, deliberately repudiate its unimpeachable qualification, and substituted therefor one based, as to its negative effects, upon racial sentiment, and as to its affirmative effects, upon family affection and patriotism of a sort most favourable to their policy – a policy furthermore, framed on an issue which has heretofore been practically tabooed in Canada?[78]

The platform of the Union Government was for a vigorous prosecution of the war, the immediate enforcement of the MSA, and the extension of the franchise to certain women. It promised measures to prevent excess war profits and to encourage cooperative management of transportation and agriculture.[79] The Union Government offered an image of "standing together" and necessary harmony. It was not an easy one to vote against.

It is also important to be aware that the election was not simply a referendum on conscription. It was a vote for or against the Union Government, and a negative vote, for many people, implied dissatisfaction with the entire war effort. In the *Canadian Baptist*, S.J. Moore of Toronto urged readers to understand that "the faults of the Borden administration are not the issue."[80] What did seem to be the defining issue was the need for equality of sacrifice, which meant that a defining issue was also Quebec. Sergeant-Major Gordon M. Philpott voted for the Union Government from a hospital in France and wrote a letter to his mother that was published in *The Chancellor's Correspondence* of McMaster University: "An officer came in to get my vote in the Dominion Election and I voted for conscription. The nurse smiled approvingly and said we should have had conscription long ago. I replied that I was not voting for conscription but against the French Canadians, and on a straight vote for conscription would vote against it."[81] Whatever their individual reasons, Canadians voted the Union Government into power on 17 December 1917. G.W.L. Nicholson credits the votes of soldiers overseas with having a significant effect on the outcome. Desmond Morton generally agrees. It seems fair to infer from his study that the soldiers would probably have voted as they did without the intervention of the Military Voters Act and that the legislation itself had little impact on the election.[82]

With the election of the Union Government, the Military Service Act finally came into force. If conscientious objection had seemed a selfish and undemocratic response before, it was even more so now, after the majority of Canadians had apparently deemed conscription necessary. The decision not to join the military seemed to many people a repudiation of the democratic consensus that had agreed on the necessity of military conscription. Even though the MSA contained a clause admitting exemption on conscientious grounds, few expressed sympathy for those who chose this route.

By the time the new Parliament met on 18 March 1918, machinery for the enforcement of the MSA had been set up under the control of the Department of Justice, as "it is not desirable that these inquiries should be conducted by the department which is to take charge of the men when they are once enrolled. These matters are rather of a judicial character until the question of exemption or liability is finally determined."[83] A Military Service sub-committee representing the Department of Militia and Defence was headed by the chief of the general staff, Major-General W.G. Gwatkin. On 3 September 1917, a Military Service Council, acting directly under the minister of justice, was created "to advise and assist in the administration and enforcement" of the act. On 15 June 1918, its duties were taken over by the Military Service Branch of the Department of Justice under its director H.A.C. Machin.[84] To judge the validity of an individual's grounds for exemption from military service, 1,395 local tribunals were set up nationwide. A man unhappy with the decision of his local tribunal had recourse to one of the 195 one-man appeal courts throughout the country. The final step was the Central Appeal Tribunal, where the merits of the case were decided by Justice Lyman P. Duff of the Supreme Court of Canada. If the military authorities were unhappy with a tribunal's decision, they could appeal it to the higher courts as well.

The slow process of setting up exemption tribunals and selecting judges began with an effort at fairness. Each tribunal had two members, one appointed by the county judge in the district concerned and one selected by a joint committee of Parliament. However, in practice, some problems did occur. The local tribunals, in general, were made up of respected local figures who represented the patriotic elements of society. A *Toronto Globe* article announcing the names of those appointed for Toronto and York County commented approvingly, "Almost all of these men are lawyers and well known in the profession, and hold the respect of citizens generally. A number of them are represented at the front by sons or close relatives, which augurs well for the strict enforcement of the act." Senior County Judge Winchester, for example, had a son wounded at the front, as did Judges Coatsworth and Denton, who would serve with him at the City Hall tribunal. E.J. Hearn, K.C., who had one son wounded and another at the front, would sit at the tribunal in the Canada Life Building. Horace G. Ramseden, who would serve in the Mount Albert tribunal, had one son at the front and another wounded and returned home.[85]

The system of local tribunals was similar to, and based partly upon, the system in Britain. The tribunals were locally based because, presumably, members would be likely to know the applicants and their situation, or their history of doing religious, social, or pacifist aid work. A September article in the *Montreal Star* explained the benefits of the system to readers: "Questions of exemption will be determined, not by military authorities or by the Government, but by civil tribunals composed of representative men who are familiar with local conditions in the communities in which they serve, who will generally have personal knowledge of the economic and family reasons which those whose cases come before them have had for not volunteering their services and who will be able sympathetically to estimate the weight and importance of such reasons."

An advertisement issued by the recruiting organization the Military Service Council also promoted this means of selection. The tribunal members' familiarity with local conditions made them "well-fitted to appreciate such reasons for exemption as are put before them by men called up."[86] One letter to the editor of the *Toronto Daily Star,* predating the implementation of compulsion, agreed with the need for locally based tribunals. The writer saw little trouble for the court in distinguishing between the conscientious and the unscrupulous objector: "A conscientious objector is altogether likely to be a marked man in the neighborhood where he lives, and to have made his convictions known long before the war. An examination of a few of his neighbors would reveal the facts, and allow the tribunal to judge his sincerity and general character."[87] Although this seems simple enough, it also illuminates the difficulty in relying on popular opinion to assess the appropriateness and legitimacy of an individual's stand. The tribunal would be assessing not just the strength of a conviction, a difficult task in itself, but also the "general character" of the neighbour in question, a decision whose results could be quite arbitrary and open to abuse, especially when the use of a phrase such as "marked man" suggests where sympathies might usually lie.

The tribunal system was not as efficient as it might have been, and Canadian tribunals faced problems with real and apparent inconsistencies in decisions.[88] Granatstein and Hitsman mention one army officer from St. Catharines, Ontario, who reported that his tribunal "is not likely to grant many exemptions, they are the hottest bunch I have seen, they will hardly excuse E-men [those of low medical category], and I believe a dead man would even have to show good reason."[89] Tribunals in Quebec, conversely, were perceived as overly willing to exempt appellants. Every student at Laval University, for example, received exemption. Borden deplored this situation, commenting in his diary that, in Quebec, "wholesale exemptions seem to have been granted."[90]

An impression of the elements of a typical tribunal, and of attitudes concerning those who claimed conscientious objection, can be gleaned from the *Toronto Daily Star* account of the tribunal of Arthur Bourgeois, a member of the International Bible Students Association (IBSA). The reporter likened the proceedings to a battle: "Bible quotations flew around Tribunal 362 Saturday afternoon like shrapnel around Passchendaele last week. The engagement, which opened with a few little preliminary skirmishes and raids Thursday and Friday, came to a general engagement Saturday afternoon and it was long after union hours when it ceased." Who represented the Allies in this contest was obvious: "Bourgeois wasn't downed without a lively battle. He spat and sputtered Biblical quotations like a Boche machine gun and gave the tribunal quite an argument before he was finally downed."[91] By the same token, though the tribunal members were identified respectfully as Mr. Irwin, Mr. O'Rourke, and Major (Canon) Dixon, Bourgeois was referred to simply by his last name.

In Bourgeois' hearing, the conscientious objector and the local tribunal shared a Christian discourse, their arguments tending to focus on how to weigh and properly interpret biblical injunction. Some of the biblical arguments that Bourgeois employed to justify his pacifist stance were used by conscientious objectors of many other religious backgrounds. He "insisted that he was not of this world" and said he followed the biblical mandate to love one's neighbour.[92] The members of his tribunal, also following a general pattern, responded with the same language and evidence, offering the biblical directive to obey laws and citing the precedent of Jesus driving the money-changers out of the temple to show that the use of force was biblically justified.

The *Star* article reported that Bourgeois had been heard discussing conscription with Clay, "another conscientious objector of the same ilk ... for a year or so."[93] The two men had been overheard declaring that they would rather be shot than go to the front. The judges did not interpret this as evidence of their sincerity. When conscription became a possibility, Bourgeois, like many Bible Students, had sworn an affidavit stressing his objections to undertaking military service. The affidavit was presented at his tribunal, but the members responded to it with annoyance: "'This is getting a bit too thick,' remarked Chairman Irwin as he examined the papers. 'Here is a Class A man, who claims that he is a conscientious objector, presenting an affidavit setting forth his objections to military service on a printed form. That looks too much like an organized attempt to evade military service. It is astonishing that such things should be permitted. This affidavit looks as if it came from England.'"[94] The affidavit challenged accepted notions about the unworldliness of the standard CO and seemed to present a dangerous level of organization. The somewhat cryptic remark regarding the document's English origin is probably a reference to the No-Conscription Fellowship in that country. This organization provided support and counsel to conscientious objectors of all religious and political affiliations, and was distrusted by most of the British government and tribunal system.[95]

Other reports suggest that the biblical discourse characterizing Bourgeois' hearing was common. In one incident, somewhat amusing given the biblical focus, a conscientious objector expressed surprise and disbelief when members recounted the episode in which Jesus drove the money-changers from the temple. They in turn were apparently shocked at his ignorance of it, but collectively could not find the passage themselves, "so their assurances had to suffice until Wilson [the CO] had time to find out for himself."[96]

Another objector, David J. Nichols, a thirty-four-year-old grocer who gave his religion as "Brethren," referred to himself as an "ambassador of Christ" and a "citizen of heaven" when he appeared before his own tribunal.[97] Twenty-year-old Arthur Clarence Guest used the same terms. These specific phrases, and the general sense of separateness from political events, were common to many objectors. In their tribunals, COs often referred to the biblical injunction to "turn the other cheek" and insisted that bellicose behaviour was not justified in the Bible or in the example of Jesus' behaviour. Hugh Roberts told his tribunal that the group with which he worshipped "followed the teachings of the New Testament to live in peace with all men."[98] Johnston Marks, too, quoted Bible verses to his tribunal judges, showing that a Christian must love his enemies. Marks, a Tunker, also defended his position using the biblical directive not to be unequally yoked with unbelievers.[99] This was a common component of conscientious refusal and a plank in the doctrine of denominations of Anabaptist origin.

The attitude of many tribunal judges showed a limited comprehension of conscientious objection, something that is understandable in such a heated atmosphere presided over by judges largely untrained in the specifics of the subject. The newspaper records show that objection often included (and includes) both a negative obligation not to kill and a positive obligation to resist the state machinery that sponsored killing, but the tribunals did not recognize this. In addition, they expected objectors to oppose all war and all violence. Tribunal judges typically asked COs how they would behave if their sister or mother were being attacked. Newspaper accounts of tribunal proceedings nearly always reported this question, treating it as if there were no difference between defending family members and participating in state-sanctioned killing. Robert Thomas Wilson replied to this ubiquitous question that he would give battle to a man attacking his mother but would not kill him.[100] In the discourse of Canadian tribunals, acceptance of any level of force under any circumstances was read as evidence of hypocrisy in claiming conscientious objection.

Many objectors argued that they could not participate even in non-combatant service, because they could not put themselves under military authority. For instance, this was a component of Christadelphian efforts to gain exemption from non-combatant service as well as from actual killing.[101] During the Second World War, provision was made for objectors to undertake work of national importance under civilian direction, but during the First World War, the makeshift character of conscription and lack of familiarity with COs mitigated against such a flexible response.

The tribunal system's difficulties in judging intangible consciences, especially at a time of such national stress, were exacerbated by the fact that it tended to sift out less-established and less-articulate believers. For many objectors, the appearance before a tribunal constituted their first public expression of their beliefs. Many, especially those from Anabaptist groups, came from isolated communities, and some had a limited grasp of the English language. The adversarial and public setting would obviously have been traumatic, especially for the youngest men. For those who claimed a conscientious objection, success depended, to a significant degree, less on the strength of their conviction than their ability to articulate it effectively.

The manner in which some men attempted to explain their position also highlights another aspect of the language problem. The account of Arthur Clarence Guest's tribunal reported his efforts to claim exemption: "In the course of a long epistle he endeavoured to show the tribunal that he did not believe in killing and said he was an 'ambassador of Christ.' He also referred to himself as a 'citizen of heaven,' and was only 'temporarily here on earth.' His religious professions availed him nothing and the court refused exemption."[102] Guest, who was twenty years old and an IBSA member, gave his profession as canvasser. He spoke for some time but seemed not to realize what information the tribunal was looking for. In the accounts of some cases, the earnestness of the objectors is touching, but in the tribunals' eyes, their energies were often misdirected. Sincerity alone would get them nowhere, even in the unlikely event that it did elicit sympathy. These men were trying to convince their judges that they truly believed they could not serve in the military. The strength of their convictions was immaterial, however, because their convictions were their own, not the established pacifist tenets of an organized church, the sole grounds on which the tribunals could accept conscientious objection.

James Patterson's statement to his tribunal offers a more formal and well-rehearsed explanation, although the grounds are similar to those expressed by Guest: "As a Christian, disciple of our Lord Jesus Christ, and member of the fellowship of God's son, I claim exemption from military service under the 8th clause of the MSA, being a member of the community for seven years. Believing that the teachings of our Lord Jesus Christ for his disciples are that as 'they are not of the world even as I am not of the world.' John 17, 16. I take no part in the ruling of this world, not exercising a vote for either municipal, Provincial or Federal Government."[103] What is interesting about Patterson's statement is that its arguments are very similar to those used by the historic peace churches. Patterson, along with men making a similar claim, differs only in that he made it on an individual rather than a group basis.

The exemption hearing of Hugh Roberts, an Eaton's salesman, also illustrates the problems faced by the judges in trying to reconcile the individual claim for conscientious objection and the limited definition under the MSA. Roberts told the tribunal that he belonged to no particular church, but to a religious, nonsectarian group that met in a house. They were known simply as Christians. The *Toronto Daily Star* reported the subsequent exchange:

> "We want some proof that you belong to this religious body," said Mr. T.W. Self, at Tribunal 371. "Is your church recognized?" "Yes, by God." "Are you organized," asked Mr. Wilkie. "Yes sir we are organized according to the New Testament. We have an overseer. The religious body meet in his home. From twelve to fifteen meet there every Sunday." "Is the overseer on salary?" asked Capt. Beaty. "No sir." "How long has this body been in existence?" asked Mr. Wilkie. "Since the time of Christ." "How long have you been a member?" "For about 5 1/2 years," replied the applicant. "Have you any doctrines?" "None but what are in the New Testament."[104]

Although the tribunal's military representative did wonder what Roberts' group would do were a regiment of Germans to come over, the judges in this case seem to be struggling to be fair and to find some way in which the group might meet MSA requirements.

It is easy to be critical of the tribunals, but important to remember that the judges faced a difficult task and were quite overworked. The tribunals were under a great deal of pressure to provide reinforcements, and Thomas Socknat argues that the judges tended to look especially askance at requests for exemption on conscientious grounds because "they and the majority of Canadians were not well acquainted with religious pacifism, and neither understood nor trusted the variety of claimants."[105] Many Canadians had never encountered these people and their beliefs before. For example, when asked for his religious affiliation, CO Clifford Leroy Fletcher told his recording officer that he was a Seventh-day Adventist. The name apparently meant nothing to the officer, who replied "I asked you what religion."[106]

IF THE GROUNDS on which these men sought exemption were unusual, the fact that they were asking for it was anything but. Once Canadian men began to report, it became evident that almost all of them were seeking exemption. On 18 October 1917, the *Montreal Star* noted that, of the 896 men who had reported in Montreal thus far, all but 59 had sought exemption, only "a trifle over 7 per cent" being ready to serve. Other cities reported similar results. By the end of 1917, when the final results of the year were available, 404,395 Canadians had reported; of those, 380,510 had sought exemption, leaving only 24,000 men who had been willing to serve in the army from the outset. In Ontario, 118,000 of 125,000 had sought exemption, in Quebec, 115,000 of 117,000. Nationally, 93.7 percent of those called asked to be excused from serving.[107] And many of them were granted exemption. By the war's end, local tribunals had heard over 300,000 appeals, granting exemption in 86,000 cases. Approximately 42,000 persons were involved in appeals before Justice Duff at the Central Appeal Tribunal, and roughly half of these were ordered to service.[108] Although the majority of Canadians had supported conscription as a means of equalization of sacrifice, they had apparently supported it as appropriate for someone else.

The Borden administration's response to this widespread disinclination to be drafted – and to the German spring offensive of March 1918, which put the Allies' backs to the wall – was to pass an Order-in-Council that cancelled all exemptions. In April 1918, all single men between the ages of twenty and twenty-three were deemed to have enlisted. This was controversial, and there was some protest that it was illegal. R.B. Bennett took it to the Supreme Court, but pacifists voiced little public protest.[109] The farmers, however, were outraged. They had been promised exemption for their sons under the Wartime Elections Act; the removal of that exemption seemed no more than government skullduggery, as well as poor policy at a time when food production should have been paramount. The cancellation of exemptions affected the traditionally agrarian peace churches in another way because many members had applied for, and received, exemption on the basis of occupation: producing food was work of national importance. Exemption on this ground was surer, and easier to prove, than on conscientious grounds. The Order-in-Council, then, had raised the stakes as far as COs were concerned.

Because conscientious objectors were members of a legally created category, they encountered the coercive mechanisms of the state more directly than did other wartime Canadians. As long as their objections could be articulated in the terms that were laid out for them in bureaucratic regulations, objectors could use the law as a protective shield. Those who did not fit the definition, and did not share the government's discourse, had a more arduous experience. The bureaucratic difficulties raised by Canada's first conscription for overseas military service were considerable. Conscientious objectors, with their intangible claims of fidelity to an alternative duty, were a problem for the tribunals and the government. In accordance with Ottawa's decision to treat conscientious objection solely as a corporate response, the following chapters will examine the similarities and differences in the experiences of conscientious objectors from various groups and of those with no ecclesiastical affiliation.

2

Days of Anxiety: Conscientious Objection within the Historic Peace Churches

THE CLAUSE IN the Military Service Act of 1917 providing exemption from military service on conscientious grounds was included specifically for the members of Canada's historic peace churches. This was a marked departure from the wording of the provision in the British act, if not from its spirit.[1] In Britain, allowable exemption on grounds of conscience had been provided on an individual basis, whereas in Canada, exemption was offered clearly only to members of specific groups. Mennonites, Quakers, members of the Brethren Church (also called Tunkers), Hutterites, and Doukhobors had received prior promises of exemption from military service, and the conscience clause in the MSA was concerned with the fulfillment of those promises. Although this simplified matters to some extent – proving membership in a group was easier than proving the verity of one's ethical code – it did not obviate the problems faced by the members of the historic peace churches. The churches were not able to present an organized front, and difficulties in the wording of the act and various interpretations by tribunals caused a great deal of anxiety and led to the imprisonment of several young men. Insecurity about their position, along with the public antipathy they faced, contributed to the emigration of several Mennonite groups after the war.

What is most interesting in the interaction between the peace churches and the government is the discourse of dissent that evolved. The tenet of non-resistance of the Mennonites, Hutterites, and Tunkers was combined with doctrines stressing obedience to authority, especially the state. Their insularity and general avoidance of civil affairs made overt political expressions of dissent even more uncomfortable for them.[2] At the same time, it was crucial to protect their pacifist principles and make their grievances known. Thomas Socknat, in his study of pacifism in Canada, makes note of the contrast between these groups' religious radicalism and their social conservatism.[3] Discussing the Mennonite response to military conscription in the United States, Susan Huxman argues that the "confrontational rhetoric generated by a group of quiet, un-assuming Christians was bound to violate the norms of how discontented groups confront the power elite."[4] An examination of this discourse of dissent and accommodation illuminates some of the idiosyncrasies of conscientious objection in Canada during the First World War.

In discussing the historic peace churches of Anabaptist descent, I will, at times, refer to them simply as "Mennonites." Although this sacrifices strict accuracy in exchange for readability, it does not do so, I hope, to an unwarranted extent, and it follows the path of other historians and Mennonite scholars.[5] Although the Mennonite Church has several branches, there is enough similarity, for the purposes of this work, in their attitudes towards non-resistance and in their self-identification to group them. Like other historians of the Mennonites, Gerlof D. Homan has also included the Tunkers, Amish, and Hutterites in his study because they closely associate themselves with Mennonites: "Their history of non-resistance and nonconformity was much like that of Mennonites, and in the twentieth century they would cooperate and identify with Mennonites in various ways."[6] Although the Society of Friends often took a somewhat different stance from that of the other non-resistant churches and had a different ethnic and social background as well, it is grouped with them in this chapter due to its status as a recognized peace church. In addition, I will sometimes draw upon scholarship from studies of historic peace churches in the United States. This is due partly to their self-identification as an international community and partly to the relative paucity of work on the specifically Canadian Mennonite experience with military conscription in the First World War.

Although they tended to avoid civil affairs, the Mennonites were not on entirely unfamiliar ground during the First World War. They had a long, though limited, history of interaction with various governments in order to gain and later protect their exemption from military service. Some Mennonites had settled in the Maritimes by the mid-nineteenth century, but most had emigrated to Canada from the United States after the revolutionary war, along with groups of Quakers and Tunkers, expecting a continued tolerance of their religious ideals. Frank Epp has shown that Mennonites in the United States had generally supported the British during the American Revolution because of Britain's earlier tolerance and their own predisposition to respect authority and government.[7] The British had a tradition of tolerance towards this form of dissent, having made earlier concessions to groups such as the Baptists and the Society of Friends.

Because the Mennonites who immigrated to Canada after the American Revolution were among the stronger supporters of loyalty to established authority, it is reasonable to suppose that they were more conservative than those who remained in the republic. The same conservative tendency seems true of the groups of Mennonites who immigrated later. When Tsar Alexander II abolished their exemption from military service, about two-thirds of Russian

Mennonites chose to remain in the country because of the promised option of non-combatant alternative service.[8] Those who could not reconcile themselves to this emigrated to North America; most chose the United States. The promise of respect for their non-resistance was a key element in the decision of the poorer and more conservative Bergthal and Kleine Geminde sects to settle in Canada after delegations from various Russian Mennonite groups toured North America in 1872.[9] A conversation between Bergthal delegate reverend Heinrich Wiebe and Hutterite delegate Paul Tschetter, recorded in Tschetter's diary, discusses the reasons for their choice. The agricultural possibilities in Canada were not as appealing as those in the United States, but that was not the prime consideration. Recounting Wiebe's thoughts on the matter, Tschetter wrote that "He said the country [Canada] did not appeal much to him and that after all the question of military service is the most important. He thought that it would not be possible to secure total exemption from military service in the United States, but that the English government would be more liberal ... He said that one should not only consider the land question but also not forget the matter of freedom, for that is the reason why we came to this country and are making this long journey."[10] Guarantees of freedom from military service were more important for these groups than the quality, quantity, and price of land. The Canadian Mennonites, then, were self-selected for their conservatism; thus, one might expect them to display both a high degree of fidelity to the non-resistant aspect of their faith and a marked inclination to obey government directives. This would make them a singular group to deal with when Ottawa instituted its first-ever conscription of men for overseas military service.

The original legislation exempting members of the non-resistant churches from military service in Upper Canada was the Militia Act of 1793, which released Quakers, Mennonites, and Tunkers from personal militia duties but demanded compensatory payment.[11] Their status was, by and large, respected in the War of 1812, during which they were generally given non-combatant duties: "The government, finding them unalterably opposed to carrying arms, required the Mennonite settlers to serve in camps, hospitals etc., and as teamsters in the transport service."[12] The problem of compensatory payment remained. In 1849, after many years of petitioning, the Legislature of the Canadas passed a bill that rejected the principle of fines as a substitution for militia service. Men were then simply required to present evidence of membership, signed by the meeting or society, to the local assessors every year. Subsequent acts retained these provisions, and in 1868, they were extended to "Any person bearing a certificate from the Society of Quakers, Mennonists or Tunkers, or any inhabitant of Canada, of any religious denomination, otherwise subject to military duty, but who, from the doctrines of his religion, is averse to bearing arms and refuses personal military service when balloted in times of peace, or war, upon such conditions and under such regulations as the Governor-in-Council may, from time to time prescribe."[13]

This was also the basis for promises of exemption made to Russian Mennonites who immigrated during the 1870s. In 1890, there was a similar Order-in-Council for the Doukhobors and one for the Hutterites in 1899.[14] Members of the historic peace churches had some grounds for confidence, then, when conscription was raised as an option during the Great War. Legal protection, however, is dependent to a degree upon interpretation and public feeling, which, during the war, was increasingly unfriendly. This had profound effects for the Mennonite conscientious objector's experience.

Despite this antagonism, it could be said that, in many ways, the COs from the pacifist sects were a privileged group. Having the most support from the Borden administration in their non-resistance, they also enjoyed the most support from their communities. Though often the focus of resentment, peace church members ensconced in their separate communities were a degree removed from the atmosphere in the rest of the country, which focused negative attention on young men in civilian clothing.[15] The relative ease with which peace church members are able to withstand pressure from the outside world is discussed by John A. Hostetler and Gertrude Enders Huntington in their anthropological case study of the Hutterites:

> Colony members strive to lose their identity by surrendering themselves to the "communal will," and attempt to live each day in preparation for death, and hopefully heaven. It is not surprising, therefore, that the Hutterites have retained their solidarity despite the persecution of surrounding neighbors ... Although the history of the Hutterites is a history of persecution, it is relatively easy for the well-trained Hutterite adult who has internalized the God-given rules to withstand persecution. The harassment, humiliation, ridicule, and torture of this people has served to reinforce the basic belief that there is only God upon whom to depend.[16]

Although it is safe to argue that members of the other historic peace churches in Canada were less isolated than the Hutterites and perhaps did not experience the feeling of persecution to the same degree, other aspects of this description do fit for the Mennonites as well.[17] The peace churches also shared an upbringing that emphasized conformity with the historic will of the group, which further served to insulate and protect them against the antagonism of Canadian society.

In addition, they could call upon doctrinal support for their non-resistance and a history that lauded pacifist martyrs. Whether the pacifist aspect of their faith remained vital in the early years of the nineteenth century is open to argument. Homan asserts that, in the United States prior to the war, sermons placed more emphasis on evangelism, missions, and pietism at the expense of teachings on non-resistance.[18] However, some evidence does reveal that Canadian young men eligible for conscription would have had a grounding in non-resistance as more than a traditional aspect of their faith. *The Scottdale (PA) Gospel Herald,* a Mennonite publication circulating in Canada and the United States, ran several articles on non-resistance in the years immediately prior to the war.[19] Ernest John Swalm, a member of the Tunker Church, recalls, "I was fortunate in having been exposed to the Biblical teaching of nonresistance from my earliest memory."[20] He found this to be a great support when he was drafted for military service.

This is not to say that the response of peace church members was uniform or completely predictable. Some Mennonites, Quakers, and Tunkers did, often at the cost of their church membership, voluntarily join the armed forces, and not only in medical or non-combatant units. Although there is no record of how many Mennonites enlisted, the records of the Canadian Expeditionary Force document several volunteers who gave their religion as "Mennonite." Among them were thirty-six-year-old machinist Abraham Rempel, who was born in Gretna, Manitoba, but gave a Los Angeles address on his attestation paper, twenty-three-year-old farmer John F. Friesen from Eunice, Manitoba, and Abraham Friesen, a chauffeur from Plum Coulee, Manitoba. Abram Harder Funk, a merchant from Rosenfeld, Manitoba, and nineteen-year-old bookkeeper Peter Funk, from Prelate, Saskatchewan, also volunteered.[21] Epp argues that as a whole, however, the Mennonites "were not easily moved."[22] The *Ottawa Journal Press* declared in 1917 that, "out of a total Mennonite population in Canada of thirty thousand, forty young men have enlisted contrary to the principles of their church."[23]

Few Doukhobors seem to have enlisted. S. Mabor, superintendent of the Department of the Interior, estimated Doukhobor voluntary enlistment at between two and three hundred, out of a population of about twelve thousand.[24] Arthur Dorland makes a similar argument about the unity of response among the Quakers. According to him, those few Quakers who did join the armed forces were only "nominal members" of the church, ones "for whom the Quaker testimony regarding war was merely an inherited tradition. They understood it, perhaps, as a beautiful ideal, but not as an active way of life in war time as well as at other times. These followed what for them was the only possible course. A few (perhaps a half dozen) joined the Canadian or British army, three or four the Military Red Cross, while the son of one prominent Toronto Friend entered the Air Service, in which he laid down his life." Although clearly sincere, this comment seems to reflect a perspective that was common when Dorland wrote his book, specifically, a general reluctance to admit that these men could have volunteered for idealistic reasons. Canadian Quakers who wished to take on some form of service often entered the Friends Ambulance Unit (FAU). Dorland places four Canadian Quakers in the ambulance units and six in the reconstruction unit in France.[25] In his history of "Young Friends" in Canada, Kyle Jolliffe adds that of the four who joined the Friends Ambulance Unit, one served in France and three in Italy. Those serving in Italy included David Pearson Rogers and J. Ellsworth Rogers. The latter trained as a fighter pilot later in the war.[26]

That volunteers to the armed forces are counted singly by these historians is not wholly a measure of their unity of belief. None of the churches to which they belonged were large. The census of 1911 enumerated 4,027 Quakers in Canada, compared with 44,611 Mennonites and 8,014 Brethren.[27] Most Quaker historians give the number of actual adherents as only about one thousand.[28] Although it is difficult to be precise about how many would have been subject to conscription, given that some peace church members were not Canadian citizens and rather more would have fallen into the "enemy alien" category than would have been the case for the general population, it is reasonable to assume that about a quarter of them would have been men of military age.[29]

If not numerous, the Quakers were influential in helping to shape Canadian ideas about religious pacifism. The denomination was founded in England by George Fox, who challenged the belief of the Roman Catholic and Anglican Churches in the necessity for, and the authority of, a hierarchical structure of priests and bishops. He claimed that everyone was able to have a personal relationship with God without having to depend on the intercessions of a priest or minister. He taught that Christ could speak to each person's condition and that the responsibility for ministry therefore rested upon all.[30]

Non-resistance is a central tenet of the Quaker ethos, which, as Peter Brock puts it, "involves an attempt to accept literally the command to love God and one another. It rules out war. It recognizes evil but meets it with that active good will which outlasts it or transforms it." Whereas Brock characterizes Mennonites and the other outgrowths of Anabaptism as "separational pacifists," he describes Quakers as "integrational pacifists."[31] Brock shows that the important difference between the Quakers and the other historic peace churches lies in their understanding of their peace testimony as being a reflection of "inner light," rather than obedience to biblical injunction. It follows that if a Friend's "inner light" advises that war is wrong, he or she should work against it, with no proscription against joining non-Christian groups in anti-war activities.[32]

Part of the Nonconformist tradition in the seventeenth century, the Quakers have long regarded politics as compatible with their pacifist stance. Even so, they were relatively quietistic until the advent of an evangelical movement, the Quaker Renaissance, in the late nineteenth century.[33] Brock argues that, whereas "their witness against war was a somewhat pallid one," it then underwent an important change, becoming more politicized and more willing to work with non-Quakers (largely within the social gospel movement) in a non-sectarian peace movement. In one Canadian instance of this revival, Quaker Ada Mary Courtice and her Methodist minister husband helped found the non-denominational Canadian Peace and Arbitration Society in 1905. Canadian Quakers also worked closely with peace organizations sponsored by American Quakers, such as the Peace Association of Friends and the Lake Mohonk Conferences on International Arbitration.[34]

This more expansive understanding of pacifism and non-resistance can be seen in the Quakers' action when conscription began to seem imminent. They sent a resolution to Prime Minister Borden in May 1917, reaffirming their opposition to bearing arms and requesting that exemptions under the Militia Act be carried over in any new measure.[35] It is significant that their resolution also urged that the exemption clause in any new act be broadened beyond recognized pacifist sects to include anyone "whose conscience forbade them to carry arms regardless of their membership in any particular church or society."[36] Curiously, despite this enthusiastic beginning, Canadian Quakers do not, in general, seem to have been a strong force against conscription in Canada, especially compared with their counterparts in Britain.

One reason for this was the fact that there were so few of them. Also, fairly consistent anecdotal evidence indicates that the population did not include many young men of conscription age.[37] Another reason was that, perhaps partly because so few of their young men seemed directly threatened by the conscription legislation, Quakers poured their energies into medical and reconstruction work instead. The Friends emphasize an active response to suffering. Whatever the cause, the weaker presence of the more integrationist Society of Friends in Canada, as compared with that in Britain, had implications for the shape of the pacifist movement in this country.

Brian John Fell argues that a further important cause for the differences between Quaker anti-conscription activism in Britain and Canada can be traced to the comparative weakness of the socialist tradition in this country. Quaker socialists, with their journal the *Ploughshare,* were an influential minority in Britain. In Canada, Quakerism was rooted in rural districts; most of its adherents were farmers or farm workers, and very few were urban dwellers. British Quakers, living in a more industrialized country, were found in all types of occupations and often in urban areas. They were active in social work among the industrial poor, and some became interested in socialism as a means of solving the ills they saw around them: "Socialist-Quakers, then, were a product of the interest of a religious group in social welfare. Canadian Quakers, because of their rural orientation, were more concerned with the social welfare of immigrants and in sending out missionaries among the new arrivals from Europe. Socialism was not an important element in Quaker thinking in Canada, nor was it an important element in the thinking of other Canadians."[38] Fell sees this absence of political radicalism within the Canadian Quaker tradition as a significant cause of their muted presence in anti-war movements.

The relative clarity of their exemption, along with a general respect in mainstream society for their pacifism, meant that very few Quakers were imprisoned as conscientious objectors. Dorland notes that "there were ... only two instances where local Tribunals in Canada failed to grant total exemption to a Quaker."[39] He does not name them but is probably referring to Thomas George Mabley and Howard Toole, about whom Dorland wrote a letter in the *Canadian Friend.* A search through the CEF records, however, shows at least one other Quaker imprisoned as a conscientious objector: Joseph Cameron Cody, a twenty-year-old farmer from Newmarket, Ontario. These three imprisoned Quakers had all been granted non-combatant service, which they refused. In Britain, for comparison, 279 Quakers out of a population of about 20,000 were imprisoned for varying terms for their objection; of these, 142 were absolutists.[40]

The Canadian Quaker objector for whom the most information is available was Thomas George Mabley, a twenty-three-year-old farmer from Ilderton, Ontario, who belonged to the Coldstream meeting. Mabley was born in Britain and had come to Canada as a boy of eight in 1904, under the Barnardo scheme. He lived and worked on the farm of the Zavitz family, who were prominent in the Quaker community, and himself joined the Friends in 1910.[41] Mabley was called before the Bryanston tribunal on 19 November 1917 and applied for exemption both as a farmer and a member of the Society of Friends; he was granted exemption because of his agricultural work. When the changes in the Military Service Act cancelled that exemption, Mabley was enlisted in the First Depot Battalion, Western Ontario Regiment, at London, Ontario. He was court-martialled on 17 June 1918, pleaded guilty to the charge of disobeying an order, and was sentenced to two years' imprisonment. After two weeks in London City

Jail, Mabley served eight months' hard labour at Kingston Penitentiary. He did farm work while in prison and "had no complaints" about his treatment by the prison authorities or guards. Mabley remembers that, in prison, he was visited by ministers of various churches who tried to persuade him to abandon his position as a conscientious objector.[42]

Less information is available for another Quaker objector, Howard Toole. Toole was the first member of the Friends to be court-martialled, on 31 May 1918. He was twenty-three, a farmer from Mount Albert, Ontario, and, like Mabley, a member of the Hicksite Branch of the Society of Friends.[43] On hearing of the intended trial, Charles A. Zavitz, clerk of the Genesee Yearly Meeting, sent two telegrams concerning Toole: one to Justice Duff, the central appeal judge, and the other to Major William Keslick at the Second Depot Battalion of the First Canadian Ordnance Regiment at Niagara Camp, Ontario. The telegrams asserted that Toole was a bona fide member of the Society of Friends and reminded the recipients of the church's pacifist beliefs. They do not seem to have had the desired effect: Jolliffe records that Toole served a sentence similar to that of Mabley at Burwash Prison Farm.[44]

The smaller numbers of Friends in this country, along with their lack of political clout compared to that in Britain, meant that they also had a more hesitant attitude about dissent. Brock Millman has described the British Society of Friends as being basically at war with the government. He cites an "ultimatum" sent to the Home Office in January 1916: "We write to inform you that if any measure having the above [conscription] for its object should become law, the opposition of our Society to it will in no sense be modified or withdrawn. Such opposition is fundamental and is based upon a conscientious objection to all warfare. We are further to inform you that if any such measure should become law the support and co-operation of Members of the Society will be available for those outside their own body whose conscientious objection is based upon the same grounds as their own."[45]

The diplomatic language of Canadian Quakers, though similarly principled, contrasts sharply with this adversarial position. As Charles A. Zavitz, clerk of the Genesee Yearly Meeting of Friends, wrote to Borden, "I sincerely ask that if there is to be compulsory military enlistment in Canada those religious denominations be exempt whose doctrines are opposed to war. I understand that this method is being followed in the United States."[46] At times, tact extended almost to tentativeness. In response to a query about Quaker chaplains visiting prisoners, Albert S. Rogers, head of the Quaker Peace Committee (1917-18), wrote that there were "scarcely any" Quakers in prison: "So far as I know only two Friends have thus far been sent to prison and they are in a remote camp in

Ontario." He then counselled his correspondent, David D. Priestman from Victoria, that official visits might be frowned upon:

> While the war lasts public opinion will continue to look with much disfavour on anything that might be interpreted as propaganda or encouragement for any members of the community to abstain from military service ... It is not at all certain that everyone who takes the C.O. stand does it from sincere religious conviction ... There has been so much indifference and even a tendency to pro-germanism in some quarters that we feel that Friends should be exceedingly careful not to compromise their own reputation for sincerity by giving any sort of encouragement to any conscientious objectors whose previous life has not demonstrated a truly religious aspect.[47]

In response to this perceived threat to its reputation, the Society of Friends in Canada and the United States had suspended the enrolment of new members for the duration of the war, intending thereby to reassure governments that men who wished merely to take advantage of the exemption from combatant service would be unable to do so. The caution of this measure is remarkable, especially compared to the forthrightness of Quaker activism in Britain. After conscription was enacted in the United States, James Wood, president of the New York Society of Friends, promised, "the door will be closed by the Friends to slackers who seek a refuge from war duties": "The Friends have framed a resolution expressing their appreciation of the exemption from military duty granted them by Congress in the Draft Bill, and they furnish a pledge that such exemption will not be abused. There is a dry recommendation to young men of conscript age to postpone application for admission into the Society of Friends until after the present emergency." The Quakers would have no truck with those who might use them to dodge their duty. Already, the various meetings had been "besieged" by young men, some of them "obvious 'slackers' seeking to hide behind the cloak of Quakerism."[48]

This reluctance to ally themselves with other objecting groups also seems to have been a contributing factor in the inability of Canadian pacifists to organize an anti-conscription movement. In Britain, Quakers were among the leaders in the pacifist movement, and wealthy Quakers provided much of the financial support for the No-Conscription Fellowship (NCF). Quakers in Parliament, such as T.E. Harvey and Arnold Rowntree, kept the question of the conscientious objector in frequent debate. Thomas Kennedy says of their constant attacks on compulsion that, "By the end of the war, the NCF had created more bitterness and caused more problems than any other group."[49]

In contrast, conscientious objectors had few defenders in Canada's Parliament. One of the only MPs willing to speak up for COs was Quaker Isaac Pedlow. When the Hutterites were emigrating to Canada at the end of the war, their pacifism, German ancestry, and communal way of life angered many people and made them question these immigrants' ability to become "Canadians." When the topic came up in the House of Commons, John Wesley Edwards, the member from Frontenac, argued against allowing them into the country and made some offensive comparisons:

> If there are in the United States or Europe people of any class, whether they be called Mennonites, Hutterites or any other kind of "ites," we do not want them to come to Canada and enjoy the privileges and advantages of life under the British flag if they are willing to allow others to do the fighting for them while they sit at home in peace and plenty. We certainly do not want that kind of cattle in this country. Indeed not only do we not want that kind of cattle, but I would go further and support the view that we should deport from Canada others of the same class who were allowed to come in by mistake.

Pedlow, the member from South Renfrew, Ontario, found his remarks insulting and rose on a point of order:

> I belong to a religious denomination known as the Society of Friends. The principles of that society are opposed to war and we are therefore conscientious objectors: We object to taking direct part in war. The hon. Member has described that class of people as cattle. Now, Mr. Chairman, my objection is to these people, who are in every other respect decent and eminently respectable and loyal citizens being referred to by the term which the hon. Member for Frontenac has seen fit to use. As a member of the Society of Friends I object to their being called cattle, and would ask that the hon. Gentleman be requested to withdraw that statement.
>
> Mr. Edwards: Mr. Chairman, I will withdraw the statement, and apologize to the cattle.

After this, the exchange became even more acrimonious. Edwards explained that, in using the word "cattle," he meant no personal insult to any member of the House. But, he added, "If I had looked more closely I might have deemed it proper to use another word describing a different class of four-footed creatures that are more distinguished for the length of their ears than their horns." Edwards was ordered to withdraw his "undignified and unparliamentary" remark, but the fact that such language was used shows the passionate antipathy that conscientious objectors faced.[50] However, it is also notable that, in 1919, Pedlow had to introduce himself as a Quaker and then explain the pacifist beliefs of his group. Like most other MPs, he had never spoken on conscientious objection or any related matter since being elected in December 1917.[51] The silence of prominent Canadian Quakers contributed to conscientious objectors in Canada being left leaderless and mute.

Canadian Friends earned justifiable admiration for their wartime efforts. They were active in medical units, quite an important part of reconstruction during and after the war, and, among other wartime contributions, donated their school, Pickering College in Newmarket, Ontario, for a hospital. They do not, however, seem to have been able to make their voice heard in extending exemption beyond the clause that protected them. In a letter to Amish Mennonite John R. Ebersol, Mennonite bishop S.F. Coffman wrote, "We have heard very little of the Quakers during these exemption proceedings, and I have wondered whether or not they have given up their non-resistant faith in this country. The Tunker brethren are very much concerned with their standing with the government and we are working with them and for them in this matter, and hope to see them enjoy the privilege of freedom from military service."[52] Quaker records of the war show a concern for more active behaviour, focusing on reconstruction, than on conscientious objection. Fell sees this emphasis as part of the explanation for the few references in the *Canadian Friend* to imprisoned Quaker COs George Mabley and Howard Toole. Only one article mentioned both men by name, and this was written by Arthur Dorland after the war had ended. The Friends had created an image of service in the eyes of the government and wider Canadian public, and they wished to keep this image as constant as possible. As Fell puts it, "While the Society had sympathy for Mabley's position it is not clear that they wanted to draw attention to it ... The two men represented views which, although consistent with the Quaker peace testimony, were not the view of the main body of the Society."[53] Most Quakers in Canada wished to serve humanity in some way while still maintaining an anti-war attitude. They considered ambulance work to fulfill these conditions and, therefore, an acceptable war service.

THE OTHER HISTORIC peace churches' dealings with the government were also markedly non-confrontational. If their promised exemption and their insularity were important components of their experience, certain aspects of the Mennonites' doctrine were also key in shaping the discourse of their dissent, especially their stress on obedience to the state. Their oldest extant confession of faith, the Schleitheim Confession of 1527, begins with the significant affirmation that the office of government is ordained by God. This article, based on Romans 13 in the Bible, holds that the state was instituted by God in response to human sin in order to punish the evil and protect the good.[54] The respectful attitude towards authority that it engendered continued to be an important part of Mennonite discourse in the First World War. One example is the clear statement by the Tunkers emphasizing their loyalty and good citizenship: "We respect our National Emblem, and in accordance with our Faith and Practice we are subject to the higher powers and obey magistrates and uncomplainingly submit ourselves to every good work for the Lord's sake ... Our opposition to war is not founded upon disloyalty to our Government, but upon the conviction that the Gospel of Christ is the Gospel of Peace."[55] Such expressions of fidelity were common; perhaps they seemed particularly needful in light of public sentiment against people of German background and "slackers" who did not enlist. That the Mennonites were vulnerable to both of these charges, and often lived in self-contained groups with little interaction with mainstream society, increased the need to assert their patriotism and otherwise good citizenship.

Similar expressions of patriotism were important components of the petitions written to the Borden administration by several Mennonite groups when conscription seemed imminent. So too were the earlier promises of exemption. A letter from the Mennonites of Manitoba and Saskatchewan assured the administration "of our true allegiance to this country and its government." It also reminded Borden gently, and after thanks for the "noble treatment" accorded them thus far, that they had come "into this country with the assurance from the Dominion Government that we should be left undisturbed in our convictions and conscientious scruples about bearing arms and participating in war."[56] In spite of some problems, Ottawa generally remembered its promises.

Some mainstream Canadians, either individually or in groups, did oppose participation in the war. Rather more disagreed with conscription, either in principle or practice. However, a separate examination of peace church dissent is worthwhile because the society that voiced it was a unique group with which to deal in enforcing conscription. Its disavowal of military service was clear, but other elements in its religious doctrine and social composition complicated expressions of resistance to conscription. Pacifist church dissent is interesting partly because of the ways in which it departed from that of other war resisters. It incorporated a generally respectful attitude to government authority and emphasized obedience to government demands. Even in retrospect, the tone is conciliatory. A Mennonite account written just a few years after the war explains the cause of the troubles faced by the group: "Most of the persecutions arising from misunderstandings with officials may be traced to the fact that some men magnified their authority, took matters into their own hands, thus proving themselves untrue to the government they represented."[57] Even for this post-war Mennonite writer, who no longer needed to fear government censure, Ottawa's actions were not blameworthy. Rather, "misunderstandings" that disrupted the smooth flow of government intentions had occurred because individuals overstepped their appropriate roles and duties, a typical Mennonite criticism. In the face of great confusion surrounding their status under the MSA and inconsistent advice as to how to receive exemption, Saskatchewan Mennonites maintained that "our faith rested and continues to rest in the successors in office of those with whom our fathers entered into a solemn contract. It is unthinkable to us that they should violate this contract and we are quite sure that it only requires a thorough presentation of our case to cause them to so act that we may again have that peace for which we long so much."[58]

The Mennonites' deference to authority and trust that the Borden administration intended to respect their non-resistant beliefs seem to have been more central to their discourse at this time than admiration for martyrs to pacifism. When S.F. Coffman, a Mennonite bishop from Vineland, Ontario, who became the key intermediary between the government and the Ontario Mennonites, was visited by an official bearing reports that his sermons discouraged recruiting and production, he was flabbergasted. "We have been doing everything possible ourselves to aid in production," he wrote, "and have had no reason whatever to discourage recruiting." He concluded that some remarks he had made encouraging his people to be steadfast in their non-resistance "were dragged from their setting and meaning and were sent to the authorities as a charge of unpatriotic sentiment."[59]

Finding themselves in such a situation, secular pacifists might well have rejected the charge of unpatriotic behaviour on the grounds that, in a country wrongly at war, their stance constituted the true patriotism. Coffman's shock at the interpretation of his sermons highlights a major difference between the historic peace churches and secular pacifists. The former had no desire to universalize their behaviour. Coffman did not see his exhortations of perseverance as unpatriotic, because they were intended solely for his congregation. War was wrong, yes, but it was part of the sinfulness of the secular world, and if that world chose to go to war, attempting to stop it was not the job of the Mennonites.

As well, the historic peace churches preferred to describe their stance as non-resistant rather than pacifist, following the biblical directive to "resist not evil."[60] Non-resistance is, self-evidently, passive. The combination of these two doctrines is a key element in the nature of their dissent and a large part of what kept Mennonites and members of most other peace churches away from any form of resistance beyond conscientious objection.[61] Although ascertaining precise numbers of COs in First World War Canada is extremely difficult, it is safe to say that the majority of them were peace church members, largely because MSA recognition of this form of objection was limited solely to them. Their passivity and separatism, then, offer a compelling, if partial, explanation for the comparative frailty of the pacifist movement in Canada.

THE DEGREE TO WHICH the historic peace churches were able, or unable, to present an organized response to conscription legislation constitutes another aspect of their doctrine and behaviour that shaped conscientious objection in Canada. Although separatist, these churches did not exist in complete isolation. Canada's Mennonite community did have connections with its counterparts in the United States. And, later in the war, it organized with other conferences and non-resistant churches for war relief. This was, however, an ongoing process, and one of the most compelling aspects of the separatist churches' wartime relations with the government is their lack of a unified voice or an organizational structure with which to respond to the demands of conscription. As Epp shows, "In organization and structure, the Mennonites were ill-prepared for the onslaught of federal legislation, administrative regulations and adverse public opinion which was about to burst upon them. They had no united approach to government authorities of any kind. Consequently, they had no common secretariat to mediate the many messages that of necessity flowed between the federal authorities and the people."[62] This obstacle in their interactions with the government, in Canada and in the United States, may have been exacerbated by their rejection of charismatic leaders. Susan Schultz Huxman describes the belief that "any attempt to call attention to one's superiority as a commanding, energetic and outspoken individual had no place in a fellowship of believers." Mennonite pastors, instructors rather than leaders, were not accustomed to acting as church spokesmen to outsiders. She puts the point clearly: "Since Mennonite leaders were most comfortable in an unassuming role, it was difficult for them to impress government officials."[63]

This is an important consideration. However, in the Canadian case, it is difficult to prove. Documents touching on the interactions between Canadian government officials and Mennonite delegations make no specific mention of any difficulties raised by Mennonite humility. Mennonite accounts of meetings with officials generally see them as promising and successful dialogues. In his memoirs, Tunker Ernest John Swalm recalls, "During World War One, D.W. Heise was considered the most able to represent the interests of the [Tunker] Church before the Canadian Government. He nobly defended the conscientious objector with statesman-like dignity."[64] Such evidence seems to suggest that

Canadian Mennonites may have fared better than their American counterparts in this respect.

Those who took on the unaccustomed leadership role of intermediaries between the congregations and the Borden administration had a great deal of work before them. The papers of S.F. Coffman, for example, are full of requests for advice in an unfamiliar and confusing situation. Letters to Coffman generally inquired about Mennonite status under the act, asked whether and how an individual should register, requested clarification of contradictory responses from registrars, MPs, and tribunals, or included the rather desperate plea that Coffman speak to somebody personally about a son or other relative. Epp shows that David Toews and Benjamin Ewart took on similar duties in the West, "not because they were appointed but because they were the most knowledgeable and, consequently, most able and willing."[65]

Coffman dealt with requests that extended beyond members of his own church. From early February 1918, he maintained extensive correspondence with John R. Ebersol, a member of the Old Amish Mennonite Church who had been asked by his ministers to "help our young Brethren in the interest of their souls about Militaryism [sic]." His small church, which had no building but worshipped "from place to place," had many members who lacked both a strong grasp of English and experience in civil affairs. Coffman seemed to offer a lifeline in the face of much unaccustomed interaction with bureaucracy. A sympathetic judge had told Ebersol that the efforts of the Amish to secure exemption would be best served if they tried to obtain an Order-in-Council passed "the same as the Mennonites of the west have." His first letter sought the advice of Coffman, whom he addressed as "brother – to a good extent of our faith," as to whether this would be the best route to take and whether the Ontario Mennonites had also pursued it. Ebersol lamented "that the Mennonites and Amish Mennonites are so very much split up," and his correspondence with Coffman, which extended into a discussion of post-war reconstruction efforts, seems to have worked towards diminishing that split and helping to pave the way for the more organized and unified Mennonite response during the Second World War.[66]

Orland Gingerich also credits the disturbances of the war with the formation of a conference structure among the Amish in Ontario. He argues further that "It can be safely assumed that World War I served to broaden the horizon of the Amish community in Canada making possible their broader cooperation with other groups and their acceptance of new ideas and new ways, especially from their Mennonite brethren. These experiences prepared the Amish for the mission and service opportunities which came their way in the years that followed."[67] Similarly, Swalm writes of the Tunker-Mennonite collaboration that evolved: "Culturally and doctrinally, we [Tunkers and Mennonites] have much in common. Our roots are imbedded in the same historic peace witness. We have united our efforts in promoting the cause of peace in this warring society. During World War I we discovered each other in a sense hitherto untried. Our mutual needs as minority groups brought into focus a desperate situation. The intolerance of war hysteria caused us to see the importance of team work in our approaches."[68] Whereas Thomas Socknat argues that the First World War tended to radicalize liberal pacifists in Canada, drawing them away from mainstream politics, it is interesting that it seems to have had a contrary effect on the members of the historic peace churches, impelling them to a closer integration, both with each other and mainstream Canadian society.[69] Thus, one element of Mennonite patterns of interaction with each other and the Canadian government, as shaped by the war, was the creation of strong leaders such as Coffman and the founding of the more unified response with which the peace churches met conscription in the Second World War.[70]

While examining issues of leadership, Huxman's study of American Mennonite newspapers between 1914 and 1918 also describes the apparent lack of any sense of impending crisis. The denomination did not try to articulate any distinctive Mennonite peace position or to establish a lobby with other peace churches. It seemed unprepared for justifying its faith to outsiders. Huxman explains that the faithful, almost by definition, were to be devoted to sacred, not secular concerns.[71] This focus further coloured the distinctive discourse of the historic peace churches during the First World War. It is important to add, however, that a lack of political agitation is not the same as an absence of reaction to the threat of enforced military service. An example of an apolitical but nonetheless active response can be seen in Ontario in 1917. Prompted by reports that the Eastern (Ontario) Mennonites would not be exempted, during a time J.S. Hartzler refers to as "days of anxiety," a letter was sent to the Department of Justice, asking for interpretation of the MSA as it affected Mennonites. Perhaps more importantly, a meeting of representatives from Mennonite and Amish Churches in the district was called in Kitchener "for prayer for help and direction from God in this time of extreme need." Prayer was deemed a suitable and active response to crisis. With timing appropriate for post-war storytelling, a letter promising exemption arrived just before the meeting. Thus, "The meeting for prayer was changed to a meeting of praise."[72] Later in the war, a letter from S.F. Coffman to the moderator of the Ontario Mennonite Conference, L.J. Burkholder, passed on the proposition of another church member: "He suggested it would be well to appoint a day of prayer in all of our churches for our young people who are liable to this call and for all others who will be called into the service of the army when their exemptions are refused. I think that this would be a good thing for us all to do. Could you, as Moderator send out such notices so that the day could be appointed or announced next Sunday."[73] The letter, which continued by issuing instructions about the choice of day, is one of several that offered prayer as a practical response to fears of conscription.

Another significant aspect of Quaker and Mennonite discourse and interaction with Ottawa was their perception of duty owed. Conscription itself, as argued by Robert Craig Brown and Ramsay Cook, among others, is as much a response to the home-front desire for equality of sacrifice as it is a military necessity.[74] The Mennonites seemed to share this perception that everyone in the country must, in some way, do their fair share. Mennonites in general and conscientious objectors in particular were disenfranchised in the Wartime Elections Act of 1917, and anyone who had voted in the 1917 election was retroactively denied exemption on conscientious grounds. Mennonites seem to have voiced few protestations about the removal of this right of citizenship, one practised by few of them anyway. On the contrary, their sense of wartime obligation was a frequent subject of correspondence. A letter from S.F. Coffman to Aaron Loucks in November 1917 considers how best to fulfill their duty: "Since we have been fortunate in securing the favorable interpretation of the Exceptions' clause in the Military Service Act, we, as a church have been contemplating some active assistance in the matter of giving relief and assisting the Government in such a way as we felt we could in accordance with our principles."[75] The letter goes on to discuss suggestions for relieving war sufferers in the devastated countries and contributing to the support of hospitals for disabled soldiers. A letter the two men sent to the prime minister that same month is more explicit in its sense of gratitude and obligation, and is worth quoting at length:

> We realize also that the Government has not assigned us any duty in lieu of military service, and therefore we are not made to share any special part of the burden which our nation is bearing. We have recognized this fact, and, while we are sharing in the national burden of trials and fears and labors, it is our purpose, by the grace of God, to undertake voluntarily some share in the sacrifices of our fellow-citizens, and by some means, the plans of which are now under consideration, express in a more substantial manner our gratitude to the Government for the Christian privileges which we enjoy under the laws of Canada.[76]

Although they were not morally able to give money to institutions under the control of the army, Coffman suggested in correspondence with the rest of the committee that their contributions would be acceptable if sent directly to the government: "We were considering the contributing of all of our funds to the Government so that we would be bearing a share of the burden which the nation is bearing. Others are giving their personal service and still others are lending money, and we are only paying our taxes with all the rest and only a proper proportion. A special contribution for some specific part of the work in which the Government is using of the nation's means was what we felt would be the most consistent way of giving public service."[77] Clearly, the Mennonites do not seem to have been immune to the spirit of obligation with which much of Canada viewed the war.[78] Because of the respectful, if distant, Mennonite attitude to civil authority, the Borden administration could serve the function of a trusted intermediary, channelling Mennonite contributions to an appropriate need.

The monetary gifts were also intended partly as a sort of "thanks offering" to the government for military exemption. One of Coffman's letters, for example, unites closely the double burden of thanking the government and relieving distress. "I am glad that we have been thus favored by the Government," he wrote, "and think that we owe them some recognition and also should now make an effort to show our readiness to take up the burden of supporting the many suffering people today in war-stricken districts. We have not been doing this to the extent that we are able to do so."[79] Ens shows that the collections raised by the Mennonites of Western Canada were sent to the government "as an expression of thanks for its considerate treatment of the Mennonites in regard to military exemption," as well as to provide relief for war victims. The organizers also observed that raising money might help to gain the goodwill of their neighbours, who would perhaps be less likely to press for Mennonite enlistment if they saw evidence of their voluntary financial sacrifices.[80]

Doukhobor communities seem to have reacted in a similar way in recognizing the need for some type of sacrifice in lieu of military service. In a meeting with Solicitor General Arthur Meighen, the author of the MSA, they indicated that they would be willing to pay a double measure of taxation and had placed as much of their land as possible under cultivation.[81] Like the Mennonites, they also sent money to the government to be used for victims of the war. In one letter, the Society of Independent Doukhobors at Buchanan, Saskatchewan, sent a donation and stated that "Our faith and conscience will not permit us to take an active part in the strife, but our sympathy and compassion for those who, though innocent and in no wise responsible for the hostilities, have been rendered homeless, indigent and destitute by its progress, bid us to at least share with them the produce of our labor applied to God's soil."[82] There were several donations, in cash and kind. For instance, the *Canadian Annual Review* for 1918 records a gift by the Doukhobors to the Military Hospitals Commission of twenty thousand pounds of jam.[83]

It would be unfair to characterize the financial contributions of the Mennonites and Doukhobors as motivated solely by thankfulness for their exemption and a sense of the need for equality of sacrifice. There was, as well, an important religious aspect to the donations, which served as an active response to the suffering caused by the war. One of Coffman's letters closed with an exhortation to his American correspondent that "We should do something to do our duty. Our hearts have the work before them and our heads should work out some plan. Our bodies we have consecrated to God as well as our means and we should use them as a living offering to God in the relief of suffering in this time of awful distress."[84] Another letter reminds Burkholder, "Some of our congregations have done fairly well but none have done more than their share towards this work. As we have opportunity let us do good to all men."[85] The sense of obligation the Mennonites felt was to their church, their nation, and the suffering world.

The generosity of the historic peace churches may also have been a response to the fact that the attitude of mainstream churches had put them in a difficult position. When the clear exemption that seemed promised in late 1917 failed to materialize, the Mennonites appeared to recognize the difficulty of the government's situation. Coffman wrote, "I believe that the Government is sincere in their desire to grant us the privilege of continuing our faith and recognizes that our faith is right, but there is so much opposition on account of the other Churches and their practices which are the opposite of ours in regard to the participation in the war that it is hard for the Government to do anything for us without incurring the displeasure of others, and inviting a more severe persecution of our faith if their decisions in our favor are too publically [sic] declared."[86] This is a sensitive response. Although the intentions of the Borden administration, as discussed in the previous chapter, were perhaps not so transparent, the peace churches faced threats posed by the attitudes of an increasingly chauvinistic citizenry and mainstream churches that saw the war as a crusade. J.M. Bliss has shown that Methodist ministers, for example, "played a leading part in alerting the Saskatchewan government to the 'Mennonite menace' and suggested that the policy of exempting Mennonites be reviewed."[87]

Furthermore, the exemption of the historic peace churches also became a thorn in the federal government's side when dealing with anti-conscription forces in Quebec. Henri Bourassa questioned Ottawa's "willingness to exempt from service on religious grounds the Mennonites, Doukhobors, and Quakers, while refusing to recognize the French Canadian sentiment against military service except in the defense of Canada."[88] In an article for *Le Devoir*, translated for English-speaking readers in a pamphlet entitled *Conscription*, Bourassa went into more detail about his attitude regarding CO status. He argued that the peace church exemption was fair but that the MSA clause should properly include French Canadians as well: "If the religious scruples of these new-comers are taken into account, by what right should the government disregard the time-honoured traditions of the oldest, the most thoroughly *national* element of the whole Canadian population? Let there be no mistake: the conviction of the French Canadian that he is only bound to take up arms to defend the soil of Canada is as true and as deeply anchored in his heart as the hatred of militarism is in the mind of the Quaker or Mennonite."[89] The public reaction to the various types of conscientious objectors will be more fully discussed below, but it is worth noting here that Mennonites were aware of the various shades of public opinion and of Ottawa's need to take them into account.

IT WAS WITH THIS tradition of religious dissent and secular obedience that the historic peace churches in Canada faced the movement towards conscription during the Great War. Most of the early agitation for conscription, as seen in the newspapers of the day, had called for the reinstatement of the Militia Act. The peace churches had clear exemption rights here. When the Military Service Act was introduced, the conscription clause also seemed to offer little reason for concern. Enclosing a copy of the letter he had received from the Military Service Branch of the Department of Justice, Coffman rejoiced that the Mennonites had "found favor with the Government through His [Jesus'] grace" and explained that "The Mennonites are recognized as a body in the Exceptions to the Military Service Act. No service whatsoever is to be required of them. Since this is the decision of the Department of Justice we may well set our minds at rest on the whole matter."[90] As it transpired, matters were rather more complicated than this. Neither the act's wording nor the intentions of its authors were completely clear; as a result, neither the conscientious objectors from the historic peace churches, nor tribunal and government officials, would be able to set their minds at rest for some time.[91]

In theory, the process of obtaining exemption was simple. A young man applying for conscientious objector status reported to the authorities, claimed exemption, and then appeared before his local tribunal to present his case and prove his membership in a recognized pacifist denomination. Exemption on conscientious grounds was probably the most difficult to obtain, partly because it was the hardest to prove. The intangibility of conscience was a serious disability to potential objectors. Exemptions based on occupation, financial dependency, or physical unfitness were by far more common and simpler to explain and defend. Most members of the non-resistant churches lived in agrarian communities, and many chose to claim exemption as farmers rather than take the less certain route of conscientious objection.[92] A letter in the October issue of the *Canadian Friend* suggested that members look carefully at the exemption clauses, for they might be able to claim exemption on grounds other than conscience.[93] Farmers, however, were not always exempted, and later, when farm exemptions were cancelled in 1918, taking this route caused further complications for members of the historic peace churches. Dorland offers this further explanation for the muted presence of the Quakers as objectors: "Since, with one exception, all of the meetings to which they [the men of military age] belonged at this time were in rural districts, by far the greater number of them were farmers who, though liable to military service, were in many instances granted exemption by the local Tribunals because of the necessity of carrying on the basic industry of the country." The same seems to have been true for the Tunkers.[94] It appears that, for all the churches involved, the exemption itself was what mattered, and taking a rather abstract and public stand for the principle of non-resistance, or the obligation of the government to honour historic promises, was less important. To cite one example, the *Toronto Star* reported the tribunal appearance of Stuart W. Starr, a farmer from Newmarket who was a member of the Society of Friends and a conscientious objector. In spite of his religious affiliation, Starr eventually received exemption on the grounds of being the sole support of his mother, his brother being in a construction battalion in France.[95] Such behaviour further complicates the effort to assess the number of COs during the war. Especially in the case of objectors outside the historic peace churches, as will be discussed in a later chapter, it is common to see multiple grounds for exemption claimed, with a bid for conscientious objection coupled with one of ill-health, the dependence of a relative, or occupational necessity. But multiple claims did not always ensure success; indeed, in some cases, they were viewed as evidence of cowardice and the possibility that, singly, none was strong enough to warrant exemption.

This double basis for exemption was not accepted, for example, from Ernest John Swalm of Duntroon, in the Nottawa military district. Swalm, who would later become a Tunker bishop, applied for exemption both as a farmer and a member of a pacifist denomination. The Ontario registrar had ruled that, because Tunkers were not specifically named in the act, they were not exempted.[96] Tunkers did, however, fall into the category of historic peace church in that they were in existence on 6 June 1917 (and had been for over a hundred years) and had tenets opposing participation in war.[97] Sider describes the confusion Swalm faced: "No one – he [Isaac Swalm, Ernest's father], his son or the Nottawa officials – could find satisfactory information on the conscription policy, nor how and on what basis he might appeal the summons. Inquiries that Swalm did make persuaded him that appeal would be fruitless. He had no alternative to obeying the summons."[98] Swalm, the first Tunker to be called up, had no idea what might happen to him. Some years later, he detailed his apprehension: "We read in the papers of several boys who were conscientiously opposed to serving in carnal warfare. They did not belong to any Peace Churches but stood firmly on personal convictions. They were maltreated by unauthorized men in the army. Some were held under a cold water pump until they died from exposure. No case was made of it as the days for the Allies were desperate and Conscientious Objectors were made victims of a patriotic hysteria that ignored law."[99] Believing that such things were quite likely to happen to him as well, Swalm's family and friends were emotional about his leaving. Swalm wrote, "Memory of her [his sister's] pathetic cries and relentless clinging to my arms haunts me to this moment. I literally dragged her out on the lawn before she let me go." In spite of this, he was "greatly strengthened" by the support of his family and church. Before he left, his father "put his arm around his son's neck" and said, "My boy, I do not know how I can get along without you here on the farm with only one arm, but I want you to stand true to God and your convictions at any price. I would rather get word that you were shot than to know you compromised your position and disobeyed the Lord."[100] In Hamilton, Swalm's father showed Major Bennett documents that pointed to certain exemption privileges given to the peace churches. The officer "emphatically told us that those treaties were all abrogated" and declared that "One stroke of the pen can suddenly remove any favours granted to persons or groups." Bennett also lied to the father and son about the kind of company the latter might find in the guard house. "There I met eight other C.O.s," Swalm remembered. "What a pleasant surprise after being told by Major Bennett there was not one other Conscientious Objector in the Battalion! He said they had all been treated harshly enough that they had gladly fallen in line."[101]

Swalm was court-martialled in Hamilton along with the other conscientious objectors, who were from a variety of sects. He was imprisoned for one month while awaiting the court martial and for another month in a St. Catharines jail after the trial. He faced "many threats and jests, including the intimation that [he] would be shot." After his second month in jail, the ruling was overturned, the Tunker Church was recognized, and Swalm was released. Epp credits this to the "persistent effort" of Coffman and D.W. Heise of the Tunker Church.[102] Several other Tunkers faced imprisonment, including John Henry Heise and Charles Wright, who were sentenced to two years less a day hard labour digging stumps in northern Ontario before they too were released.[103] In spite of their eventual success, the trials of these men added fuel to the fears of other pacifist groups that their legitimate claims would be ignored.[104]

Furthermore, a certain lack of clarity existed as to exactly who was recognized as a Mennonite under the act. Most Mennonite young men were not baptized until they reached twenty or twenty-one years of age, and legal induction into the army occurred when a man was eighteen. The Mennonite delegation sent to Ottawa in 1917 had been assured that the children of Mennonite parents would be considered Mennonites by the government. But, as public attitudes grew less tolerant, the *Winnipeg Tribune* reported that military exemption would be reserved for baptized members only.[105] After Abraham Dyck, a Mennonite who had not yet been baptized, was inducted in Winnipeg in June 1918 as a test case and the Manitoba Appeal Board accepted the explanation of area bishops as to the membership of unbaptized members, the situation seemed resolved, although some problems persisted in Saskatchewan.[106]

The baptism issue was a complex one. In his study of Old Order Mennonites in Ontario, Donald Martin shows an unusually large baptism class for 1918. For the previous seven years, the number of boys entering the church had ranged between twelve and twenty-one; in 1918, eighty-four were baptized. Martin offers no explanation for the size of the class, but it caught the attention of military officials. An investigating officer from the London district went to the Elmira meeting house, examined the eighty-four boys, and "was satisfied that there were no draft dodgers present."[107]

Epp writes that "the proper identification of Mennonites and Tunkers was not the end of their troubles."[108] Choosing a narrower and more easily proven definition of conscientious objection than its British counterpart, the Borden administration faced further confusion caused by ambiguities in the MSA and the claims of the Mennonites and Doukhobors who had been encouraged to emigrate by promises of protection for their non-resistance.[109] It was unclear, for example, whether the exemption clause applied to all Mennonites or solely to the Russians who had emigrated in 1873 under specific promises of exemption that were designed to encourage immigration. Whether the Mennonites were exempted *under* the act or *from* the act was also unclear. This was an important distinction in that the Military Service Act made no provision for absolute exemption, only for the option of non-combatant service. If Mennonites were exempted *under* the act, they still had to face a tribunal and at best would be conscripted into the army in some non-combatant capacity. If they were exempted *from* the act, they had only to prove that they were Mennonites to be allowed to return to their daily lives.

In a "confusing and inequitable" policy, the Western (Russian) Mennonites were at first granted complete freedom from any service and sometimes even from registration.[110] Protected by an Order-in-Council of September 1872, they were deemed exempt *from* the act and had only to carry a card signed by a bishop or elder that vouched for their church membership. The Ontario, or

Eastern, Mennonites, though longer established in Canada, at first faced induction and were permitted exemption from combatant service only. This generated much anxiety among them.

The confusion caused by miscommunication and overly ardent tribunal members was thus exacerbated by regional differences. The Eastern Mennonites spent much of the war trying to convince officials that they merited the same unqualified exemption given their Russian brethren in the West. In the West, despite the comparative clarity of Western Mennonite exemption, official reaction to their claims varied according to province. Further disparity occurred on the district level. Local tribunals were not always aware that these people were exempted from, rather than under, the Military Service Act. Ens shows that "in the large block settlements in Manitoba and in those Saskatchewan communities where the Mennonite leadership became personally acquainted with members of the local tribunal this did not present a problem."[111] But individuals living outside the Saskatchewan Mennonite communities were frequently inducted.[112] The same disparity occurred in other provinces. Martin argues that, in Ontario, officials differed in their interpretation of the law: "The London tribunals continued to hold that the Mennonites of Ontario were excepted from the Military Service Act while other tribunals viewed the Mennonites as needing to seek exemptions ... through the tribunals."[113]

Due to a combination of Mennonite protest and the actions of sympathetic government officials, the greatest inequities were erased by the end of the war. Although Ontario Mennonites were still considered to be subject to noncombatant service throughout the war, in practice, a compromise was worked out. An Ontario Mennonite, upon presenting a certificate of church membership to military authorities, was issued an open-ended "leave of absence" that permitted him to return to his peacetime occupation and "allowed the tribunals to avoid the question of exemption and exception."[114] The relevant Routine Orders of the Canadian Expeditionary Force read as follows: "2. Any draftee ordered to report for duty who produces proof that he is, by virtue of the 'War Time Elections Act, 1917,' or Order-in-Council (P.C. 111), of the 17th January, 1918, exempted from combatant service, shall, on his request be struck off the strength as 'erroneously ordered to report.' 3. Draftees so dealt with shall be given a certificate of leave of absence (MFW 160) 'for 20 days from date, subject thereafter to confirmation by Registrar,' and will be instructed to apply to the Registrar asap for a certificate of exemption in exchange therefore."[115] J.S. Hartzler argues that, through this "leave of absence" plan, "Canada finally solved the religious objector question better than most other countries engaged in the war": "By the leave of absence plan the nonresistant young men were allowed to remain at home, and thus were among Canada's best producers instead of being con-sumers only and accomplishing no immediate good as so many were forced to be in camps and guard-houses because they could take no part in the war." Janzen was also impressed with the "remarkable flexibility" of both Canadian government officials and Mennonites in working out this alternative.[116]

Although this approach offered a greater equity among Mennonites, it did not always seem fair to outsiders. An editorial in the *Manitoba Free Press* saw rampant abuses of church membership certificates:

> It would seem on the face of it, as if the Department of Justice ... has opened wide the door for not only the slacker, but also the grafter. Under present regulations, any ordained minister of the Mennonite church can sign exemption certificates for any of his flock, or any one else's flock for that matter ... How such a wide-open instrument placed in the hands of a lot of Mennonite pastors and ex-pastors – it does not seem to make much difference what their status is, in respect to church or general honesty – is subject to abuses, can well be imagined.[117]

The piece went on to chronicle cases of non-Mennonite defaulters who had somehow acquired exemption certificates and to inveigle against the bribery that the author saw as necessarily facilitating this. Among clergymen, Bishop David Toews was singled out in the mainstream press as "one of these one-man exemp-tion tribunals," an official who would sign certificates indiscriminately.[118]

Requiring a person seeking exemption to produce a certificate signed by the authorities of his church, as William Janzen has noted, could pose a problem in that it gave considerable power to those church leaders.[119] Difficulties arose in the Doukhobor community, which had divided into two groups: the Christian Community of Universal Brotherhood and the Society of Independent Doukh-obors. Peter Veregin, the leader of the Community Doukhobors, was outspoken about his position that the Canadian government ought to distinguish carefully between the two groups: "At the present time, I Peter Veregin, the representative of the Doukhobor community, do not recognize the second party as Doukhobors and consider that these people must be liable to be conscripted for military service on the same basis as other citizens of Canada."[120] The government did not follow his advice. Arguing that the Independent Doukhobors had emigrated to Canada in good faith that they would be exempted from conscription, Ottawa agreed that both groups were excepted from the act and "appear to have en-countered few problems during the war."[121]

The nativist reaction against these groups was not immediate. Due to the fairly clear government intention to exempt the Mennonites, their relative isola-tion, and frequent expressions of duty and thanks, this kind of conscientious objector aroused less controversy than those of other backgrounds. In the first months after the enactment of conscription legislation, Mennonites were almost invisible in most Canadian newspapers.[122] This changed in 1918, when, fleeing conscription in the United States and encouraged by the exemption of their northern brethren, a fresh group of Mennonites arrived in Western Canada. It is difficult to ascertain their numbers.[123] Concerned members of the House of Commons spoke of sixty thousand immigrants; thirty-five thousand actually crossed the border. James C. Juhnke estimates the number of Mennonite immigrants who actually stayed in Canada at a conservative eighteen hundred.[124] Their arrival was important in terms of public attitudes to conscientious objectors, and it is worth taking a moment to look at what brought this group to Canada.

Even though the United States had enacted conscription earlier than Canada, entering the war with a policy of compulsion, Mennonite thoughts about migration evolved slowly, according to Allan Teichroew, because of the "dilatory manner in which the [American] government clarified its policy toward conscientious objectors." It seemed presumptuous to plan to emigrate while hope remained that pacifist principles would be safeguarded. Teichroew also reveals Mennonite fears that talk of migration would handicap negotiations with the Wilson administration, although Huxman shows that threat of emigration had always been a traditional part of Mennonite rhetoric.[125]

For American Mennonites uncertain about their position, Canada seemed an appealing destination because of its proximity, land and job opportunities, and the presence of their co-religionists. It seemed to offer security. However, the new Mennonites met with a storm of negative public opinion. The *Manitoba Free Press* reported, "Groups of Mennonites or members of a sect closely resembling them, in any event slackers or people who profess a religion that prevents them from taking on their fair share of the responsibilities of Government, are reported to be trooping over the border into Canada and are settling in the Prairie Provinces." The writer, albeit unenthusiastically, saw the need to honour Canada's "contract" with the Mennonites who had arrived before the war, but not with these newcomers: "People of peculiar religions, living in colonies and clinging to an alien tongue and to racial habits are from every point of view – except that of production, perhaps – undesirable settlers ... The country wants citizens in the full meaning of the word, and not a lot of slackers who are fully prepared to pile up wealth at someone else's expense, but to whom the obligations of government mean nothing."[126] The assumption that this "alien" group would not bear its share of the military burden easily accommodated the charge that it would become wealthy in a time of stringency. A later *Free Press* article remarked that

Unless something is done to stop these people from coming in ... they are going to be a grave menace to the south country, and at the same time steps must be taken to bar them from their customary habit of forming self-centered communities, with little or no connection with the outside world, for while they persist in so living they will not make good Canadian citizens ... It is self-evident that "white folks," be they Scotch, Irish, English, American, or just plain Canadian, do not want to reside in the neighborhood of a colony which speaks the enemy language, adopts the costumes and customs of enemy countries, and professes itself free from military or other duties of State that have to be recognized and obeyed by Canadian citizens.[127]

When it was customary to see the war as uniting the disparate elements of the country, the persistence of a group living separately and clinging to a "peculiar" religion infuriated many Canadians. Worse still was its German background and refusal to fight. Antagonism to the conscientious objector status, in contemporary newspapers, was very often paired with anger at the separatism of the historic peace churches. Non-resistance, in this view, was merely further evidence of the group's not being sufficiently Canadianized.[128]

Despite this hostility at the end of the war, the historic peace churches seem in general to have benefited from the support and sympathy of several Cabinet members, such as Arthur Meighen and J.A. Calder, MPs such as F.S. Scott and W.D. Euler, and officials such as E.L. Newcombe and R.B. Bennett.[129] Janzen summarizes the variety of factors that may have contributed to the comparatively favourable political climate encountered by the churches: "This sympathy may have been prompted by the character of these groups, or perhaps by the principle of conscientious objection, which had a long history in Britain. In several instances, the sympathy seems to be related to the importance of honouring historic promises ... The military authorities seem to have responded to the argument that these people would not make good soldiers anyway."[130] Although no one would argue that the experience of peace church members as conscientious objectors was easy, it was less harsh than it might have been and certainly less harsh than that of objectors from outside this group. Although the peace churches, especially the denominations of German origin, did encounter a degree of public antipathy, their difficulties with Ottawa seem to have arisen more from bureaucratic problems than from any real government desire to penalize them.

The tendency of peace church members to avoid expressions of individual dissent is important in the development of pacifism in Canada, in that it corresponded with the way in which the Canadian government prepared for, and reacted to, conscientious objection in the First World War. Although conscientious objection is by definition an individual response, provision was made only for members of certain churches that had historic promises of recognition for their non-resistance – in other words, for the conscience of a group.[131] That those thus recognized also tended to deprecate individualism and treat objection as a response necessary to retain membership in the group accorded with this definition. This agreement about what constituted conscientious objection further increased the isolation and impotence of the individual who was not a Quaker or a Mennonite and served to weaken the base of support for a politically organized body of objectors similar to the No-Conscription Fellowship in Britain.

The Mennonite response to military conscription in the First World War, then, called upon traditional modes of rhetoric in dealing with the government. Mennonites held prayer days, wrote letters, and sent delegations to Ottawa. They made large donations that served as public thanks for their exemption, as expressions of their sense of obligation in community with the rest of the country, and as charity. Despite some agitation from the Society of Friends, accommodation, to the limits of their ideals, tended to be a more important part of their discourse than protest. Their quietism and disinclination to link their non-resistance to secular pacifism or that of other religious denominations helped keep a strong pacifist anti-conscription movement from taking hold in Canada. Organization was further discouraged by the relative clarity of their exemption, as compared with that in Britain. Their experience during the First World War also sees the beginning of a greater organization that presaged a readiness to work with the government and other non-resistant groups during the Second World War.

3

An Insidious Enemy within the Gates:
Objection among the Smaller Sects

IF THE HISTORIC peace churches in Canada faced many "days of anxiety" due to confusion over the limits and mechanics of their exemption, they enjoyed greater security than members of the smaller pacifist or millenarian churches who also sought exemption, including the Christadelphians, Plymouth Brethren, and International Bible Students Association (IBSA). In certain respects, the beliefs of these sects were similar to those of the peace churches, especially in the biblical grounds for their non-resistance. However, the former were handicapped by their size, by not being specifically named in any previous Order-in-Council, and by public attitudes that ranged from ignorance to acute antipathy. Members of these denominations faced an uphill battle. Some few, such as the Christadelphians, finally succeeded in their efforts to be recognized as pacifist churches. Most did not, so that many of their adherents suffered harsh punishment and imprisonment for failing to obey military orders. Perhaps partly because they provoked the widest antagonism, the Bible Students faced probably the greatest obloquy. The experiences of these COs reveal that their treatment was closely tied to perceptions about their denomination's respectability, including its history, ties to Britain, and ability to present itself as well organized.

The group that arguably had the most trouble with the Military Service Act was the IBSA, also known as Millennial Dawnites or Russellites, after their founder, Charles Taze Russell, and today more familiar as Jehovah's Witnesses.[1] Russell was a businessman from Pittsburgh, Pennsylvania, who rebelled against the doctrine of eternal torment for the wicked that had been part of his Presbyterian upbringing. In 1872, he formed a class with a few friends interested in studying the Bible to learn more about Christ's Second Coming, and they became convinced that the Second Coming would be invisible except "with the eye of understanding." Russell expressed these views in his first pamphlet, "The Object and Manner of the Lord's Return," and began publication of the *Watch Tower* in 1879.[2]

Like members of the historic peace churches, Bible Students are strict biblicists. They also share a common belief in the sinfulness of the world and avoid accommodation with it in matters such as voting. However, they have a much stronger view of the iniquity of present conditions, seeing "the world around them as satanically ruled, and the religious, political, and economic institutions which support it as deserving of destruction."[3] Also like peace church members, they generally refuse military service. However, Bible Students are not pacifists in the strict sense, in that their objection is not to bearing arms per se, but to doing so in an earthly army: "When the time comes to fight for God, no Jehovah's Witness will conscientiously object."[4] Theirs is an apocalyptic religion, and adherents believe that Christ returned invisibly to the earth in 1914. This element of doctrine acted to intensify both their religious zeal and their unpopularity. During the war, the imminence of their expected Armageddon increased the fervour of their proselytizing and the consequent irritation of their neighbours.

Canadians were probably annoyed less by the Bible Students' canvassing than by their condemnation of many doctrines, institutions, and practices integral to mainstream Christianity. Their unpopularity, especially in Quebec, stemmed mostly from their strong anti-clericalism and the fact that they attributed the current debauchery of the world in large part to Satan's working through the Roman Catholic Church, although the Protestant Churches were also implicated.[5] During the war, two of their publications, the *Unfinished Mystery* and *Bible Students' Monthly,* were outlawed under Canadian censorship regulations because of their attacks on organized religion in general and Catholicism in particular.[6] However, according to James Penton, individual Bible Students initially did not suffer much for this attitude, which tended to focus on their leadership.[7] As the war dragged on this changed, due to a dangerous concatenation of factors: Bible Students' increasingly vociferous message coincided with their adamant refusal to participate in a war that was not only popular, but seen as just and Christian. The coupling of their religious beliefs with their conscientious objection seems to have led to the hardening of public attitudes.

Although increasingly notorious, they were not a large denomination. The 1901 census recorded no International Bible Students in Canada and only 518 in 1911. At one tribunal appeal during the First World War, a lawyer acting for the sect estimated its membership as "in the neighbourhood of one thousand students or members scattered throughout the various large centres of population."[8] By the 1921 census, 6,678 Canadians gave their religious affiliation as International Bible Student. This growth may have had an influence on the sect's perceived threat.

From the beginning of the First World War, Bible Students were some of the most visible objectors. Quite often the first direct discussion of conscientious objection in Canadian newspapers concerns an affidavit that Bible Students of military age signed in 1916 and then filed with the commanding officer in each military district in the country. The affidavit was widely quoted: "I am averse to bearing arms or rendering personal military service under conditions as subscribed by 'An Act Respecting the Militia and Defence of Canada.' I make this affidavit for the purpose of exemption from liability to service. I rest my claim for exemption as follows; I am a Christian and the religious doctrines I believe and hold preclude me from bearing arms. I am a member of the International Bible Students' Association and subscribe and am in harmony with its doctrines."[9] Although the Military Service Act had not yet been promulgated, the Militia Act included provision for compulsory military service. The IBSA seems to have foreseen conscription and probably that its own exemption status would be uncertain. Conscription in Britain, and the inclusion of an exemption clause on the grounds of conscientious objection to military service, had been widely reported in the newspapers, and it is likely that the Bible Students were preparing for a comparable situation in this country. They were also aware of exemption given to the historic peace churches, as it had been discussed in Russell's *The New Creation.*[10] More plainly, the 15 November 1915 issue of the *Watch Tower* had published excerpts from the Canadian Militia Act of 1906, showing that it entitled conscientious objectors to exemption from military service. In the 15 February 1916 issue of the *Watch Tower,* the editor, obedient to a directive from Russell's legal advisor, Joseph Franklin Rutherford, advised Bible Students between the ages of seventeen and a half and sixty to submit a letter and an affidavit to their local commanding officers of militia.

A sworn affidavit seemed to offer protection in the language of the government. Rutherford, an American, was an attorney who had occasionally acted as a judge, and this seems to have affected the character of IBSA relations with government both during and after the war. The litigiousness of the Jehovah's Witnesses, and their success in legal challenges, has been frequently remarked upon: "The Witnesses have been masters at appealing to Caesar. Although they regard the political process as fundamentally immoral, they have been quite willing to use certain democratic rights to gain their ends."[11] Their greater comfort in the world of the courts was another signal difference from the relative unworldliness of the historic peace churches.

However, whatever the legality of their position, it did not accord with popular opinion. W.H. Chittick, a London, Ontario, justice of the peace, wrote to the minister of militia and defence about being asked to witness the affidavits: "I have the honour to call your attention in being called by telephone to a law office to administer the oath to a number of persons who are taking advantage of the Militia Act, which, I am sorry to say, allows such persons, especially in time of war. Had I the authority, I would much prefer to sit on a Court Martial and to try them on a charge of disloyalty ... It is certainly an unpleasant duty for me to swear in such a class of men who should be offering their services on behalf of the Empire."[12] It is interesting that, despite his personal misgivings, the justice of the peace also saw the IBSA stance as legally protected. H.J. Ross, a Montreal justice of the peace, was somewhat gentler. He referred to the Bible Students as a "cult" but wrote to Brigadier-General Wilson, the commander of Military District 4, that "I am, as a Public Officer, bound to swear any one desiring to make deposition. It is not my right to reason why. As a Retired Captain of the Militia with some sixteen or seventeen years service at my credit, and with two sons at the front, one being away over a year, I may have my own opinion about this affair, but these men may have theirs as well, even if it does not agree with you and me."[13] Wilson was more heated in his reply: "There is no necessity for these forms being sent in, as none of these blackguards have been asked to enlist, nor is there any probability of conscription being enforced. I wish that we were going to have conscription and I would take damn good care that every one of those fellows would be enlisted."[14] It is curious, especially in view of such an assertion, that none of the Bible Students whose affidavits to Wilson are included in the Department of National Defence file devoted to "IBSA COs" are recorded as being drafted into the CEF.[15] The men were from Montreal, and the climate in Quebec may have been more congenial to those who objected to the war on any grounds, although they probably would have come before English rather than French tribunals. Also, simply defaulting may have been easier there. However, the fact that those who filed affidavits with the officer commanding Military District 4, nearly a dozen men, supplied their names and addresses would seem to make them easy targets for those rounding up defaulters. Probably, it was simply decided that the intransigence of pacifist IBSA conscripts made drafting them more trouble than it was worth.

The existence of this group of objectors would also seem to weaken the conclusion of the post-war "Report on the Administration of the Military Service Act in Military District No. Four (Montreal)," which reported of COs that "very few draftees of this class were encountered in this District – probably not more than a dozen in all; and these were very easily disposed of by the Officer Commanding the Depot Battalions – a short period of detention in each case producing a complete cure."[16] The presence of at least one group of COs that the government and military authorities chose to ignore also complicates the problems of defining them and determining their numbers in Canada.

The Bible Students' assertion of their pacifism, made in advance of being actually compelled to take up arms, may have been intended to prevent their refusal to enlist from being seen as the knee-jerk reaction of the slacker. Mainstream

Canada did not read the legal document along these lines. "Fears of conscription have awakened some half-dozen eligibles to the fact that they have a conscience," reported the *Toronto Globe*.[17] The signing of affidavits was also clearly an organized action, generally a good and necessary attribute in assessing whether an exemption on the grounds of conscience could be made. However, in the popular imagination, the degree of organization possessed by the Bible Students, rather than lending credence to their claims, took on a sinister aspect. The *London Free Press,* perceiving German roots and influence at work, commented,

> It is thought by certain military men that the propaganda has an ulterior motive, and that it emanates from pro-German quarters, and is an attempt to injure recruiting. However this may be, the military authorities regard the International Bible Students' Association as an insidious enemy within the gates, which needs watching. The affidavit forms used by the conscientious objector are legally drawn up and witnessed by a Magistrate. They are specially printed for the purpose for which they are designed. This fact is regarded as significant of a determination to spare no expense in a propaganda to spread a spirit of craven and hypocritical piety among those who are eligible for military service.[18]

Already marginalized, the Bible Students simply aroused suspicion in their attempts to avail themselves of the law. Legitimate conscientious objectors, it seems, were supposed to be unworldly.

The *Free Press* saw a further danger to the Canadian war machine. The IBSA affidavits presented "a splendid opportunity to the slacker, as all he will have to do is to become a member of the International Bible Students' Association, and he can face a battalion of recruiting sergeants with impunity."[19] In a letter to the *Toronto Daily Star* protesting the paper's sarcastic description of the trial of IBSA member Arthur Bourgeois, L.S. Ward reacted to this reading of the situation. Aware of the low social status of the Bible Students, his letter also responded, ruefully, to the "splendid opportunity" that joining the denomination offered to those wishing to avoid war service: "No one need be afraid of the town being full of followers of Pastor Russell, not even to escape going to war."[20] For Ward, the unpopularity of the IBSA was such that membership could not appeal to any significant number of Canadian men, even if it seemed to promise exemption from conscription.

Ward also defended religious COs more generally, asking, "Why should a religious conscientious objector be sneered at in a free country like Canada? There is as much difference between a religious and a political conscientious objector as there is between two poles."[21] Although he did not mention the historic peace churches directly, Ward apparently wanted the Bible Students to be accorded the same recognition and sense of legitimacy that some, especially the Quakers, had – as good Christians adhering to unorthodox but understandable beliefs. For him, the political objector belonged in a different category: it was he who was being selfish and ungrateful to his country. In Canada, the nature of the Military Service Act, in specifically offering exemption to members of particular churches, worked to isolate COs of various religious and political stripes, encouraging partisanship and keeping an organized movement from coalescing.[22]

Like any man unhappy with his tribunal decision, a Bible Student who was refused exemption could resort to appeal tribunals. The appeal of David Cooke, a thirty-six-year-old wood machinist and Bible Student from Winnipeg, became the test case for whether this group could claim exemption under the MSA conscience clause. The first objector to have his appeal rejected by the appeal courts, he was sentenced by Sir Hugh John Macdonald to two years in Stony Mountain Penitentiary. The *Manitoba Free Press* recorded that "he received his sentence smilingly, stating that he obeyed the law of God in refusing to fight against his enemies and recited several passages of scripture to prove that he had done right."[23]

Cooke then appealed his tribunal verdict to the central appeal judge, Supreme Court Justice Lyman P. Duff, who set the precedent for further decisions by supporting the judgment of the lower court. One problem, for Duff, was the fact that the IBSA had no written creed or articles of faith through which to ascertain its beliefs about non-resistance and military service. Instead, its lawyer, Mr. Davidson, offered the affidavits and some works by Russell, "which are expositions of the Bible as he expounded them and the doctrines set forth in these works are generally accepted by the adherents." Justice Duff did not find the evidence presented to him to be "entirely self-consistent," in terms of "whether a member of the association might conscientiously under the compulsion of legal necessity, engage in combatant military service."[24] Pastor Russell's proscription against military service was not unilateral; ultimately, he left the decision up to the individual.

However, Duff rejected the appeal on different grounds: "The evidence before me does not justify the conclusion that these groups or associations so-called, either individually or collectively come within the description – 'organized religious denomination existing and well recognized in Canada' within the contemplation of the Military Service Act."[25] Duff found "much room for doubt" about whether the primary purpose of the association was for a common worship, and he was further perturbed by the lack of conditions for membership.

The Bible Students were deemed ineligible for exemption under the clause because they were simply not recognized as a religious organization.[26]

The difficulties encountered by the Canadian Bible Students were not peculiar to their place or time. They faced similar situations in the United States, Australia, and New Zealand, and their objection was likewise not recognized in the Second World War. Such consistency seems to go beyond distaste at their religious idiosyncrasies. In "The Nation State and War Resistance," Nigel James Young argues that conscientious objection can be granted to small quietist groups because they do not challenge state sovereignty. This describes the situation in First World War Canada. We have seen, for instance, the respectful Mennonite attitude regarding government authority, the Quaker denial of new members during the war, and Ottawa's general willingness to tolerate their non-resistant stance. The Bible Students were different and problematic. Young shows that they could be seen as the thin edge of the wedge: "Active conversionist and absolutist, they are not good citizens in other respects, and draw straight from the working class."[27] This argument seems to hold true for Canada during the First World War. Although an analysis of the socio-economic background of Canadian Bible Students is beyond the scope of this book, the newspaper reports of tribunals, when they list occupation, show a definite working-class base. (See Table 1 in the appendix for occupations of conscientious objectors.)

Like the IBSA, the other churches that were refused exemption on the grounds that they were insufficiently organized seem to have lacked either a unified or unilaterally pacifist response to military conscription. The absence of church archives for most of these denominations, along with the destruction of tribunal records, severely hampers efforts to gain a clear picture of, for instance, the Church of Christ or Disciple of Christ objector, or the prevalence of objection within these groups.[28] Frustratingly vague newspaper articles give only hints of their response. One account in the *Manitoba Free Press,* for example, mentions that "Numerous cases of conscientious objectors are now coming before the tribunals. In practically every instance however, the claims are being disallowed. It is stated that a number of such applications have come from members of the Pentecostal mission."[29] However numerous these claims were, the churches do not seem to have wholly supported them. When Reverend Joseph MacKenzie from the Church of Christ was refused a chaplaincy, apparently on the grounds that "the brotherhood had been remiss in sending its quota of men to the Front, and that it had a number of conscientious objectors," church members drafted a letter of protest. Not wanting to be put down as "slackers," they objected to being treated "as one of the fancy churches that did not count."[30] Despite the presence of pacifists within the denomination, the Church of Christ in general seems to have joined in the spirit of wartime rivalry among Canadian churches, who competed with each other in their loud support of the war and the number of their members who enlisted.[31]

THE PLYMOUTH BRETHREN, which also drew largely from the working class, likewise failed to receive the hoped-for exemption. Reverend John Nelson Darby founded the sect in 1830 in Plymouth, England, and though it is older than the IBSA, it too subscribes to millenarian beliefs. Like many other denominations seeking exemption on conscientious grounds, the Plymouth Brethren saw themselves as "in the world but not of it ... they have been called upon to be a separate people unto God, pilgrims in a foreign land."[32] They take the Bible literally and, like the recognized historic peace churches, place much emphasis on the directive not to be "unequally yoked with unbelievers." Also like the peace churches, they downplay leadership, a problematic factor in their dealings with government: "They do not, therefore, allow one man, however good he may be, or however much he may have been owned of the Lord as a servant of his, to take a place of authority in the assembly for worship, for by doing so they would hinder the free operations of the Spirit of God."[33] They were also a small denomination. As is the case for the other, more loosely affiliated denominations, arriving at precise membership figures is difficult. The 1911 census records 3,438 Plymouth Brethren, a number that grew to 6,482 by 1921 – although reliance on these figures is rendered problematic because of its repudiation of denominational labels.[34]

When conscription legislation was the talk of the day, two Plymouth Brethren wrote to Prime Minister Borden, thanking him from refraining thus far from implementing it. Unlike the petitions sent him by other denominations, this was not signed on behalf of a group: instead, its signatories described themselves merely as "Christian Canadian Citizens." Linking their problems with those of other patriotic Canadians, who probably did not want to kill anybody either, they put the dilemma of conscientious objection simply and eloquently: "We are aware that in taking the stand which we have some will consider us to be 'shirkers' but this is far from being the case. Some are bound by what seems like a tragic fate to take the lives of our fellow-men whilst they only wish to give their lives for their country – on the other hand some of us are bound to appear the enemies of our country for conscience sake when we wish to serve her with all our powers."[35]

The signatories of the petition, David D. Priestman and George Arthur Wigmore, reminded Borden that exemption on conscientious grounds had been permitted in Britain and hoped that "the liberty of individual conscience" would be similarly protected in this country. It was not to be, at least not on the individual grounds the two men anticipated. Wigmore was drafted on 16 May 1918.

He was twenty-one, married, and working as a bookkeeper in Victoria, British Columbia. He accepted non-combatant service and left Vancouver on Boxing Day 1918 for Siberia, as part of the Sixteenth Field Ambulance.[36]

Thirty-one-year-old Robert F. Elliott became the test case for whether this denomination's pacifism would be recognized. When his local Calgary tribunal rejected his claim of CO status, he appealed to the Central Appeal Tribunal. Elliott had applied for military service exemption on the grounds that he was a minister of the gospel in the Plymouth Brethren Church. Commenting that, if he were a minister, he would not come under MSA jurisdiction and would thus be exempt from service regardless of his denomination, Justice Duff found the Plymouth Brethren not to have sufficient grounds for exemption. Although Duff credited Elliott with presenting the Plymouth Brethren case "with great clearness as well as obvious sincerity," he based his refusal on the fact that Elliott "Did not dispute that the taking part in combatant military service would not, according to the corporate views of the Plymouth Brethren, be regarded as a disqualification for membership; wickedness alone, he said, would be a ground of exclusion, and that would not necessarily be regarded as wickedness in all circumstances."[37] The church, then, was not included in the exemption clause because it did not impose harsh enough, or consistent enough, penalties on those who transgressed its pacifist tenets. Adherents of sects with such flexibility made up the largest part of unrecognized conscientious objectors; along with the Plymouth Brethren, these included IBSA and Pentecostal Assemblies members.[38]

Several Plymouth Brethren persisted in their objection despite not being recognized. Sydney Mitchell was a twenty-one-year-old farmer from Forest, Ontario, who, after the failure of his appeals, was sentenced to two years in Kingston Penitentiary. The *Toronto Globe* reported his trial: "Mitchell was brought before a court a couple of weeks ago, but was given another chance. He claimed that he is a Plymouth Brethren member, and, as such, he would not take up arms against his fellow men. When his uniform was issued to him at Ordnance Stores he refused to accept it, and his humiliation and sentence before the paraded battalion at Queen's Park Camp followed."[39] Tunker Ernest John Swalm was detained with a Plymouth Brother while awaiting trial for his refusal to obey military orders. In his memoirs, he recalls the difficulty caused by this group's reluctance to take on a denominational label:

> "What church do you belong to?" asked the colonel.
> "The Church of Jesus Christ."
> "Do you have a creed?"
> "Yes, the Bible," replied my friend.

"Where do you originate?"

"At Calvary."

"But where are your headquarters?"

"Heaven."

"Don't get smart, kid," snapped the officer.

Although the officer's frustration is understandable, given that he was apparently looking for the evidence of organization required to exempt the young man, Swalm explains that "the colonel did not know that the Plymouth Brethren boy was answering sincerely in the tradition of his accepted belief."[40] In repudiating denominational labels, the Plymouth Brethren ran up hard against the Canadian government's decision to base recognition on denominational, rather than individual beliefs. That it had strong pacifist principles is evident, but its deliberate lack of structure and organization was a serious handicap in a wartime society impatient with the nuances of radical Christianity.

RADICAL CHRISTIANS LIKE the Plymouth Brethren, the Seventh-day Adventists also had proscriptions against worldly military service. The denomination grew out of the Millerite movement of 1844, when a group of as many as fifty thousand Americans believed that they would witness the Second Coming of Christ and be delivered from the destruction awaiting the world. It was officially organized in 1863 by Ellen Harmon White and her husband, James White.[41] Like the other denominations with prohibitions against military service, Adventists base their pacifism on biblical proscriptions against killing. They focus on the Ten Commandments in particular. A declaration made during the American Civil War by the executive committee of the General Conference of Adventists explained, "If there is any portion of the Bible which we, as a people, can point to more than another as our creed, it is the law of the ten commandments, which we regard as the supreme law, and each precept of which we take in its most obvious and literal import. The fourth of these commandments requires cessation from labor on the seventh day of the week, the sixth prohibits the taking of life, neither of which, in our view, could be observed while doing military duty. Our practice has uniformly been consistent with these principles."[42] Like the millenarian IBSA, the group had a strong missionary and publishing focus. That it was recognized whereas the IBSA was not seems to have been due to its willingness to participate in non-combatant military service. The focus, for the Seventh-day Adventists, was on obeying the commandments rather than biblical proscriptions against being unequally yoked with unbelievers or enjoining non-resistance to evil, so they were willing to participate in medical non-combatant units. The historian of Canadian Adventists, J. Ernest

Monteith, explains that Seventh-day Adventists prefer to be known as "conscientious cooperators," thus emphasizing the positive and active aspects of their response to conscription.[43]

This too was a small group: when the war broke out, there were only about three thousand Adventists in Canada. When conscription threatened, H.M.J. Richards, president of the Ontario Conference, had sent a petition to Borden outlining their beliefs: "Seventh-day Adventists are a denomination of Christians duly organized in all the Provinces of Canada. They believe in salvation through faith in Jesus and accept the Ten Commandments construed in their most literal and obvious sense in the light of the teachings and life of Christ as their rule of faith." Mentioning their organization, the petition also emphasized their good citizenship and their doctrines stressing respect for authority. This combination of submission and dissent resembled that of the Anabaptist churches, and marks a clear and recognizable aspect of Canadian pacifism during the First World War. As Richards went on, "The same conscience that makes them [Seventh-day Adventists] willing to endure any sacrifice in order to obey the moral law of God as they understand it, also requires them to support civil government in all its divinely appointed sphere of authority and to loyally and willingly fulfill all the requirements of citizenship if not inconsistent with their hope of eternal life."[44] He called upon several precedents of recognition for religious pacifism. It is somewhat curious that, unlike for the IBSA, the degree of familiarity with the legal system that this entailed did not rouse public or government suspicion. Justice Duff recognized the sect as sufficiently organized, and with sufficiently strong prohibitions against fighting, to earn its members exemption on conscientious grounds.[45] However, several young men were nonetheless ill-treated and imprisoned.

Three of these were from Alberta and managed to stay together as a group for much of their ordeal. James Bennett Wagner, at twenty-six years of age, was the oldest. "I suppose that is why it became my lot to do more of the talking than the others," he recalled. On his army attestation paper, he gave his occupation as "student for mission work," which meant he was also probably better versed in explaining his denomination's stance than the other objectors with whom he was drafted. Only a year younger was Max Popow, a Russian-born farmer from Lacombe, Alberta. At twenty-one, Floyd Edwin Jones was the youngest of the group and another farmer, from Strathcona, Alberta.[46]

The young men were drafted into the army training camp at Calgary on 15 April 1918. When they informed the sergeant-major of their principles, he first replied that "that [would] be all right" but later put the men into military detention when they refused to drill on their Sabbath (Saturday). Wagner records that the three men "tried to persuade those in authority to transfer us to the

Medical Corps, where we could conscientiously help the sick on the Sabbath; but no, they would not do that, for we were all in good health, and they wanted us as common infantrymen." The military later made the concession. Wagner spent six weeks in jail at Lethbridge before he was transferred to the Medical Corps, where he met Jones, who had been transferred there earlier. The three Adventists faced yet more problems: their refusal to do unnecessary work on their Sabbath had annoyed the sergeant-major, who complained "I haven't time to be running after you all the time." Other soldiers expressed their frustrations more violently, as Wagner recalled: "One night [after] Floyd and I had gone to sleep, into the tent came a mob of disguised soldiers. They jumped upon us, beat us, and smeared us with axle grease ... A few days later we were mobbed again in broad daylight. When they slipped the canvass bag over my head and carried me out of the tent, I did not resist them, but only offered a silent prayer to the God whom I was serving. Without any injury to me, after smearing my body with tar, they set me free."[47] A few days later, the two were released from the army.

ANOTHER GROUP THAT managed to gain exemption, at least to a degree, was the Christadelphians. This small denomination was founded by a doctor named John Thomas in the United States just prior to its Civil War. It consisted of small groups called ecclesias, who met informally in adherents' houses. When asked what Christadelphians should do if war broke out, Thomas replied that they should avoid the violence: "Our conviction is that Christians should leave the devil to fight his own battles; and that if he sought to compel them to serve in his ranks, they ought to refuse to do so ... Let the potsherds of the earth strive together and Christians stand aloof."[48] The outbreak of the American Civil War prompted the group to incorporate itself. In the North, the law gave exemption to those "who belonged to a denomination conscientiously opposed to the bearing of arms." Specifically in order to gain this exemption, Thomas gave the group a name, basing it on the Greek Christou adelphoi, meaning "Brethren of or in Christ." He signed certificates for men of conscription age, verifying that they were members of this sect and that "the denomination constituted of the associations or ecclesias of this Name, conscientiously opposes, and earnestly protests against 'Brethren in Christ' having anything to do with politics in worldly strife, or arms-bearing in the service of the Sin-powers of the world under any conceivable circumstances or conditions whatever; regarding it as a course of conduct disloyal to the Deity in Christ, their Lord and King, and perilous to their eternal welfare!"[49] That the very reason for the incorporation of the denomination was based around non-resistance and conscientious objection underscores the importance of this position for the Christadelphians.[50]

In his study of Christadelphian teaching concerning the proper relationship with the state, E.R. Evans explains the reasoning behind the sect's refusal to join the military. Like other non-resistant groups, Christadelphians focus on biblical directives against killing but also advance a more theological argument. Christadelphians do not believe in the immortality of the soul. In this belief system Jesus conquered death through the Resurrection. Through belief and obedience to God, humanity shares in this victory and consequent immortality. If one does not participate in this salvation, then the consequence is death, which is seen as God's just punishment of sin. "Thus if a Christadelphian kills another man in battle – a man who has not responded to the call of the Gospel – he has deprived that man of any hope, whatsoever, of eternal salvation. Moreover he places his own salvation in jeopardy."[51]

Like the Mennonites, Christadelphians faced a problem when it came to proving denominational membership. They attend a Sunday School at their ecclesia until they feel ready to be baptized. This is an individual decision, not to be affected by age or any "exterior influence or pressure." Recalling the wartime situation, John Evans remarked, "It was therefore deemed advisable under the circumstances to recommend to these senior students subject to call up, that if they were contemplating baptism in the indefinite future and if their convictions were such that they, in any event, would take a stand as a conscientious objector to military service, they should consider baptism in the immediate future in order not to place themselves in an unnecessarily difficult situation."[52] Although the sharp rise in baptisms experienced by Ontario's Old Order Mennonite Church in 1917 does not seem to have been repeated here, the war years were marked by the baptism of a proportionately large number of Christadelphians. E.R. Evans explains, "The Great War was indeed a unique event which stirred the Christadelphian body in depth. Of the one thousand and two Canadian members alive during the war years, two hundred and seventy (27%) were baptized from 1914 to 1918."[53] It is impossible to judge whether this occurred because baptism offered them the chance of exemption, or, less cynically, because the world crisis moved them to embrace their faith.

Also like that of the Anabaptist peace groups, Christadelphian dissent was shaped by tenets emphasizing obedience to government strictures: "The Christadelphians are a law-abiding people. They not only obey the laws of the land but they also promote obedience to the law, both by advocacy and example. They do not engage in acts of civil disobedience nor in public demonstrations; nor do they engage in the stirring up of social unrest."[54] This point was frequently reiterated in their correspondence with the Canadian government. A letter to the prime minister, written when the conscription bill was introduced, emphasized "that they are a peace abiding folk and loyal subjects of His Majesty the

King: submitting themselves to all Laws and ordinances in perfect good will."[55] The Christadelphians' tendency to be "good citizens" outside of wartime, their offer of other forms of service, and their use of the obedience and duty discourse that typified their more bellicose fellow citizens contributed to their ultimate exemption.

The way in which they proceeded and the reasons for their success illuminate Ottawa's attitude regarding conscientious objection. The Christadelphians have rather helpfully (since many government records have been destroyed) kept a comparatively well-documented record of their response, as an organization, to the conscription legislation. Their first reaction was alarm: the exemption on grounds of conscience was conditional only, something to which they felt they could not accede:

> It was seen at once the Act fell away behind the English Army Act No. 2., whereas we had felt assured Canada would not enact provisions inferior to those of the Mother Country. The Canadian Act, as it stood, provided the granting of absolute exemption from all military service for all and every consideration but religious conscientious objection; which, from a Christadelphian standpoint, means there was to be no exemption at all, for it is a well-known fact, that in the army, non-combatant service is a misnomer, every man is a soldier and must fight when called upon to do so.[56]

This sense of crisis impelled the Christadelphians to launch a well-organized lobby aimed at the federal government so as to strengthen their position. The Canadian group was quite small; thus, as it lobbied for exemption, it was able to append a full roll of its membership, complete with ages, addresses, and occupations, to its correspondence with Ottawa.[57] A later report from their standing committee, which had been formed to interact with the necessary authorities to gain exemption from military conscription on conscientious grounds, indicates that only seventy-three Christadelphians came under the operation of the act. Of these, forty-nine were exempted from combatant service – some because of religious belief, some because their occupations were considered of national importance, and some for medical reasons. Interestingly, the report simply notes that the men were exempted on these three grounds, without specifying further. The Christadelphians seem to have followed the general trend among Canadian conscientious objectors of accepting whatever grounds for exemption they could get. Two, A.V. Buck from Manitoulin Island and Allen F. Smith of Toronto, renounced their faith to join the army.[58] Two accepted non-combatant service and were excommunicated. Nineteen were imprisoned for varying terms. Two of those imprisoned – John Evans and Louis Alexander Cotton – were among those Canadian objectors shipped overseas, a policy that represented the nadir of government treatment of COs. At the front, disobeying an order, likely behaviour from a CO, was grounds for being shot.[59] Two died, one of influenza in jail, and one after being taken out of jail to an asylum.[60]

Unlike the Bible Students or the Plymouth Brethren, the members of the standing committee quickly recognized that the best means of gaining exemption lay not in efforts to establish the verity of their objections, but, rather, the authenticity of their organization: "This seemed to us extraordinarily important, because the Act shows that a man's own individual conscientious objection to combatant service would not avail him anything unless he was a member in good faith of a recognized religious denomination; so that every means we knew had to be bent to this end particularly." They were somewhat perturbed by this, as "we had no organization such as is common to religious bodies." But they were able to respond in an organized manner. And, like the members of the historic peace churches, they pleaded their case in terms that showed a sensitivity to the government's dilemma:

> A careful record is kept of all our members. It is not easy to become a member of our body; candidates must have a studious knowledge of the Old and New Testaments, and be well grounded in Christadelphian doctrines. The man who shirks his duty to his country cannot find unworthy shelter by joining our body. He has to appear before a competent Board of Examiners after we have knowledge he has been a Bible student, or educated in the home of a Christadelphian, or is one of our Sunday School scholars. There need not, therefore, be any fear that the enforcement of the Military Service Act will add unusual numbers of adherents to our body.[61]

Although they did not go as far as the Society of Friends, who suspended the creation of new members for the duration of the war, the Christadelphians promised that their beliefs would remain confined to a very small minority and would not affect the war effort. A letter to Borden emphasized that their position presented no danger to the status quo: "The Christadelphian Church collectively nor individually are not in any way affiliated with any 'conscientious objectors' movement nor are agitators against conscription or any governmental measure whatsoever."[62] Certainly, a strong and organized pacifist movement could not be based upon reactions such as these. Although this approach succeeded in keeping Quakers and Christadelphians relatively safe, it deprived other objectors of leaders and support.

Before the implementation of the Military Service Act until after the Armistice, the Christadelphians sent delegations to anyone they thought could help their campaign for exemption. Their petitions showed an awareness of parliamentary language and procedure. They also found a well-placed and sympathetic ear in Lieutenant-Colonel H.A.C. Machin, the director of the Military Service Branch of the Department of Justice: "The real friend of the genuine conscientious objector was Lt.-Col. H.A.C. Machin. He spoke firmly in his opinion as to what ought to be done on their behalf, and deplored the tardiness which had arisen in bringing about necessary provisions for alternative works of national import-ance." Machin helped the standing committee by impressing upon it the amount of work the government faced and advising it that unless it pressed its case at Ottawa, it would be "snowed under and forgotten."[63]

His sympathy was neither unique nor overly controversial. In one of the only House of Commons debates about the conscientious objection clause in the Military Service Bill, members discussed who would be included. Solicitor General Arthur Meighen and Minister of Justice C.J. Doherty explained the intentions of this exemption clause to the MPs. In response to a query about whether the local tribunals would be adequately versed in the theology of the various sects to determine legitimate exemption, the following exchange took place:

> *Mr. Meighen:* It is not a question of theology, but merely of the existence of the denomination and its recognition in the community. It is a question of fact which the local tribunals will decide in the first instance.
> *Mr. Marcil:* My understanding is that this relates to the Mennonites, the Doukh-obors, and the Quakers.
> *Sir George Foster:* And the Christadelphians.
> *Mr. Meighen:* These would be included; there may be more.[64]

That the Christadelphians were mentioned by name, and by a Cabinet member – Sir George Foster was minister of trade and commerce – anticipated their success at gaining recognition where other sects failed. The Christadelphians were aware of this and sympathized with those who did not garner equal gov-ernment support:

> Whatever we may say, or our critics may think, our young men, on the whole, have been better treated in camps and in the hands of the military generally than most other conscientious objectors. The "Plymouth Brethren," "The Disciples," "The Christian Brethren," and the "Bible Students" have a very dark chapter to record. The light was always with us. It was always recognized wherever we went that the Government intended to make some provision for us. There was not one of us who went to Ottawa but was treated with the greatest respect, and at

the time the armistice was signed, our labor with the Government had come to a fruition, and had war not concluded, our young men imprisoned would have been released in accordance with the conditions of the Order-in-Council prepared to meet cases like ours, and those to be called would have been given the option of work of national importance.[65]

Although one cannot definitely say whether this prediction would have been fulfilled, the Christadelphians' confidence seems firmly grounded. Their sense of being better treated than most other conscientious objectors seems to have held true in Britain as well.[66]

The Christadelphians in Canada were further helped by their British connections, upon which they drew for support and precedent. After the passing of the MSA, they sent a petition to the governor general in which they frequently referred to the successful efforts of their British counterparts in gaining recognition for their non-resistant beliefs. They appended a copy of the exemption certificates issued Christadelphians by the British authorities. They also included a copy of an Australian Christadelphian magazine, the *Shield,* "to emphasize our statement that Christadelphians everywhere were actuated by the same characteristics and disposings towards governments."[67] Whereas the international connections of the IBSA seemed suggestive of a pro-German conspiracy, the Christadelphians' British presence appears to have been read as indicative of a reassuring historicity and stability. If the mother country had seen fit to exempt members of this denomination, surely it was incumbent upon Canada to do the same.

That the Christadelphians were more successful in their quest for recognition than some of the other groups could also be credited to the fact that they could call upon a relatively well-documented history. Ensuring that Ottawa knew this was the initial point in their first petition.[68] Having a long-standing organization, and one recognized by previous and other national governments, put them nearly into the category of the historic peace churches and made the Borden administration more comfortable about allowing their objection.

In January 1918, the Christadelphians gained recognition under the MSA. After this date, as far as Christadelphian COs were concerned, tribunals confined themselves to two questions: whether an appellant was a bona fide member of the denomination and whether he had a true objection as an individual.[69] The denomination did not succeed, however, in its effort to make a certificate of church membership sufficient grounds for exemption in and of itself, or to gain exemption for those who joined the church or reached age nineteen after the Military Service Act was passed. These had been granted to the historic peace churches, whose ranks, at least implicitly, the Christadelphians were anxious to join.

Like the peace churches, the Christadelphians emphasized that a British citizen had a duty to fight for his country. They saw their own civic responsibilities as different only in terms of military service. Christadelphians tried to make their patriotism and awareness of the duties of citizenship as public as possible. Elder Edwin Hill sent a circular to exemption tribunals, the contents of which were reported in the *Toronto Daily Star:* "Our church in Canada has put itself on record, as was done in England, Australia, New Zealand, offering, if granted total exemption, to be ready to go to the ends of the earth to honor the King and his councillors in works of benevolence and mercy for our country and to do any work of national importance, under civilian conditions in trades and manufacturing and agriculture."[70] The Christadelphian Standing Committee made repeated requests that the Canadian government institute work of national importance in which conscientious objectors could participate, as had been done in England and the United States. Toronto brothers Arthur and Alfred Hill, both Christadelphians, declared to their tribunal that "they were taught to flee from harm, and that there was no combination of circumstances which would induce them to fight," but they were willing to do work of national importance.[71]

The Christadelphian belief that no earthly justification excused participation in warfare meant hardship for some young men. John Evans, a Christadelphian, was imprisoned for subscribing to it. E.R. Evans, John's son, published an account of his father's experiences as a conscientious objector, *Test Case for Canada '3314545.'* Called up in late 1917, Evans had been refused total exemption and was assigned to non-combatant service. When he refused to cooperate, he was subjected to a series of arrests, courts martial, and military detentions until he was finally discharged on 12 January 1919. During that time, he was subjected to some very harsh treatment. He was severely beaten on a number of occasions, spent nearly a month on starvation diet, and was threatened with death among other punishments.[72] His experience is instructive, for members of the churches discussed in this chapter were involved in the most public instances of coercion and brutality involving COs.

Probably the most widely reported case of the alleged mistreatment of conscientious objectors involved two IBSA members – Robert Litler Clegg, aged thirty-two, and Henry Naish, twenty-one – as well as a Pentecostal, Charles Matheson. Clegg and Naish, clerks from Winnipeg, had been called up on 18 January 1918, their requests for exemption from military service denied. All three suffered abuse at Minto Street Barracks in Winnipeg. For not obeying an order, they were held twice under an ice-cold shower until they either accepted military discipline or collapsed. Matheson broke down and agreed to obey orders. Later, testifying before a court of inquiry, he described the experience:

> [The water] was very cold, and as I stood under it, it got colder, till it became icy cold. My whole body began to heave ... when I would stand with my back to it, he [Provost Sergeant Simpson] would make me turn around and face it, and make me turn my face up to it. I was shading my face with my hand ... he made me take my hand down ... I was beginning to get dazed, and I was tumbling around ... He asked me, "Will you give in now?" I said no. He put me in again ... This went on three or four times ... He said "we will either break you or break your heart" ... I was put into my undershirt and things, and I was dragged away. My body was wet, my hair was wet, I was taken up to the guard room and put in there.[73]

According to his sworn affidavit, which was published in the *Manitoba Free Press,* Clegg's shower apparently lasted for about fifteen minutes, until he fell unconscious and had to be hospitalized. He charged that he was stripped of his clothes and "subjected to a violent treatment of ice-cold water, which was from time to time directed at my neck, shoulders, spine, kidneys, forehead, chest." He was then "violently lashed dry" and subjected to another cold shower treatment: "I was in a semi-conscious state during the greater period of the second treatment, and when taken out, I was seated upon a cold stone slab, which caused me to lose control of myself and become absolutely incapable of any control of my limbs or muscles ... While still wet and in a condition of complete nervous prostration, and helplessness, I was dressed ... dragged on the concrete floor upstairs, through the drill hall, to the place of detention ... Subsequently, while unconscious, I was removed to St. Boniface Hospital."[74] The incident was corroborated by Private Paul Case, who reported that the soldiers of the barracks were "highly incensed over such cruel treatment and have questioned if even Germany can beat it ... We, as men, regret there are those so debased who would tolerate such treatment on human beings when it would be unlawful to mete out such treatment even to a dog." The commander of the depot battalion, Lieutenant-Colonel Osler, played down the event, stating that the matter had been "very much exaggerated." Another "prominent officer who is familiar with the case" compared the incident to "schoolboy pranks" or "ragging."[75]

MLA Fred J. Dixon, one of the few voices of anti-war protest in Canadian politics, brought up the incident in the Manitoba Legislature and promised that he would follow the case very closely.[76] In a letter to T.A. Crerar, the federal minister of agriculture, he suggested that the minister of militia and defence, Major-General S.C. Mewburn, issue a general order about the treatment of conscientious objectors. Dixon wrote, "The day of torture should be past. If there is no other way of dealing with these men, it would be more humane to shoot them at once than to submit them to torture which endangers their reason."[77] The *Manitoba Free Press* published an editorial entitled "Stop It!" cautioning Canada to avoid the "serious mistakes" in Britain's "physical coercion" of its conscientious objectors. The editor refused to credit the claims regarding schoolboy pranks: "It is idle to pretend that, in cases like this, the hazing is the result of spontaneous indignation by the companions of the recalcitrant; these things happen because some one in authority is desirous that they shall happen."[78]

Brigadier-General Ruttan ordered a district court martial to investigate the non-commissioned officer, Provost Sergeant G.J. Simpson, for his part in the hazing, but the court found the charges to be "absolutely groundless," and he was acquitted.[79] Despite some efforts, civil charges were never laid. The court of inquiry took no action regarding the treatment of COs beyond ordering that, in the future, objectors who refused military orders were to be sent to civil prisons.[80] Major-General Mewburn supported his subordinates at Minto Street Barracks and concluded that the affair had been blown out of proportion.[81] Clegg, Naish, and another Bible Student, Francis Wainwright, were convicted by district courts martial and sentenced to two years at Stony Mountain Penitentiary.[82] Later, they were shipped overseas to England.

In describing the brutal treatment, Clegg's statement also makes clear the extent to which he refused to submit to military authority, including refusing to dry himself when wet and freezing because he had been ordered to do so. Probably due to their stronger support structure, "absolutist" COs like Clegg seem to have been more common in Britain than in Canada, but they occasioned the same frustrated, baffled, and sometimes violent response in both countries. When discussing the hazing incident, the registrar under the MSA, E.R. Chapman, said that the three COs were adopting "a most unreasonable attitude." Had they simply shown reason and explained their objections to killing, some other work could surely have been found for them. He remarked that "The best men among the conscientious objectors meet the situation half-way."[83] His was a common attitude; objectors who were willing to take on non-combatant service seemed to accept the same ideas about civil duty and responsibility as their compatriots. Absolutists were often seen as merely stubborn, rather than as men unwilling to negotiate their principles.

The case of David Wells also attracted much attention. Refusing to report when called up for service, he had been charged with desertion. His two-year sentence was intended as something of a deterrent for others contemplating the same course of action. Captain Goddard, the assistant provost marshal who conducted the prosecution, referred to Wells, a twenty-four-year-old Pentecostal who worked as a teamster, and a Bible Student, Charles H. Edwards, as "religious fanatics who attempted to hide behind their religion." The two men were equally adamant in their defiance. When asked to plead, Wells responded, "I plead guilty before man, but not before God."[84] Whereas his rather cocky absolutism earned him a brief newspaper mention, he drew wide notice when he died in Selkirk Asylum a month later. The *Manitoba Free Press* summarized: "Wells became a raving lunatic four days after being taken to the penitentiary on January 24. On February 11 he was removed to the Selkirk asylum, and died on February 18."[85]

A great deal of publicity followed his death – and a great deal of argument over who was to blame. Members of the Pentecostal mission to which Wells belonged claimed that they had been denied admission when trying to visit him at Stony Mountain Penitentiary and that he had entered it a healthy man.[86] The Justice Department reported that Wells was a manic-depressive who had been overcome by shame. Members of his church seem to have blamed his death on intolerable social pressure more than on any sort of ill-treatment in prison. The *Manitoba Free Press* spoke to his pastor: "Rev. Mr. Sweet stated that the death certificate, when he saw it, hinted that probably Wells was wrong mentally for some time. This, according to Mr. Sweet, is not borne out by facts. 'What is the use of a government doing men to death in this fashion?' he said. 'He was sentenced by a judge who knew absolutely nothing about his private life and who was influenced by what he was told by other people.'" The mention of Wells' private life apparently refers to the fact that he was evidently supporting his mother in England, that his father had served a long career in the navy, and that he had two brothers in the British army. Comparing this situation to that of the absolutists in the Minto Street Barracks case is instructive: Charles Matheson's mother made a statement to the *Manitoba Free Press* supporting his position: "I would much rather have my boy put up against that wall and shot than he have to go and fight. He is standing up for his Lord and he will keep on doing so. These boys have suffered for their Lord and will still suffer and then they will not fight."[87] Clearly, Matheson had support at home for his absolutist stance; Wells did not. What his mental state was when he entered prison, we cannot know; the speed of his decline is certainly shocking, whatever his mental health. But his stance was a very lonely and unpopular one, and it seems that he could not sustain the confidence with which he faced his tribunal. Although Wells' physical and psychological isolation from his family would have been at least somewhat mitigated by the support of his church, guilt and worry over his mother's support probably added to the strain. One CO in Britain described the pressure and isolation he and his fellow pacifists faced: "No normal person likes the prospect of being sentenced to death, but the prospect caused infinitely less anxiety and mental anguish to the C.O.s than the fact that they found themselves up against the war-fever – not only of their countrymen at large, but of their neighbours and even some members of their own families."[88] The lack of an organization along the lines of the British NCF meant that, in Canada, COs, unless they had some church support, were isolated from each other as well.

Although a CO's church could offer him spiritual and emotional backing, often it could do little to protect him from military coercion. Wells' church, not yet organized into the Pentecostal Assemblies of Canada, could offer slight defence. When, following Wells' death, the *Manitoba Free Press* asked Reverend H.C. Sweet whether the Winnipeg "Pentecostal Missionites" would take action, he replied in the negative: "The Pentecostals are not united on this question of objection to military service ... Some of them are believers in war and others are not. They are not a unit, and therefore I don't think the matter will be discussed by them as a body."[89] Leaving the matter of conscience to the individual, rather than making non-resistance a point of doctrine, forced an objector to rely upon his own convictions, which could be quite difficult, especially when he had few other resources.

The wide public outcry at Wells' death acknowledged the isolation faced by objectors outside the historic peace churches. Supporters campaigned to have them treated equally to those from recognized religious groups. William Ivens, a radical pacifist clergyman, wrote to T.A. Crerar, urging that individual conscience be accorded full and proper respect: "It may be that his death was necessary to convince the Government that there are Conscientious Objectors in the Dominion outside of Pacifist Churches and Organizations who are prepared to die for their convictions rather than submit to perform military service."[90] The Winnipeg Trades and Labor Council wrote to Prime Minister Borden, requesting an immediate investigation into the treatment and death of Wells and the treatment of COs generally. It criticized the unequal treatment of objectors under the MSA, concluding, "We request that the Act be so amended as to apply equally to all bona fide Conscientious Objectors and that those Conscientious Objectors now suffering incarceration under the Act be immediately released by being placed in the same category as those belonging to the recognized sects."[91]

These protests had no noticeable effect on the Borden administration. In March 1918, the Military Service Branch ordered that conscientious objectors sentenced to civil prison were to be sent overseas. Refusal to obey a military order at the front (which was deemed to include England) was grounds for being court-martialled and shot by firing squad.[92] The first group, sent over on the troopship *Melita,* included Clegg, Naish, and Wainwright, along with two more Winnipeg Bible Students, a car checker named John Gillespie, aged thirty-four, and Claudius Brown, a porter aged twenty-seven. It also included a Baptist, twenty-three-year-old bookkeeper Nicholas S. Shuttleworth from Brandon, Manitoba, and two Plymouth Brethren: a twenty-three-year-old driver from Regina, Albert Edward Bagnall, and E.W. McAulay. The second group, which sailed on 20 June 1918, on the *Waimana,* was composed of two more Bible Students, twenty-two-year-old salesman Oliver K. Pimlott from Belleville, Ontario, and Sydney Ralph Thomas, from Haliburton, Ontario, who was twenty-seven and who worked as a farmer and stonemason. Three Christadelphians were also transported overseas. One was a twenty-three-year-old sewer "constractor" from Hamilton, John Evans, who left Halifax aboard the SS *Metagami* on 9 April 1918.[93] The other two, whose date of departure I have been unable to determine, were Frederick Hiley, a twenty-one-year-old farmer from Norwood, Manitoba, and Louis Cotton, a thirty-four-year-old miner from Rossland, British Columbia. There were also two objectors from outside these denominations: Joseph L. Adams, aged twenty-four, a newspaper man from Peterborough, Ontario, who gave his religion simply as "Christian" and Vernal Running, a Pentecostal farmer from Lansdowne, Ontario.[94]

Most of the men were sent to Seaford Camp in Sussex, England. Although information about that time is scarce, those who did leave accounts report brutal punishment. Pimlott recounted that, in an effort to make him obey military commands, he was dragged around by the feet, beaten over the head, and kicked with heavy boots until he lost consciousness.[95] The other men mentioned similar experiences. Thomas claimed that he was "dragged, shoved and kicked several miles into the country to the edge of a 150 foot precipice and threatened to be thrown over." He also charged that "ten officers took turns in beating him, threatened to bayonet him ... shoved him against a target and fired at him from the other end of the range, tried to shoot him at close range and cursed because the gun wouldn't go off."[96] When Nicholas Shuttleworth wrote to his father, A.N. Shuttleworth, about his imprisonment overseas, the latter responded with an angry missive to Borden condemning the "torture" that his son and the "seven other Christians" sent from Winnipeg were enduring: "My son had a chain twitch put on his arm and twisted up until the blood oozed out. One other had boxing gloves put on him and had his head taken under an officer's arm and was punched in the face until his nose was broken. They have all been put at times on bread and water, been kicked until they were blue and subjected to the most inhuman treatment possible." Shuttleworth advised

Borden that these actions were being watched by "the God of Justice" and that he "would be obliged to appear some day before him for Judgement."[97]

Evans had been court-martialled on 6 August 1918 for "disobeying a lawful command given by his superior officer in the execution of his office" – refusing to fall in on parade upon being ordered to do so. His statement, compared to that of other court-martialled COs, was fairly terse:

> In Canada I belonged to a society known as the Christadelphians. Before the Military Service Act came into force in Canada our standing committee approached the Government as regards our members being exempt from Military Service on the same grounds as exemption had been granted to our brethren in England. I was called up for service on the 19th February 1918. I declare that I am a Christadelphian and a conscientious objector of good standing. My society is purely religious and non political and I am willing to take up work of national importance in a civil council and serve the government.[98]

It was a well-rehearsed statement. Evans did not try to explain his personal views, choosing instead to emphasize his membership in a religious group, in conformity with the legal provisions of the MSA. Nevertheless, he was found guilty and sentenced to twelve months at hard labour. Louis Alexander Cotton, the other Christadelphian court-martialled at Seaford Camp in Sussex, also stressed his membership in the sect and added a statement of his personal views: "I am a member of the Christadelphian Church of Canada, whose religion forbids me to join in any form of military service. By doing so I greatly endanger my future welfare and my rights to everlasting life. Therefore I must refuse to take any part in military service."[99]

John Evans reported being "beaten up, pushed down a flight of stairs, and flogged with a rope" for refusing to obey orders while in England.[100] He described one of the beatings that took place when, in Wandsworth prison after his court martial, he refused to obey a sergeant's order to parade:

> Infuriated by my refusal, he began to curse and commence a violent physical attack. He struck both sides of my head simultaneously with his hands, attempting to produce pain by suddenly increasing the pressure on my eardrums. Then he banged my head against the brick wall, struck me in the stomach with his fist and continued battering me around the cell until he was exhausted. His object was to try and make me fight. If I had retaliated he could have either accused me of being a traitor to my cause, or otherwise, depending upon his disposition, he could have called for reinforcements which may have cost me my life.[101]

Evans offered no resistance, although, in a humanizing moment, he admitted that "my actual urge to kill him was very great." There were other beatings, one with a rope that left "my back as green as grass. I looked like I had gangrene."[102]

International Bible Students Robert Clegg and Henry Naish were also court-martialled at Seaford for failing to obey a military order. In their respective statements, both men made somewhat fuller explanations than did Evans. They used their statement of defence to explain their views and to chronicle their experiences and the various punishments meted out to them as conscientious objectors. They described their filing of affidavits, their failure to gain exemption at local and appeal tribunals, and their steadfast refusal to submit to military authority in a variety of situations. Naish emphasized this: "I have never been officially informed that I was being sent to England or my consent asked as to my desire to become a soldier ... I have never accepted any regulations or signed any papers." Clegg insisted, "I am not obligated in any way to render military service because my religious principles do not allow me to take part in that service."[103] Naish and Clegg also called upon witnesses to testify to their good character and to their IBSA membership. In his trial, Clegg called Naish as a witness.[104] However, both men were found guilty of "Disobeying in such manner as to show a wilful defiance of authority a lawful command given personally by his superior Officer in the execution of his office" and were sentenced to eighteen months' detention, remitted to twelve months.[105]

The conscientious objectors were transferred to Wandsworth prison, where they were housed with "common criminals." Evans recalls that he was kept in a cell measuring twelve by seven feet and endured seven weeks on a starvation diet of bread and water.[106] He could not write to let his wife and family know where he was, and in August 1918 he was told he was being sent to France. He managed to write to the Christadelphian Standing Committee in London; "it may have been due to their intervention that the order drafting him to France was cancelled at the last minute."[107] He was then transferred to Pentonville prison, where he suffered poor conditions similar to those at Wandsworth.

In Canada and Britain, protests were raised about the policy of sending Canadian COs overseas, and, on 22 April 1918, the Military Service Council issued a new order to the effect that conscientious objectors would no longer be sent overseas. Instead, they would be obliged to serve in Canada with the Canadian Engineers, Army Service Corps, Army Medical Corps, Canadian Ordnance Corps, or in clerical capacities.[108] One group, including the IBSA objectors, arrived back in Canada on Armistice Day and "shortly thereafter" was given a dishonourable discharge.[109] Evans remained overseas for the duration of the war and was shipped back 2 December 1918 on the liner *Aquitainia* with other returning soldiers. Still held under open arrest, he was first threatened with further punishment but was then allowed leave and eventually received an honourable discharge.[110]

It was no coincidence that the reports of mistreatment of conscientious objectors tended to involve members of these smaller denominations. These groups were unfamiliar. The Bible Students were actively conversionist, with beliefs that threatened the status quo. They also seem to have had the strongest tendency to be absolutists, an intransigence that mainstream society found difficult to understand. Unlike for most of the historic peace churches, especially the Quakers, IBSA wartime idiosyncrasies were not mitigated by otherwise model citizenship. Conscientious objectors also seem to have been predominantly from the working class. The Christadelphians, who were able to present their case successfully, did so by proving their sect's stability and organization. They exploited their ties to England and had supporters in government. They also stressed, publicly and repeatedly, that they shared their countrymen's sense of duty and that their scruples regarding its fulfillment were limited solely to military service. A denomination's success in gaining exemption from military service seems to have been closely connected to perceptions regarding its respectability, including its history, its ties to Britain, and its ability to present itself as well organized. For men whose claims to exemption were not recognized, membership in these sects offered protection, however small, in the face of government bureaucracy and a public unwilling to understand community and obligation outside nationalism and war. But even this shelter was denied individuals who, for reasons of conscience, could not participate in war but did not belong to a religious organization, or, worse, were members of a church that supported the war.

4

Exemption from Religion on Religious Grounds: Conscientious Objection outside Pacifist Denominations

IN HIS VALUABLE study *The Quaker Peace Testimony,* historian of pacifism Peter Brock argues that, "In World War I, as in the Second World War, absolute pacifism found support in Canada chiefly among the Quakers and other peace sects like the Mennonites and Doukhobors."[1] This refers partly to the failure of secular liberal pacifism during the wars; but it also underlies the difficulty of maintaining a pacifist stance, particularly a conscientious objection to military service, outside of those groups. Popular belief about the necessity of the war, combined with government intolerance of dissent, made pariahs of those with pacifist beliefs who did not belong to the peace churches. Their stance was also a challenge in terms of the Canadian government's long-standing tendency to treat rights and obligations in group, rather than individual, terms.

In recording its attempts to gain recognition for its conscientious objection to military service, the Canadian Christadelphian Standing Committee mentioned an incident that took place while its members were waiting for a meeting with H.A.C. Machin, the relatively sympathetic director of the Military Service Branch of the Department of Justice:

> While we were waiting our turn a Major called us aside and showed us a very pathetic letter from a church minister on behalf of one of the members of his congregation; the Major remarked that their hands were tied to do anything for a genuine religious objector who was a member of a church which did not have a tenet enjoining its members against participation in war; he remarked, You are all right, but Col. Machin feels there is a great injustice here which should be remedied, in which we concurred. The same feature had been spoken between us and Justice Duff.[2]

The major had touched upon a real problem. Men who would not accept military compulsion on ethical grounds, but were not members of a church that clearly prohibited military service, were granted no protection under the conscience clause of the Military Service Act. Their objection was not recognized, and they tended to suffer greater vilification than members of the acknowledged pacifist denominations. The men who persisted in their refusal, despite the intense social and moral suasion of a country at war, despite the restrictions of the law, and despite the solitude of taking a stand at odds with almost all of their friends and family, did gain the sympathy of some individuals and groups. Conscientious objectors from the historic peace churches, for instance, often expressed compassion for these lonely men. And later, editorials began to protest the harsh sentences handed down to COs even after the war had ended, especially in contrast with the comparative leniency accorded men who had deserted or failed to register. But, for most of the war and from most people, they met with confusion and antipathy. Their country had agreed that the war was a righteous one, a war for Christianity and democracy, and the major churches more than concurred. The energy with which Canadian churches supported the war made the pacifism of any of their adherents seem nearly incomprehensible. At best, these men, and those who claimed no denomination, were deemed deluded and stubborn, at worst, dangerous cowards.

Their isolation was partly due to the successful efforts of the Borden government to limit recognition of conscientious objection. Support for absolute pacifism outside the peace sects suffered a serious blow from the wording of the Military Service Act. Brock Millman has shown that the provision in Britain of alternative service for all but absolutist COs was designed to "drive a wedge between religious and political objection."[3] Although it is not certain whether the Canadian government shared this objective in providing military service exemption to members of well-recognized peace churches, it was certainly the effect. Furthermore, the limitations of the Canadian act also drove a wedge between the members of those churches and individuals from other denominations who had scruples against military service.

In some ways, the lack of support for COs who did not belong to the peace churches might seem rather surprising. Pacifism had been an international movement in the 1910s and had a wide religious and political acceptance. J. Castell Hopkins reported that in 1914, "peace had become a habit of thought with many minds in Canada and, in some cases, was almost a religion."[4] The Toronto Baptist Association, for example, passed a motion in 1914 to commemorate one hundred years of peace between the United States and Canada, concluding it with "the hope that this good will may continue and that these two peoples may be leaders in the abolition of war as a means of settling international disputes throughout the world."[5] The anti-war sentiment was such that some people found it worrying. Principal Maurice Hutton, of Toronto's University College, warned a Toronto audience that "the air is so full of pacifism that it is necessary to urge upon the country the duty of national defence."[6]

In offering an explanation for the pacifist wave, Hopkins also revealed one reason for its speedy demise. Since pacifist rhetoric was "difficult to oppose and hard to discuss," it was "easy of presentment and popular acceptance."[7]

Pacifism in theory was clearly a good thing. But what people were so readily accepting was a rather vague notion of international goodwill, one that offered no agreed-upon course of action should war in fact break out. Thomas Socknat makes a compelling case for why Canadian pacifism, at such a high tide at the outbreak of the Great War, ebbed so quickly almost to invisibility. What the liberal pacifists tended to be advocating so clearly was actually "pacificism," a term he borrows from Peter Brock, which argued mainly for the use of international arbitration and an international court to achieve order and stability in the world. Socknat asserts that, though many Canadians thought of themselves as pacifists, "they gave little thought to the ethics of war and failed to penetrate the relationship between war and the economic order. Rather than pursue the roots of war into the structure of society or formulate a proper response for pacifists in a time of war, the pre-war pacifists merely erected a superficial façade which quickly shattered upon impact with the Great War."[8] J.M. Bliss makes a similar point: "Ripples from the world tide of peace sentiment increased the volume of pacifist rhetoric in Edwardian Canada. They did not produce a serious re-examination of the ethics of war."[9] Another point of weakness was that, though it condemned the disastrous results of war, "pacificism" believed that it was justifiable and necessary under certain conditions. Such pliability meant that pacificism could fairly easily accommodate the presentation of the conflict as a "just war." This flexibility stands in contrast to the pacifism of religious groups such as the Society of Friends, which was more resilient because the Friends believed that war was always inherently immoral.

Author and social reformer Nellie McClung offers a convenient example of the shift in attitude. A member of the Methodist Church who was strongly pacifist before and during the early part of the First World War, McClung later became an ardent proponent of the war effort. Her book *In Times Like These*, published in 1915, offers "a classic formulation of the contemporary feminist pacifist position."[10] Like many feminists of the time, McClung held that war was a masculine construct. In a chapter entitled "What Do Women Think of War? (Not That It Matters)," she explains that the disparity in violent attitudes is apparent even in childhood: boys are always breaking girls' dolls. Men, to her understanding, fight because they like it: "The masculine attitude toward life was: 'I feel good today; I'll go out and kill something.'" Women, on the other hand, were healers: "Men make wounds and women bind them up."[11] Pacifism seemed a natural outgrowth of her maternal feminism. In *In Times Like These*, one mother, while knitting for her soldier-boy, ruminates on the changes the war would have brought about in him:

He was to have been a great doctor, a great healer, one who bound up wounds, and made weak men strong – and now – in the trenches he stands, this lad of hers, with the weapons of death in his hands, with bitter hatred in his heart, not binding wounds but making them, sending poor human beings out in the dark to meet their Maker, unprepared, surrounded by sights and sounds that must harden his heart or break it. Oh! Her sunny-hearted lad! So full of love and tenderness and pity, so full of ambition and high resolves and noble impulses, he is dead – dead already – and in his place there stands "Private 355" a man of hate, a man of blood.[12]

In McClung's view, war was a masculine construct that should be opposed because it dehumanizes people and wastes their abilities.[13]

By 1917, however, she had become a vociferous supporter of the war. She describes the evolution of her attitude in *The Next of Kin:* "When I first saw the troops going away, I wondered how their mothers let them go, and I determined I would not let my boy go." But the propaganda about German atrocities, especially the sinking of the *Lusitania,* led her to re-evaluate her views: "Then I said that we were waging war on the very Prince of Darkness ... I knew that it would be better – a thousand times better – to be dead than to live under the rule of people whose hearts are so utterly black and whose process of reasoning so oxlike – they are so stupidly brutal. I knew then that no man could die better than in defending civilization from this ghastly thing which threatened her."[14] The extremity of her new views was not unusual. Because of her earlier pacifism, participation in the war could be acceptable only if the war were holy, fought "against the Prince of Darkness himself."[15] The pre-war acceptance of pacifist ideas itself, then, could be partly to blame for the religious fervour with which the First World War was promoted. Other reformers who attempted to retain their pacific attitudes, such as editors J.E. Atkinson of the *Toronto Star* and J.A. Macdonald of the *Toronto Globe,* were similarly affected. Both began with a certain amount of criticism for the war and ended as its ardent proponents.[16]

The shift occurred not only on an individual level. In spite of their earlier preaching about the value of peace and the pacifist aspects of Christianity, the established churches in Canada, as in all the belligerent nations, became some of the most strident supporters of the war. Mark Moss attributes much of the responsibility for this change to "the press, personal accounts, and government reports," which, he argues "recast the war in terms [the Protestant Churches] could relate to: it became a holy war."[17]

In "Religion, War and the Institutional Dilemma," sociologist Toyomasa Fusé offers one explanation for how "institutionalized religion proscribes killing and violence, and yet always rationalizes and supports institutionally organized killing by its national community."[18] Fusé contrasts church and sect: the church sees itself as part of society; the sect perceives itself as separate from it. According to this definition, non-resistant groups such as the Mennonites, Doukhobors, and Christadelphians would be classified as sects. Fusé argues that conscientious objection is more common in sects than in churches due to this tendency of adherents to see themselves as properly set apart from secular society. Members of churches are less likely to object to war because they are more clearly part of the society that is waging it. Fusé suggests that churches use the chaplaincy system to "resolve the value conflict in favour of society in a manner to support the values of the socio-political system in war." Although he neglects the role of the crusade and the "just war" in the Christian tradition, which at least partially accounts for bellicosity apart from socio-political considerations, Fusé offers a neat explanation for the variation in conscientious objection according to different denominations.[19] He also concludes that a church's stand on social issues depends largely on the mood and sentiment of its parishioners, rather than solely upon its own religious values.[20]

In his historical and sociological study of pacifism, David A. Martin refines these definitions and carries them a step forward. Martin draws upon Reinhold Niebuhr and Ernst Troeltsch for his discussion of the differing social roles played by church, sect, and denomination. For him, the *church* is a "socially inclusive institution that adapts the absolute law of God to the relativities and necessities of politics as well as tempering its demands to average possibilities." The church functions as a means of conservation and unification, whereas the *sect* regards itself as an elect minority, "proclaiming or embodying the imminence of a new society and a new judgement in the world."[21] For Martin, the *denomination* is a dissenting, reformist group, including those of Nonconformist origin – Baptists, Presbyterians, and Methodists.[22] His argument resembles that of Fusé: that pacifism belongs to sectarian religion more than to its ecclesiastical counterpart and is associated with religions that reject the world to some degree. Although he posits that only sects can be truly pacifist, denominations are more tolerant of pacifism than churches because they accord greater importance to individual conscience: "The denomination never, as an organization, adopts pacifism, which belongs to the sects and to their complete absorption of Nature in Grace, but it does adopt a pacific optimism which becomes an important political factor in those countries where denominationalism is widely disseminated."[23]

In his study of the British government's dealings with dissent on the home front during the First World War, Brock Millman examines the religious provenance of British pacifism and its connection to liberals and Nonconformist churches: "Whatever political form anti-war dissent might take ... all were rooted in the traditional abhorrence of large portions of British nonconformity for war of any kind, and distrust of the state both as foreign policy actor, domestic oppressor and in and for itself ... In significant ways their dissent was as much a product of their religiosity as a response to the circumstances of the day."[24] The "pacific optimism" of the denominations is similar, and often linked, to liberal pacifism and internationalism. That it dwindled away when the war broke out could possibly be traced to the same tendencies that led to the failure of liberal pacifism in Canada. It is also interesting that, for Martin, "any social group which embodies the religious or political variety of dissent" is a denomination, so that the Independent Labour Party in Britain, which did include several conscientious objectors, is also classified as such.[25]

DESPITE THESE CONNECTIONS between pacifism, liberalism, and Nonconformist religion, and the popularity of pacifism before the war, all the mainstream churches in Canada supported the country's war effort. That this stance conflicted with their pre-war attitude did not go unnoticed at the time. A weekly columnist for the Anglican *Canadian Churchman*, who signed himself "Spectator," raised the issue in October 1918 as one he felt ought to have been addressed at the recent Anglican General Synod. The delegates had passed a resolution approving of the objective and methods of the war in which the British Empire was engaged, but at the same time had noted that "The Gospel of Christ is generally interpreted as a Gospel of peace and good will among men. How are these things to be permanently and logically harmonized? It is absolutely essential that the Church should at once come to a clear and sound understanding upon the subject, when and how far shall we go in the advocacy of war." "Spectator" discerned a serious problem in the fact that, before August 1914, the church had been opposed to armament, but "When the blow fell we at once threw ourselves into the promotion of war. Were we right or wrong before the war? Is it the policy of the Church to cry peace in time of peace and just as lustily clamour for war when war is upon us? ... We have been sending conscientious objectors to prison, but are they not carrying to a logical conclusion the doctrines we taught them in time of peace?"[26] "Spectator" was always a vocal supporter of the war effort; this article was an unusual recognition of the difficulties and inconsistencies of the Anglican Church position, and would probably have been more difficult to make earlier in the war. Although he offered no answer to the question of "What will the Church do when the war is over?" in terms of whether and how it might return to a pro-peace position, he pointed out the need for some settled principle of action, one that would resolve the tensions between preparedness, a just war, and peace.

Earlier in the war, the Reverend James Thayer Addison, another *Canadian Churchman* writer, offered counsel to Anglicans who were confused by the apparent paradox. In an article titled "Christianity and Non-resistance," he addressed the issue in terms of ideas about courage and sacrifice, attempting to resolve the "pitiable state of confusion" concerning the demands made of Christians, and specifically of Anglicans, by their religious allegiance in wartime. Addison used two images from the Bible, one of resistance (Jesus driving the money-changers from the temple), the other of non-resistance (Jesus submitting to the crown of thorns). He argued that the apparent contradiction between these was nothing of the sort:

> No word or act of Christ urges us to non-resistance when we see in peril the institutions we honour, the traditions we revere, or the safety and welfare of those we love. In their service and for their sake He calls us to exert ourselves, to spend ourselves, to sacrifice ourselves. When non-resistance means the deliberate purpose of yielding ourselves that through our sacrifice others may gain, then non-resistance is at once noble and Christian. But when non-resistance means standing by to watch the dishonour of our temple, our country, or our friends, then non-resistance is only another name for the ignoble selfishness of saving ourselves at the cost of losing what is greater than ourselves.[27]

For Addison, as for many Canadians, the central issue was the value of sacrifice. The Anglican who felt conflicted about whether to join the military should enlist, because this involved a greater self-sacrifice than did conscientious objection.

The Methodist Church also recognized the place of pacifism in the Christian tradition and the apparent contradiction in its denunciation of modern conscientious objectors. For the *Christian Guardian,* a Methodist publication, Reverend C.D. Baldwin remarked that "The heroes of our faith who won our heritage of religious liberty were 'conscientious objectors.' The martyrs were such, and by their valiant defiance of public opinion bequeathed to us the right to worship God in purity. We cannot afford to sneer at conscientious objection, yet we feel that modern conscientious objectors cannot be classified with the martyrs." According to Baldwin, modern COs were simply paying lip service to conscience and were most concerned with their own comfort. As a result, the church did not accord them the respect and admiration in which it held earlier objectors. He added that these men "refuse to risk anything for the peace they profess to honour and whine over inconveniences ... If love of their brethren prompts their decision how can they better convince their critics than by flinging themselves into ministries of mercy and succour? ... If brotherhood is so real to them, why do they shrink from sharing the common risks of their contending brothers?"[28] Baldwin argued that, by refusing to put themselves in danger, those men who rejected non-combatant service were revealing that they were not true conscientious objectors at all. As a corrective, he praised the Society of Friends for its members' non-combatant work as stretcher-bearers and minesweepers. This idea, that sacrifice constituted the only real proof of conscientious objection, pervaded the discourse on the subject throughout the war years.

Many Canadians reconciled the contradictions between a church or individual's earlier pacifism and later support for the war by making the soldiers themselves into the ultimate peacekeepers. The purpose of the war, as popularly understood, was to protect democracy and freedom from German militarism. By this reasoning, only by going to war could real peace be preserved.[29] The theme was apparent in a sermon given by the Reverend Henry Cody, of St. Paul's Anglican Church in Toronto, at a memorial service for Sydney McWhinney who, though only seventeen years old and technically not eligible for military service, had died of wounds received at the front. The sermon was published in late July 1916 in the *Canadian Churchman:*

> In what nobler cause could any man lay down his life? Our youths by their sacrifice are defending their homes, their loved ones and their country. They are upholding the best traditions of the Empire. They are maintaining freedom for the generations that are to be. They are avenging the unspeakable outrages perpetrated on the helpless. They are restraining brute force from violating international law, the great bond of brotherhood and peace among the nations. They are striking a blow for mercy, justice, humanity and peace among men. They are making possible a better age in the days to come.[30]

The ways in which Canadian participation in the war was praiseworthy were seemingly illimitable. By offering themselves in such a cause, the soldiers were imitating the best example of sacrifice in the Christian tradition. Indeed, in a great deal of wartime art and writing, they became Christ figures themselves. Marjorie Pickthall's poem "Marching Men" illustrates this particularly well:

> Under the level winter sky
> I saw a thousand Christs go by.
> They sang an idle song and free
> As they went up to calvary.
>
> Careless of eye and coarse of lip,
> They marched in holiest fellowship.

That heaven might heal the world, they gave
Their earth-born dreams to deck the grave.

With souls unpurged and steadfast breath
They supped the sacrament of death.
And for each one, far off, apart,
Seven swords have rent a woman's heart.[31]

Such an argument seemed to take the ground from beneath the conscientious objector's feet. In these terms, military service was the ultimate expression of Christian sacrifice. It was incomprehensible to stand aside from a holy war for reasons of conscience. The *London Free Press* expressed this idea clearly in its apparent bafflement at the IBSA affidavits claiming conscientious objection. They seemed to be "claiming exemption from religion on religious grounds."[32]

Such views made objection difficult for men outside the historic peace churches, because they encountered strong antipathy from their congregations and the wider community. Despite the Canadian government's limitation of exemption to members of non-resistant churches, conscientious objection in itself is one of the few forms of protest that does not require the mobilization of a group.[33] However, group membership provided the support necessary to maintain an objection in the face of considerable social pressure. A signal difference between conscription in Canada and Britain was the existence in Britain of the No-Conscription Fellowship (NCF). Although the decision to refuse combatant service was, of course, an individual matter, many NCF members speak feelingly in their memoirs about the necessity of the organization.[34] In an atmosphere of isolation and unpopularity, NCF membership formed a lifeline. Its members attended tribunals, recording insults and inconsistencies to be published in their newspaper, the *Tribunal*. They also visited prisons, lectured, wrote letters to newspapers and MPs, and distributed pamphlets. British CO J.P.M. Millar was certain of its utility: "There is no doubt whatever that the existence of the NCF enabled considerable numbers of individuals to hold fast to their principles."[35] The organization gave support in a climate of tremendous social pressure and made its adherents feel less isolated.

Canadian objectors, who did not have such support, strongly felt its lack and the need for some sort of community backing in the face of the hostility of Canadian society. Joseph L. Adams, a twenty-four-year-old newspaper man from Peterborough, Ontario, who gave his religion as "Christian Brethren," was one of these. Sent overseas, he was court-martialled there for refusing to obey an order to go on parade. His statement of defence gives a short history of the events that followed his exemption claim, including his response when informed of the penalty for his stance. When asked if he understood that the consequence of refusing to obey a military order was two years' hard labour, and whether he had any choice as to punishment, Adams had inquired "if I could serve my term of imprisonment with some 18 or 20 personal friends from Toronto (with whom I had previously lived) and who, taking a similar stand, had been sentenced to two years hard labour." His request was denied. In London, England, Adams had been a member of "an assembly of Christians gathered unto the Name of the Lord Jesus Christ (commonly known as 'Brethren')" since 1907 and had "continued with similar assemblies in Ontario, since he emigrated in 1910."[36] The fellowship he found in this church was obviously very important to him, and the support it provided for his beliefs strengthened his ability to cope with their unpopularity in Canadian society generally.

Some COs gained a measure of support from mainstream society. The severity of Christadelphian objector John Evans' experience seems to have been mitigated by occasional intervention from those who had known him before conscription. On the ship transporting him to England, the orderly corporal was an acquaintance from back in Hamilton: "He covered me for the first ten days of our fourteen day passage. He would answer my name on parade, while I kept out of sight. In this way I could avoid being called upon for various duties, which I would have to refuse to do in any case, and risk severe penalties for refusing to obey orders. I could see no point in asking for trouble if it was unnecessary."[37] Evans also recalls other instances of assistance. After returning to Canada, Evans encountered an "old school chum" by the name of Laing who was acting as sergeant of the guard. Laing gave Evans advice about the camp commandant, who was coming on an inspection tour the next day: "If I were you, I'd be prepared to give him a little talk. He's not a bad head, and it might not do any harm."[38] Evans took this counsel, spoke to the commandant, and got his first leave to go home and see his wife. This level of support and recognition, however slight, was important to him. Such sympathetic contact with friends and acquaintances already in the army would have been largely denied members of the separatist peace churches.

Frederick Arthur Benson, a thirty-year-old streetcar motorman from Norwood, Manitoba, also had something of a support system that helped him maintain his objection when he was subjected to strong ostracism. This was especially vital because Benson was one of the few Anglicans recorded as a conscientious objector. Although his request for exemption was grounded in the fact that he provided financial support for his parents, Benson told his tribunal, "I am personally opposed to fighting. I conscientiously believe that it is wrong to take up weapons. I have been brought up to think so."[39] He added that he had a cousin in England who had been jailed because he refused to fight. Although Benson belonged to a church that loudly supported the war, his familial support seems to have been sufficient to allow him to persist in his objection. He was later sentenced to two years less a day in prison. To support his individual beliefs, which ran counter to the official voice of one institution to which he belonged – his church – Benson had invoked the principles of another, his family. But, while society was decrying the selfish individualism that permitted one man to "let another do his fighting for him," loyalty to a different corporate institution such as the family was also deemed insufficient grounds for exemption.[40] Christopher Joseph Capozzola makes a similar point about conflicting loyalties in his discussion of obligation, voluntarism, and citizenship in the United States in the First World War. Like that of Canada, this was "a culture organized around obligation and responsibility to a group," which made the individual claim for exemption from public duties difficult to stake.[41]

Because Benson was an Anglican Church member and because the Canadian government had decided to accept the corporate conscience of that church as a proxy for the conscience of its members, his objection was not accepted. The Anglican Church was a strident supporter of the war. Upon learning that Anglicans had apparently constituted a disproportionately high number of CEF enlistments, "Spectator" was well pleased: "That surely means whatever may be the faults and follies of the old Church, however we may criticize her activities or inactivity, whatever may be said of her worldliness or coldness, one thing emerges with proud prominence, she has shown herself to be Mother of men – real men." Although the figures cited were unofficial and other factors explained the higher numbers of enlisting Anglicans (many were British-born), these were not widely remarked upon at the time. According to Spectator's view, the high numbers stood as the best testament to the vitality and purity of a church, and to the manliness of its male adherents. In doing their national duty, volunteers were also performing their religious and manly duties: "A Church ... is expected to develop the spirit of live manhood in her sons and teach them to face their duty, great or small, when it confronts them. If when the crisis arises and the call for suffering and sacrifice is made and the men step gallantly forward and lay their lives at their country's feet, surely it is an indication that the Church has still the power to instruct and guide and inspire."[42] The conscientious objector's response to war, according to this perception, would not only be individually ignoble and unmanly, but also reflect badly on his church and his country. The monopoly the fighting men seemed to enjoy on both manly heroism and self-sacrificing piety left little to be envied in the CO stance for anyone contemplating such a role.

ROMAN CATHOLICS WITH pacifist inclinations faced a similar situation. Archbishop Alfred Arthur Sinnott of Winnipeg, for example, spoke to his synod following the issue of a war bond, urging his parishioners in no uncertain terms to participate in the drive: "He who willingly and knowingly refuses such aid must be condemned as ungrateful and recreant in his duty to that country whose protection, prosperity, and liberty he has and enjoys, and therefore, false to the teachings of holy religion."[43] Here, the religious and political duties of a Catholic and a citizen have been completely conflated. There was not much room for an individual Catholic to adopt a position that differed from this status quo and claim a conscientious objection to military service on religious grounds.

Despite one writer's complaint to Prime Minister Borden that "there are millions of Catholics in Quebec which call themselves 'conscientious objectors,'" few Catholics took this route.[44] Given the political opposition to the war in Quebec and Ireland, it is perhaps surprising that Roman Catholics made up such a small proportion of conscientious objectors. Perhaps Catholics who held anti-war views understood and expressed them more easily in political language. They may also be under-represented among Canadian COs due to their efforts to distance themselves from Quebec's opposition to the war. As a minority, and one including a large number of new immigrants, Catholics were also likely to use the war in the same way that other minorities and immigrant groups did, to attempt to prove their loyalty. Mark McGowan makes this point in his examination of Catholics in Toronto: "The First World War provided an opportunity for the Catholic hierarchy, religious press, Church associations, and the Catholic laity of Toronto to demonstrate proudly their loyalty to Canada and the Empire. Their participation, both in the trenches and in the campaigns on the home front, marked the culmination of their community's decades-long process of integration into Canadian society and an effort to come to terms with English-speaking Protestant Canada without surrendering their Catholicity."[45]

Very little has been written about Catholic opposition to the First World War on religious grounds. An interesting exception is Torin Finney's biography of Ben Salmon, one of only four Roman Catholic COs in the United States during the First World War. Finney discusses the extent to which Salmon was isolated and scorned as an embarrassment, even a threat, to the faith. His most vocal opponents were the clergy and laity of his own church: "In the eyes of his fellow Catholics, to refuse such service on pacifist grounds made the culprit suspect of succumbing to the influence of 'heretical' sects or radical, if not subversive, political movements and ideologies."[46] Non-resistance was not seen as a viable reading of Catholic doctrine. Salmon called himself a "practical Catholic," by which he seemed to mean that he agreed with Catholic dogma and doctrine except for one aspect – the just war theory.[47]

In an article for the *North Atlantic Review,* Sidney Webb praised the Catholic hierarchy for urging upon its parishioners a close scrutiny of what they supposed to be conscience: "The Catholic Church, whilst admitting the supreme authority of Conscience, reminds the objector of the necessity not only of a wholesome humility in face of all the complications of the issues, but also of an adequate knowledge of the circumstances of the case to which he is with so much presumption applying his private judgement." We see here again the aversion to the conscientious objector's perceived lack of humility and his presumption in "applying his private judgement" to an issue better left to the more "experienced" church. Webb, and the priests, argued that one should not be too quick to identify the hesitation to perform some task as being conscientiously motivated. The true voice of conscience was not always easy to discern:

> Would it not be well, the experienced Church warns him, not immediately to assume that the stop in your mind is the authoritative verdict of a divinely inspired Conscience, but humbly to reflect, with prayer and fasting, whether it may not be, unconsciously to yourself, the outcome of some natural reluctance to abandon the course of action to which you are prone, it may be even some natural shrinking from the sacrifice that is demanded, obscured by a measure of that self-conceit from which no human heart is exempt. There is, too, such a thing as self-will, an obstinate resistance to a command, merely because it is a command; and this may enter into what seems to be conscience.[48]

What seems to be conscience may actually be stubbornness, or fear, or even merely a suspicion of change. That conscientious objectors were indeed merely mulish, fearful, and set in their ways was a widely held stereotype. Webb found the tradition of obedience within the Catholic Church, which worked to diminish fealty to such a misplaced understanding of conscience, highly commendable.

THE METHODIST CHURCH was equally unfriendly to conscientious objectors. Reverend C.D. Baldwin compared them to mushrooms – ephemeral and insubstantial, harmless when "genuine" and as "deadly as German gas" when not. He also compared these men's response to conscription with another popular evil that the Methodist Church was fighting hard to eradicate – alcohol: "Alcohol has its proper use and place, but wood-alcohol is sometimes a dangerous substitute, and notoriously produces serious disorganization of the organs of vision. So conscience is a good thing and to be cherished above all; but a spurious, merely imitative conscience is harmful, and destroys those functions of moral vision which it is the office of a genuine conscience to clarify and preserve."[49] His argument resembled that of Anglican reverend Addison – that, in spite of the Christian tradition honouring conscientious objection to insupportable government demands, *these* conscientious objectors had no right to such honour, because *they* were not truly ruled by conscience. Only from the safe distance of history could dissent be seen as courageous independence rather than stubborn and presumptuous selfishness.

In late November of 1915, the Army and Navy Board of the Methodist Church, chaired by Reverend S.D. Chown, had assumed responsibility for the church's wartime duties and decisions. It officially supported conscription, the Manitoba Conference even voting itself non-exempt in order to be on the same basis as everyone else.[50] Among its duties, the board took on the task of recruiting and urged ministers to "do everything in [their] power in pulpit, pastoral work and all other ways, both within the congregation and throughout the community to assist every movement that is launched there to secure recruits." In its first letter to the individual churches, the board made an equally clear request of their ministers: "Would you kindly intimate (on a separate sheet of paper) whether there are men in your community who should respond to the call. It would help to direct the activities of recruiting officers and leagues. This valuable information would be properly used without revealing your name. The Board would also request that you take a deep personal interest in the work of recruiting."[51] That ministers were expected to double as recruiting officers was certainly not unique to the Methodist Church, but it made conscientious objection among Methodists a difficult claim and increased the hostility directed at men who did so.

In spite of this militancy, especially of its leaders, Methodists who voluntarily enlisted in the CEF seem to have been outnumbered by members of other mainstream churches. Although unconfirmed by Ottawa (and challenged by historians) the 1916 figures that reached the press showed that Methodist recruits numbered between 30,000 and 35,000, compared with 165,000 Anglicans, 70,000 Presbyterians, and 52,000 Roman Catholics.[52] "Spectator" contemplated the possible causes for the poor Methodist showing: "Can it be that they are too proud or too good to fight? Is it possible that they are worshipping a God who bids them refrain from shedding blood while they enjoy the privileges bought at the price of their neighbour's blood? ... The good name of Methodism is on trial and they that share in the privileges must also bear their fair share of the responsibilities of citizenship."[53] To mitigate the stigma incurred by the publication of these figures, the Army and Navy Board of the Methodist Church set itself the ambitious task of securing an accurate estimate of the number of

Methodists enlisted in the CEF.[54] The lower rate of Methodist enlistment can be traced to a wide number of factors. One often cited by the board was the fact that, for the first part of the war, the British term "Wesleyan" rather than "Methodist" had appeared as the religious category on recruits' attestation papers. It is also just possible that the church's earlier strong advocacy of pacifism contributed to its lower enlistment rate. At least a few individuals seem to have retained their earlier beliefs and were more outspoken than members of other mainstream churches. J.S. Woodsworth, who left the Methodist ministry partly because he disagreed with the leadership's recruiting for the war, is a notable example. In his letter of resignation, he expressed his misgivings: "The devil of militarism cannot be driven out by the power of militarism without the successful nations themselves becoming militarized ... For me the teachings of Jesus are absolutely irreconcilable with the advocacy of war ... Apparently the church feels that I do not belong and I have been reluctantly forced to the same conclusion."[55] The possibility that some support for pacifism remained within the Methodist Church is suggested by the fact that, more than the other church journals, its *Christian Guardian* was a forum for a certain amount of correspondence about the rights of conscientious objectors, especially after the passage of the Wartime Elections Act. The journal itself enthusiastically approved the war, as did most letters to the editor, but it did give some space to those who dissented. S.D. Chown's cousin, Alice, was one of these.[56] Another who wrote frequently in support of conscientious objectors was Reverend Charles Bishop from Bow River, Alberta. He argued that antagonism towards COs, and "the whole character of the campaign for recruits," was unfair to "those of us who are not convinced that to take up arms is our Christian duty." He remarked,

> It is assumed on every hand that the method of physical force is the only method available to a Christian nation to defend, not merely its national existence, but its very Christianity. In fact, to put it bluntly, God is dependent upon the number of recruits we can raise and the amount of munitions we can manufacture ... We cannot see clearly just in what way the bloody warfare which now prevails – which is costing the nations so much of noble young life, and which is making life dark and hopeless for so many more – is going to evoke a better spirit in the German people or is going to minister to what is best in our own national life.[57]

The anticipated, then actual, disenfranchisement of COs brought other letters to the *Christian Guardian*. In his letter to the editor, A.W. Keeton quoted Lord Hugh Cecil, who spoke in the British Parliament against the vote there to disenfranchise objectors. Cecil had advised his fellow members that they were fighting to preserve "Christian civilization" and that forcing a person to transgress his beliefs was antithetical to the very values they sought to defend. Keeton added, "It is so fatally easy in our excitement to trample underfoot the liberties of thought and conscience, our priceless heritage and our glory. When among an almost unanimous people there appear individuals of peculiar and unpopular views, it is hard to bear with them and not accuse them of aiding the enemy; but we ought to remember how much we and our race owe to just such peculiar and independent thinkers, just such staunch followers of the dictates of conscience who have dared to walk 'unmoved by fear or favour of the crowd.'"[58] Although he believed conscription itself to be temporarily necessary, Keeton, like Bishop, argued against the "Prussianism" of putting the state above the individual conscience. The pacifist position was denounced by the editor and other correspondents to the *Christian Guardian,* but these letters reveal that at least some Methodists supported it. The young Methodist men who did not voluntarily enlist, however, do not seem to have chosen the path of conscientious objection in any great numbers either. I have found that COs who identified themselves as Methodists only marginally outnumbered those from other mainstream churches – not enough to show a significant Methodist tendency to non-compliance with conscription on conscientious grounds.

At least some of those who did object had supporters. Reverend Fred F. Prior, pastor of the Free Methodist Church of St. Boswell's, Saskatchewan, wrote to the minister of militia and defence in support of one member of his congregation who had pacifist beliefs. The unnamed parishioner was "an intelligent, consistent-living young man, objecting a hundred times more intelligently, and with far more conscience in the matter than many members of exempted Churches." Prior felt that it was a tragedy that young men such as this were forced into either "the category of criminals" or "treason against Jeasus [sic] Christ."[59] Two other young members of the Free Methodist branch of the church, Wilson and Harold Calma, were imprisoned for their objection. Brothers from Housey's Rapids, near Owen Sound, Ontario, the two were tried as part of a general court martial for six conscientious objectors on 16 and 17 July 1918.[60] The younger brother, Harold George Calma, worked as a painter and had not yet reached his twentieth birthday when, called before his local tribunal, he claimed exemption from military service on conscientious grounds. He had refused both to wear the uniform and to be inoculated. The *Toronto Globe* reported that he justified his behaviour by referring to the Bible injunction "Thou shalt not kill." Furthermore, "He had never seen anything in the Bible permitting revenge, and because he was a follower of the meek and lowly Jesus he refused to take up arms." At his tribunal, Harold asked whether he could take on the sentence of his brother as well as his own. This request was refused, the judge stating, "You will have all you can do to handle your own sentence ... you will be kept busy."

His older brother appeared before the same tribunal the next day. Wilson David Calma, twenty-five years old, kept a grocery store in their small town. Like Harold, he refused the uniform and inoculation on biblical grounds: "Because the Lord's word tells us not to take any part in the things of this world, I object to perform any kind of military service."[61] Neither man had registered, and both refused to sign their attestation papers. Both were sentenced to life imprisonment in Kingston Penitentiary, reduced to ten years by Order-in-Council. The Calma brothers were discharged, on grounds of misconduct, on 28 February 1919. The Free Methodist church to which they belonged placed a strong emphasis on the authority of scripture and would have been likelier than the more organized main branch of the church to tolerate individual dissent on conscientious grounds.

LIKE THE OTHER mainstream denominations, the Canadian Baptist Church supported the war, and conscription. One editorial in the *Canadian Baptist* used rather moderate language but was nonetheless quite clear about its approval for the end of the voluntary system: "It would not be difficult to name churches and communities in Ontario, as well as in Quebec, from which relatively few have enlisted. We are not going to say that we rejoice at the prospect of conscription, but we shall not be grieved if many of those who are quite eligible to join the colours, but who so far have been 'slackers' should be forced by conviction, or by the Militia Act, to do their duty to the State and to humanity."[62] The editorial expressed pride in the number of church adherents who were "doing their bit" but was ready to sanction compulsion against those who did not recognize their duty. A letter from Reverend W.H. Porter employed biblical quotations to argue that there were no solid grounds for conscientious objection to "defensive and righteous war." Citing the example of the archangel Michael fighting against Lucifer, he contended that "Holy angels only do what is right. It depends entirely how, and for what we fight, whether it is wrong or right. It was wrong for the devils to fight, for they were fighting against God, and good, and what would heaven have become had not Michael and his angels fought? Pretty much what this world would be, were all the Allied people conscientious objectors to fighting. 'The Lord is a man of war.' 'In righteousness doth he make war.'"[63] Edward John Stobo Jr. agreed: "Sometimes God ordains war as the only means of advancing righteousness and putting down oppression. If ever there was a righteous cause that cause is ours." Further, he argued, Baptists should not seek exemption, because "It is the Christian's duty to answer the call of the State, for the authority of the State has Divine sanction."[64] This emphasis on the propriety of Christian submission to state authority was an obstacle for many seeking exemptions on religious grounds.

One Baptist who did not take Stobo's advice was George Henry VanLoon, a CO from Brantford, Ontario. He was twenty when he was called up from his farm, had his claim of conscientious exemption from military service rejected, and was sentenced to ten years in Kingston Penitentiary. Another Baptist CO, Nicholas Shuttleworth, perhaps partly due to lack of support from his church, converted to the IBSA while court-martialled in England.[65] Despite the fact that the roots of the Baptist denomination lay in individual dissent, conscientious objectors in this church faced denunciation like that expressed by other mainstream Canadian churches.

One development that probably diminished sympathy for the COs, especially those from mainstream churches, was the fact that ecclesiastical religion was taking the moral high ground at home as well as in the prosecution of the war. Pacifism had been a major tenet of the social gospel movement before the war.[66] When it was repudiated and the conflict was transformed into a war for peace, most social gospellers became more extreme than they had been in fighting for other aspects of Christianity's social program.[67] The changes in the Methodist Church program give the clearest example of this. At the Methodist Conference of 1918, the Army and Navy Board presented a report on "lessons learned by the war." Essentially, the report was an agenda for Canada's complete social reconstruction, the centrepieces of which were public ownership and economic democracy. The conference accepted the report with only four dissenting votes.[68] J.M. Bliss argues that, "More clearly than any other group in Canada, the Methodist Church of 1914-1918 synthesized militarism with a radical social critique."[69] This radicalization of at least one mainstream church is an important factor in the perception of COs and conscientious objection in Canada because it took away from the credibility of pacifist religious groups. COs were not seen as the vanguard of the social gospel, carrying its pacifist aspects to their logical conclusion: instead, they were regarded as laggards; in their selfish, backward-looking individualism, they were simply impeding the new kingdom of heaven on earth that would unfold after the war.

AMONG THE RECORDS decrying or supporting COs, few reveal what the men themselves felt and thought. Except for a few peace church members, they tended not to publish memoirs. This silence is even more complete for COs who had no organization to advocate for them. The tribunal records are not extant, and though newspapers did cover tribunal proceedings, their discussions have obvious limitations. The journalist rather than the objector chose what would be said about him, basing that choice on space, readability, and the paper's politics and market. One forum available to COs was the statement of defence to their court martial. Such documents are particularly useful with respect to unaffiliated objectors, and those belonging to smaller, rather ephemeral groups, who were among those sent overseas in a final effort to make them change their minds. In his statement to his court martial at Seaford Camp in England, Joseph L. Adams, who gave his religion to the court martial as "Christian Brethren," described the process he went through:

> I was ordered to report for duty at Kingston, Ontario in April 1918, and, my claim for exemption being finally disallowed by the appeal of the Judge, I returned this order to the Deputy Registrar, and stated my case to the Civil Police Chief in Peterboro' where I was taken under escort to Kingston next day and on Wednesday, April 24th I refused to sign Attestation Papers and was placed in detention and on June 13th I was Court-Martialed at Barriefield Camp and sentenced to 53 days detention. My civilian clothes were then taken from me and the uniform forced on me and I was removed to Fort Henry Detention Barracks and was there working on the road until Tuesday, June 18th when with about 15 minutes notice I was returned to Barriefield Camp and prepared for overseas next day and left Kingston that night, Wednesday June 19th, 1918.

Adams was one of the few COs who refused to sign their attestation papers, marking him as something of a hard-liner, an "absolutist." He was willing to work as a civilian, but his religious views, which he explained to his court martial, would not permit him to undertake military service: "I have been a child of God through faith in Christ Jesus for twelve years, becoming such by the exercise of a personal appropriating faith in His finished work on the Cross of Calvary, and as such to be consistent with my belief in and devotion to Him and His Word I am unable to, in the first place, engage in combatant service rendering it necessary for me to bear arms and do contrary to His Word – under somewhat similar circumstances found in John 18-36. 'If my kingdom were of the world then would my servants fight.'" Adams also called upon the Bible to explain his inability to take on non-combatant service: "For me to engage in non-combatant service renders it necessary for me to place myself under military rule thus involving an 'unequal yoke' which for one of God's children is contrary to II Cor. 6.14-18, this scripture including the world in all its phases, Religious – social – Political or military, so that my responsibility as a Christian will be clearly seen to use the language of Acts 5.29, 'To obey God rather than man.'"[70] Avoiding being "unequally yoked" with unbelievers was a motivation cited by several conscientious objectors and a plank in the Anabaptist churches' platform of separatism and non-resistance. Like Adams, absolutist COs often rejected non-combatant service so as to avoid being put in the position of having to obey military orders.

Another CO who was sent overseas and court-martialled for refusing to obey a military order was Oswald Peacock, a farmer from South River, Ontario, who was thirty-one when called up. Not a member of any ecclesiastical denomination, he refused to "render military service because I am a Christian and endeavour to live and act in harmony with God's Divine Word." Using biblical citations, Peacock offered six reasons for his non-compliance. According to his reading, the Bible forbade a Christian from taking part in "fleshly warfare," using carnal weapons, and exacting vengeance. It also compelled him to "render evil for evil to no man" and reminded him that Christ's kingdom was "not of this world." Peacock closed his argument with the commandment "Thou shall not kill."[71]

Also sent overseas to Seaford Camp and tried there by court martial for refusing to obey a military command was Vernal Running. Like many of these men, he was a farmer before being drafted, and his statement when court-martialled reveals a lack of formal education, though not of commitment:

> My reasons for refusing to obey military rules are. five years ago I gave my life to God for his service. Since then I have been obeying Gods law and keeping his commandments. he says in his word we can't serve both God and man. God says my kingdom is not of this world if it was why my servants would fight. Thou shall not kill. If we disobey one commandment we are guilty of all I am willing to suffer all that comes my way for Jesus. If we suffer we shall reign with him I am persuaded there is nothing able to seperate me from the love of christ which abides in my soul.[72]

These court martial documents reveal that, with each other and with COs from other religious groups, these men shared a focus on the Bible as a source of direction. Unlike some peace church COs, who relied upon the biblical exegesis of their leaders, unaffiliated COs preferred to interpret scripture for themselves. Another link was an obvious problem of language. Although, to some extent, all conscientious objectors were on unfamiliar ground in the sudden interaction with governmental, legal, and military apparatus that their stance had instigated, unaffiliated COs seem to have been most affected by the great gap between what they wished to communicate and what the government required of them. There is an obvious distinction between Vernal Running's attempts to articulate internalized beliefs in such an unfamiliar and adversarial setting and the language with which a group such as the Christadelphians lobbied the government.

A certain pathos figures in these court martial records. Like many peace church members, Running was a farmer: "The man that looks after the agricural [sic] told me and my father if I had not been a C.O. I would have got of[f] for I was the only man on my farm. I helped to support my father and mother and have one brother that served nearly three years in military. He believed in fighting. He is in london."[73] Whether Running meant that, had he known of this ground for exemption, he would have applied for it, or whether he wished simply to demonstrate the strength of his convictions in refusing to do so, is unclear. The latter seems more likely, as he was willing to be sent overseas rather than deny the promptings of his conscience.

Like Vernal Running, Oswald Peacock was his parents' sole source of financial support and would probably have received at least a temporary exemption on the grounds of their financial dependence: "I was the only son left to support a father of 75 years and a mother of 70 years also to aid a sister and child who were forced to return home because of a husband's lack of support. My parents having no property and no bank account it took my weekly wage of $18 to support the home."[74] To the stress of his imprisonment, then, would have been added anxiety about the welfare of his family. Had he enlisted, they would have received his assigned pay, as well as payments from the Canadian Patriotic Fund.[75] In Britain one of the roles taken on by the NCF was to make payments, however provisional, to the families of conscientious objectors.[76] COs in Canada had no such means of support. Soldiers received no pay while in prison, although this would probably have made little difference to Running and Peacock, who, like other conscientious objectors, accepted no salary from the army.[77] Familial support was important, not only because of the unpopularity of conscientious objection, but also because, in real economic as well as emotional terms, the family of a CO suffered for his stance along with him.

MEN SUCH AS Running and Peacock took a public position when they claimed the right of conscientious objection. There were undoubtedly a number of men who, on pacifist grounds, did not countenance the war but who simply did not register, especially knowing that the privilege of conscientious exemption was limited to members of the historic peace churches. Probably the most famous of these was Albert "Ginger" Goodwin, who remains a controversial figure because of the circumstances of his life and death. He is also important in the context of this study because he had a greater familiarity with leadership and dissent than did Canadian objectors as a rule and was one of the few who might have become a public figure after the war.

Born in Yorkshire to a coal-mining family, Ginger Goodwin immigrated to Nova Scotia in 1906. He moved west to British Columbia in 1910 and was an active union man who participated in several strikes. Goodwin ran for the Socialist Party for Cumberland, Vancouver Island, on a pacifist platform, in the September 1916 provincial election. He did not neatly fit the definition of a conscientious objector, for he opposed the war most obviously on political grounds. But, according to Susan Mayse, associates described him as a pacifist.[78] Refused exemption, Goodwin and a man named Arthur Goodman took refuge in the rugged country west of Cumberland. Mayse quotes one unnamed friend of Goodwin: "I remember, Father asked him, 'What are you going to do? Are you going to shoot back if they corner you?' They both [Goodwin and Goodman] said, 'No we're up here because we wanted to get away from war, and we're not going to start a private one of our own.' They were pacifists, they didn't want to go to war. They didn't want to kill people."[79] In the summer of 1918, Goodwin was shot and killed for supposedly offering resistance to capture. There was, and is, controversy over whether his death was premeditated and the degree to which the government was involved. He was a popular figure: his death was followed by a general strike in Vancouver so that people could attend his funeral in Cumberland. The absence of potential leaders such as Goodwin was a factor in the inability of anti-conscriptionists, pacifist and otherwise, to organize.[80] Given that neither radical unionism, which did not support the war, nor the Quebec anti-conscription movement were willing to join with religious pacifists, the lack of an organized movement in support of conscientious objectors was a foregone conclusion.

In forming a picture of the conscientious objector within the established churches, then, we see a man without a strong political base or reliable organizational support. Those who refused to participate in the war, censured and ultimately rejected by their larger communities, were unable to form a foundation of support amongst others of similar beliefs through which to counter this. It would seem that, in Canada's conservative mosaic, concerned as it was with respect for established churches over personal vagaries of conscience and for the identity and freedom of groups over those of individuals, these men had probably the most difficult experience of all Canadian conscientious objectors.

5
Holier than Thou:
Images of Conscientious Objectors

CONSCIENCE IS A personal matter. Conscientious objection is an individual step. A variety of men took the stance of ethical objection during the First World War, and each had his own reasons for doing so. To some extent, reaction to COs acknowledged this diversity. Lacking organization and alienated by their own frequent insularity and the divisive wording of the Military Service Act, conscientious objectors in Canada were not seen as the great threat they were in Britain, although some feared objection as a kind of contagious disease that might spread if not quickly isolated. Negative attitudes predominated but were neither universal nor static. A claim of conscientious objection was a response vilified by most and defended, albeit rather quietly and belatedly, by some. Furthermore, Canadians did not view all COs in the same light. The government had accorded the right, or privilege, of conscientious objection to individuals meeting strict criteria regarding membership in a pacifist denomination. The wider Canadian public, in general terms, followed this judgment, according religious objectors greater respect than political dissidents or those unaffiliated with a particular church. There were, however, significant differences in perceptions of different religious groups. Canadians had specific ideas about who could legitimately object and about what qualities and characteristics such a man ought to possess.

Most Canadians viewed participation in the First World War as a national duty, and many saw it as a privilege. Statistics implying that a smaller percentage of the Canadian population had enlisted than those of Australia, New Zealand, and South Africa were treated as evidence of a serious national failure.[1] Regions and religions vied with each other concerning the numbers of their men who enlisted. In this environment, the relative paucity of comment elicited by conscientious objectors is perhaps surprising. Angry derision at the COs' unwillingness to join in the great national crusade was less prevalent in Canadian newspapers than in British. This seems to have been at least partly due to a real sense that the anti-war French Canadians and, to a lesser degree, the socialists were the true threat to national unity, not the pacifists. The danger posed by unorganized and unaggressive COs seemed much less than that of the passionate and sometimes violent anti-conscription movement in French Canada, which divided the country. Animosity against the Canadian conscientious objector, however, still ran high.

The first reactions in Canadian newspapers to conscientious objectors were responses to claims made under the "conscience clause" of the British act. A poem, titled "Fetch Him Out" and written by a Mrs. Wyse, appeared in the *London Free Press* before conscription legislation had been introduced in Canada. It spoke clearly of its author's attitudes to COs:

> Is there a man who is too proud
> To help to fight the Hun
> Whose conscience will not let him handle
> Bayonet or gun?
> There is no room in our dear mother-
> Land for such a son
> Fetch him out.

Although the author did not use the term "conscientious objector," she obviously had the CO in mind; the poem neatly introduces several themes that recur in discussion of COs throughout the war. In its entirety, it focuses on three specific flaws in such an individual. First is his cowardice and unmanly weakness in not going to war. Second is his pride: the character in the poem is several times castigated for being "too proud to fight." Conscientious objection in Canada was frequently associated with a lack of humility. To be so certain of oneself that conscience could be a sufficient guide, even when it stood counter to the course of action passionately advocated by one's peers and the law, seemed a clear and presumptuous arrogance. Connected to this flaw is the protagonist's sorry failure to join in with his "comrades" who need him: "Tho' he's too proud to share the hardships of this fighting grim / He's not too proud to let his brother do his bit for him." One argument used by pro-conscriptionists was that conscription was democratic in nature. Herein lay the third flaw: the objector, according to this reasoning, was anti-democratic – not willing to take on the tasks of his compatriots but accepting the benefits and protection earned by them. The poem ends with advice on how to treat such a man:

> And when he stands convicted,
> Not knowing where to turn,
> And England's brave defenders
> Turn on their heels and spurn,
> Make him don the khaki

And honour's lesson learn –
Send him out.[2]

The conscientious objector should be spurned, forced into uniform, and sent
to the front. If he would not do the right thing voluntarily, he must be coerced
into honourable behaviour. William Buchanan, Liberal MP for Medicine Hat,
Alberta, made a similar recommendation in the House of Commons a year
later:

> I do not want the men who, I feel, are neglecting their duty at this time, to have
> an opportunity of saying whether they should stay at home or not. I want to see
> these men go forward and serve their country. They have refused to go under a
> voluntary system, and they must go under some other system. And if these men
> go forward under a system of conscription, go to the front and perform their
> duty, they will come back to Canada, I believe, thankful to this Parliament that
> they were sent forward, even under compulsion, because they will feel in after
> years proud of the fact that they participated in this war, and we hope they will
> participate in it to save liberty, justice, and democracy and to prevent the domina-
> tion of the world by the Germans.[3]

Buchanan hoped that, even if the conscripts did not go to the front voluntarily, they would later be glad of the measures that sent them there. The first references to COs, then, instituted a trend that continued throughout most of the
war, linking them with "slackers" in their perceived unwillingness to accept the
hardships of military life, sacrifices that the rest of the country had agreed upon
as necessary and a national duty. As in Mrs. Wyse's poem, the antipathy directed
at the objectors also maligned them for a certain snobbery. Not joining in, insisting on the primacy of their own personal code of ethics, seemed pretentious.
It was probably also irritating because it implied a negative judgment of the
bellicose behaviour of the rest of the country.

William Lacey Amy, a Canadian writer and journalist, promoted such enmity
and was equally antagonistic towards the British COs. For a time during the
war, he was a British correspondent for *Saturday Night* and the *Manitoba Free
Press*.[4] His articles disparaged objectors in England, those who supported them,
and equally the Asquith government, partly because he saw it as pandering to
"the men with their turgid consciences."[5] In an article devoted to COs, Amy
gives an especially clear presentation of one other perspective advanced in several
newspaper articles, that conscientious objection was a kind of disease. The
disease was physical, mental, and "a form of hypochondria." The objector's
hidden malady "was an ingrown affectation of a neurotic conscience that has

become cancerous by constant irritation": "There is a lunacy of conscience as there is a lunacy of mind, and it is the duty of the State to protect society from both. The disease is commonly induced by morbid introspection, as heart trouble results from worrying over the vascular system. Even children contract toothaches from sucking at a sound tooth. The cure is to get their minds off it. Dodging 'Jack Johnsons' is guaranteed to do that – or failing, how about a high-walled asylum with the other dangerous lunatics, or an isolation hospital?"[6] The account in the *Toronto Daily Star* of Toronto IBSA member Arthur Bourgeois' exemption tribunal also raises the idea of conscientious objection as a kind of invisible physical malady. One tribunal judge remarked that "Regular exercise and soldier's food will probably effect a marvelous cure." And, when noting that the tribunal of Clay, Bourgeois' roommate, would come up later in the week, another commented, "When you see him you will see as healthy a looking man as you will find in Toronto ... I expect he will have a weak stomach too, by the time he gets here."[7] Pacifism in this vision is a hidden and dangerous condition, but one that could generally be healed by partaking in the bracing military life and associating with sensible soldiers. What the objectors needed most was simply to be distracted from their introspection; the most ready cure for thinking too much was action. Should action not cure the self-made invalids, they must be locked away to prevent contagion.

Although the disease was a hidden one, the *Saturday Night* article's description of the COs' "veiled eyes ... soft hands ... [and] ... fat stomachs" also reveals that the conscientious objector was a recognizable physical type. Lacey Amy elaborated: "They're a long-haired, weak-chinned, narrow-shouldered, open-jawed lot. Physical development has been retarded by the overwhelming demands of mental turgescence. The only evidence of physical growth is in their hair ... The spiritual exaltation induced by such a mass of airy-fairy inflation enervates the other muscles by disuse. The conscientious objector is a human fish – largely air-bladder, without need for arms and legs."[8] The objectors were portrayed as physically weak and unappealing, and their inability to partake in robust physical activity was obviously part of their decision not to participate in the war. Their apparent over-intellectualism was both the cause and the result of their debility. This image resembles that put forward in many British newspapers regarding COs in that country. A news article in *Punch*, for example, read, "A woman at West London Police Court has been sentenced for 'masquerading as a man.' Several C.O.s are now getting nervous on sighting a policeman."[9] And the *London Daily Mail* described the fifteen hundred delegates who arrived at an NCF meeting as "mild-faced creatures, mostly thinnish and large-eyed, with rakish untrimmed hair ... and ... thin apostolic beards."[10]

In April 1917, the *British Citizen and Empire Worker* newspaper ran a full-page article by Bart Kennedy that elaborated on the distinctive physical appearance of the CO: "The conscientious objector is a young gentleman with liver and ideas. Pale is his face, high is his forehead, unobtrusive is his chin. He wouldn't even injure the feelings of a fly. He is one of the nicest and the choicest. If you were in a fight, to have him along would be cruel. It would be a great shame. You would be doing the thing that was unworthy." Many articles in this newspaper use the same sarcastic tone when discussing the conscientious objectors, but it is the physical description that is most striking: "His head sags forward slightly because of his heavy-weight brain ... His eyes as a rule are slaty blue. They never seem to be looking at anything in particular. His hair is quite often the colour of the hair – or if you like, fur – that adorns the hide of the small and elusive mouse. His manner is at once assured and nervous. His hands are charming and his profile – but I will refrain from describing it. Sufficient is it to say that it is not of the eagle brand."[11] The conscientious objector even looks different from other men. He has all the traditional physical attributes of cowardice: the pale face, the weak chin, the profile "not of the eagle brand." Indeed, he resembles a timorous mouse. Despite the sarcastic references to gentleness earlier in the article, his objection to war is based largely on weakness and timidity. He also thinks far too much. His over-large brain makes his forehead bulge and his head sag, rendering it an impediment. His body is a machine more for thinking than for fighting, for ideas more than actions, and as such is a thing to be mocked.

Even the pseudo-compliments are derogatory. What real man would be proud to own "charming hands"? Only a woman, or a decadent, effeminate male, would be gratified by such flattery. This, the failure to fit the standard definition of British masculinity, is the second key theme in the image of the CO. According to this vision, his pacifism also makes his masculinity suspect, and women know it: "He develops every trait that is the reverse of masculine. When I say that he is a feminine male, I mean no insult to the ladies. The ladies care little for such."

Finally, the CO's intellectualism is mocked as an obstinate attachment to obscure causes and schools of thought. Before the war, "he might have been orthodox, or he might have been heterodox. He might have specialised in monogamy or polygamy. In fact, it has been rumoured that he was not a complete stranger to polyandry. Sometimes he was an Anarchist; that is to say a philosophic Anarchist."[12] The implication here is that the conscientious objector is obsessed with words and labels, and ideas that have no place in the real world.

This portrayal of the objector as physically degenerate and effeminate is not surprising, but it is important to note in light of recent changes in ideas about appropriate British and Canadian masculinity. The Victorian ideal of masculinity had been promoted by, among others, Dr. Thomas Arnold, at his influential school at Rugby. He equated manliness with intellectual energy, moral purpose, and sexual purity. John Tosh shows that "Arnold's code of manliness came to epitomize the values of the governing classes."[13] In a slightly different vein, Thomas Carlyle promoted a more aggressive version of manliness, which stressed the superiority of will and independence over the Christian virtues.[14] Despite their differences, these expressions of the Victorian ideal of manhood shared an emphasis on intellectual as well as physical independence and strength.

This changed towards the end of the Victorian era, with the growth of a "cult of manliness." Many historians theorize that, among men of this generation, the shift was both a protest against the "domesticated masculinity" of their fathers and the result of growing up in a succession of all-male institutions. Mark Moss connects the crisis in masculinity with social changes in industrializing Canada. J.A. Mangan and James Walvin demonstrate that "between approximately 1850 and 1940 the cult of manliness became a widely pervasive and inescapable feature of middle-class existence in Britain and America." They also show that it was consciously disseminated down to the working classes through churches, philanthropic organizations, children's literature, and schoolbooks.[15]

In his study of the socialization of boys and young men in Ontario, who were taught to accept specific notions of manliness and the propriety of military service, Moss argues for the pervasiveness in Canada of this new ideal, with its emphasis on the martial and anti-individualistic virtues of obedience, loyalty, and conformity:

> This patriotism was supplemented by a vast array of role models, codes of conduct, and manufactured traditions that young men had to respect if they wished to be seen as upright, steadfast, and manly. The pressures to conform in this way came from numerous sources: the family, the school, the various levels of government, the playing field, the press, even the toy shop. The common thread linking these agencies together was the conscious decision to teach impressionable young men what it meant to be a proud representative of Ontario, a good citizen of Canada, a patriot of the Empire, and a manly warrior.

W.L. Morton sees the cult of manliness as a principal feature of late Victorian Canada.[16] The intellectualism and self-sufficiency valued in earlier Victorian ideals were markedly curtailed. The emphasis was now on physical masculinity, of a type where, ideally, action superseded thought.

In his examination of race, masculinity, and empire in England, Jonathan Rutherford indicates that the change came about partly as a result of widespread notions about the superiority of the British "race." He describes the transition: "The rising popularity of imperialism and the influence of social darwinism cultivated manliness no longer dependent upon soul-searching, but upon subordination to the national ideal and an enthusiasm for being 'normal.'"[17] This marked a vast difference, and the ramifications of this new understanding of masculinity were, quite arguably, one of the root causes for the nature of the abuse that public opinion visited upon conscientious objectors.

In failing to behave like other men, then, COs were not simply being cowardly or lazy: they were privileging an individual, contemplative response over one of group loyalty and action. This, and the encouragement of conformity that wartime promotes, amplified the Canadian public's suspicion of those determined to assert an individual voice, the stubborn conscientious objector among them.

Appropriate manliness is contrasted not solely with effeminacy, but also with childishness, for the CO was refusing to accept one of the public responsibilities of manhood. The popular idea that manhood equalled the ability to fight for one's country was succinctly expressed by British soldier Ted Francis, who reminisces, "I suppose I only felt a man when I joined up, became a soldier. Otherwise I was a giddy young youth who was up to everything people of my age would be and I never gave it a serious thought about being a man. But especially when I had a uniform and especially when I had a gun, then I felt like a man."[18] The war simplified the transition from youth to manhood: being a soldier clearly meant being a man. This led to an ambiguity about those who could not be called boys and would not be called soldiers.

Conscientious objectors, then, had to contend with gender ridicule as well as challenges to their patriotism. Frances Early's discussion of American feminist and pacifist resistance to the First World War shows that several conscientious objectors presented their stance as one of manly resistance and separated themselves from other objectors whom they perceived as less masculine.[19] Gerald Shenk's study of the US Selective Service Act, which examines gender identity in relation to the state and to war making in First World War America, argues that, though a particular vision of "true manhood" did link masculinity, state power, militarism, and war making, it was not hegemonic and that responses to the draft revealed contesting discourses on masculinity.[20]

The linkage between participation in the First World War, ideals of manliness, and religious virtue was an important part of the discourse of the war. An article in the *Canadian Baptist* predicted that "One of the results of the war will be the injection of virility into the Christian life." The author cited the apostle Paul, who, "When he would illustrate the ideal which he would hold before those to whom he writes, says 'Suffer hardship with me as a good soldier of Jesus Christ.' In other words he tells them that to be a Christian is a man's job."[21] The conflation of masculinity, righteous Christianity, and military service is a key element in making the CO stance difficult both for an individual to adopt and for the large part of Canadian society to understand.

LATE IN 1917, *Saturday Night* published a caustic and unattributed "Conscientious Objector's Creed":

> I believe in peace and in the determined obliteration of all feelings of wrath and indignation for crimes against humanity and civilization. I believe in a supine endurance of all insults, and in a cringing compliance with the forces of bestiality, destruction and lust. I believe in opening our gates to madmen and leaving our homes defenceless. I believe that if a war is to be fought, it should be fought by someone else. I believe in milk and water, in namby-pambyism and flapdoodle, in gush and bunkum, in veiled eyes and soft hands, in mealy mouths and fat stomachs, in the encouragement of cowardice, and in slavery everlasting, for the forgiveness of everything rotten, Kaiser's sake, Amen.[22]

The apparent passivity of these men, in the face of what many believed were the inhuman cruelties of the German kaiser and his army, was intolerable. This quotation unites several elements of the popular image of COs. They were cowards. They were lazy. They were selfish. They were effeminate. And they were rather silly men who talked too much and acted too little.

The negative portrayal of the conscientious objector also focused on his apparent hypocrisy. In answering the question "Should a Christian go to war?" Edward John Stobo Jr. displayed little tolerance for those who did not answer in the affirmative:

> It has been rather annoying to members of exemption tribunals to have certain individuals apply for exemption on the ground that they are "citizens of a better country, even a heavenly," and therefore have no duty to Canada and the Empire. Yet these same men are ready to take advantage of the laws of a country, whose right to rule over them they deny, saying that they owe allegiance to one King, even Jesus. The only time they ever recognize the right of the State to make a ruling is when they appear in court to obtain permission to be "slackers," and while claiming to be citizens of the heavenly country, to gather all the filthy lucre of the earthly

one that they possibly can. They make the average man pretty tired, and give a very wrong impression concerning the Christian teaching regarding the State.[23]

The objectors, to Stobo, were hypocritical in their avoidance of civil affairs except in the preservation of their own privileges. Their façade of piety masked self-importance and avarice.

In exemption tribunals, judges nearly always asked objectors how they would react should someone, typically a burglar, enter their home and attack their wife, mother, or sister. If the CO said he would not employ violence to resist this attack, he simply showed himself to be a coward, and most likely a liar. If he admitted that he would resort to force, he revealed the falsity of his anti-war stance, and thus his claim for conscientious objection was deemed spurious. The courts made no distinction between organized killing and the use of physical force. Furthermore, they refused to recognize that the stumbling block for many COs was joining the army and taking military orders, not a blanket disavowal of all violence. Conscientious objection, at least the absolute type that main-stream society had the most trouble comprehending, consisted not only of the negative obligation not to kill, but also the positive obligation to resist the state machinery that organized such killing.

The apparent dishonesty and hypocrisy almost inevitably generated by the attempts of COs to answer tribunal questions were coloured by other defects. Writing about British COs, William Lacey Amy conflated them with those who had avoided conscription on occupational grounds and credited them with an impossible list of vices:

One was arrested for skipping his board, one for picking pockets. At least one of the benedicts among them is living with a woman not his wife, and one nearly paid with his life for a similar exhibition of conscience when the woman's husband returned unexpectedly from the front. Two got into a drunken street row with the police. A forged military certificate was found on one, a half dozen were dis-covered by the tribunal to which they were appealing for exemption to be evading the income tax, and a score were dismissed from the factory for sheer laziness and loafing.[24]

One sure way, it seemed, to prove a conscientious objector wrong was to show that, at other times, his conscience was not a reliable compass for his actions.

The objectors were also suspected, predictably, of being pro-German. The *Manitoba Free Press* reported that one member of a local tribunal thought it prudent to bring the case of two (unnamed) COs to the attention of the registrar, "the arguments presented by them being the work of an attorney in the United

States with a distinctly German name."[25] This was exacerbated by the fact that many of the non-resistant churches spoke German and were of ethnic German background. Interestingly, however, no one seems to have worried that objectors were in league with the nationalist opposition to conscription in Quebec.[26] The *Free Press* later published an editorial titled "Conscientious Objectors," quoting a letter that had ostensibly come from someone who signed himself "A Conscript:" "My prayers shall be should it be God's will that any nation shall be victor by force of arms that German arms shall be the victor and rule the world."[27] Although there is no proof that "A Conscript" claimed any sort of conscientious objection to military service, the editor made the imputation, and no later letters to the paper criticized him for doing so.

This reading of COs as pro-German also occurred later in the war. The warden of the Provincial Gaol at Lethbridge, J.S. Rivers, wrote to the deputy minister at the Department of Justice for direction on how to treat the eleven conscientious objectors who had recently been sentenced to his institution for refusing to obey military commands. The warden wanted to know the Department of Justice attitude to these men and the treatment the minister expected them to receive in civilian prison. He was annoyed by their various "conscientious whims," which threatened what he saw as the egalitarian nature of prison life: "In the past we have had only one rule – Everybody sentenced to hard labour worked every day in the week except Sunday – if he is physically fit – We said when and where they are to work – one rule for all and a square deal for every man. Do you wish us to continue this course or shall we begin to accede to the conscientious whims of these apparently pro-German Prisoners?"

Although members of various sects were represented, he did not seem to favour one over the other: "One of them is a Seventh Day Adventist who refuses to work on our Saturday, because of his religious belief. Another is a Christadelphian, who does not believe in War and will not don the Khaki because he does not want to kill anybody. Another belongs to the Associated Bible Students [sic] (Russellites) and his conscience will not let him do certain things."[28] Rivers was bothered by the objectors' focus on following their own particular beliefs, which seemed to him foreign and dangerous not only to wartime Canada but also to the effective working of peacetime institutions such as the jail: "I am sorry these men are being sent here – I think they should be sent to the Front and made to take their share in the defence of our Country or as an alternative sent to the Detention Camps and herded with kindred spirits there. I wish you would order their removal from this Jail if possible, and stop any more of this kind from coming to a respectable jail."[29] That the COs were much less than welcome in "a respectable jail," even to serve out a term of hard labour, is strong evidence of the feeling against them.[30]

The suspicion that conscientious objectors had secret German sympathies was often connected to their ethnicity. The fact that members of several historic peace churches spoke German, for example, increased distrust of their motives in refusing military service. Frances Early has shown that, in the United States as well, "although nearly 90 percent of the objectors were native born, in the 'crowd-mind' they were dangerous foreigners or at least pro-German."[31] Furthermore, in both countries, the Mennonite objector was also sometimes derided not because of his racial ties to the enemy, but because of the perceived characteristics of his own ethnic group, as explicated in *The Conscientious Objector,* written by Walter Guest Kellogg, a member of the United States Army Judge Advocate Branch and one of the three-member War Department Board of Inquiry in that country.[32] The board travelled to every major military institution where conscientious objectors had been encamped and interrogated them briefly to determine their sincerity. Kellogg published his findings in *The Conscientious Objector,* in which he categorized the men imprisoned for their objection and discussed the typical representative of each category. The Mennonite variant, according to Kellogg, was of singular appearance: "His hair and beard are unkempt ... His trousers open only at the side and do not button, but hook together. He wears no jewelry of any kind. He shuffles awkwardly into the room – he seems only half awake. His features are heavy, dull, almost bovine."[33] The Mennonites were portrayed as almost bestially boorish in appearance, manners, and intelligence. Kellogg decried their inability to speak English "with any degree of even colloquial fluency," their lack of formal education and interest in voting or, apparently just as shocking, even in good roads. They knew their Bible well, but Kellogg was appalled at their ignorance of topical matters such as the sinking of the *Lusitania* or the identities of General Foch or Edith Cavell. To him, their isolation from modern society made them alien and anachronistic: "Civilization, apparently has passed them by."[34] This image of the obtuse religious objector, whose refusal was apparently based on his isolation from everything healthy in mainstream society, became an important aspect of ideas concerning the Canadian CO.

For Kellogg, the most important result of Mennonite behaviour and attitude was that it created poor citizens: "It is difficult to realize that we have among our citizenry a class of men who are so intellectually inferior and so unworthy to assume its burdens and its responsibilities." The key to transforming "backwards" Mennonites into good citizens was education, "not more in the rudiments of schooling than in the inculcating of the social and national spirit."[35] For this writer and many who published in Canadian newspapers, pushing these Anabaptists into schools where they would be indoctrinated with "Canadian" and nationalist values would eradicate the troubling discrepancies between them and mainstream society.

These arguments about the value of education as a means of assimilating minorities into British Canadian culture had been going on for some time, and the conforming pressures of the war brought them to the boiling point.[36] In its outline and the passion it evoked, the conflict over the "Mennonite schools question" was similar to that concerning French schooling in Manitoba and Ontario, which unfolded during the same period. As was the case for French Canadians, the threat that Mennonites might be deprived of the right to educate their children in their own language exacerbated their conflict with both conscription and the Anglo-Canadian society that demanded it. Local Mennonite histories of the war years generally spend more time addressing the conflict regarding education than on conscientious objection.[37] Mainstream Canadian society, especially in the West, was equally disturbed. Like the French Canadians, Mennonites, though living in Canada, seemed not to have become Canadian or to be fulfilling the responsibilities of citizenship, most obviously that of military service. The great good of the war, as it was going on, was generally seen to be the unity it brought to Canadian society. This perception sharpened criticism of anyone who refused to be fully drawn in and increased calls to educate non-resistant groups in the values of good Canadian citizens. Pushed by the threat of losing control of their schools, and their less than clear exemption from conscription, some six thousand Canadian Mennonites emigrated to Paraguay after the war.[38]

Conscientious objectors also faced censure for the singularity of their apparently anti-social behaviour. Their objection was suspicious simply because it seemed so different from the responses of the rest of the country. Asserting the superiority of individual morality in determining behaviour was especially difficult at a time when society was lauding the unanimity of purpose instigated by participation in the war. In a July 1917 *Saturday Night* article, author and journalist G.K. Chesterton commented on the incomprehensibility of objection: "Short of the disruption of definitely military discipline I am in favor of allowing the Conscientious Objector to talk at large. I cling to the hope that, if he talks long enough and large enough, he may at last tell us something intelligible about his conscience. At present the attempt to discover what he means brings us no further than a doubt as to whether he can possibly mean what he says."[39] He argued that, simply because a man had a conscience, it did not follow that he ought to be permitted to obey it if doing so resulted in anti-social behaviour. Further, for Chesterton, the idea of an individual conscience at odds with what the mass of society perceived as conscionable was a contradiction in terms: "The sanctity of conscience consisted in its being the voice of God, which must be universal ... If a particular man's opinion is not the voice of God, is not common sense, is not what men call morality, then his conscience is no more necessarily sacred than his nightmares." Chesterton argued that morality was a norm generally agreed upon by society and that if an individual's ideas of right and wrong did not conform to that norm, they should not be obeyed. He turned the objectors' pacifist argument on its ear by comparing the inscrutability of their consciences to that of the "militaristic" Germans: "For the Prussian is the supreme and typical Conscientious Objector. His whole position is poised on the idea of a new conscience, incomprehensible to the common conscience of men. He has a conscientious objection to the Red Cross, a conscientious objection to the white flag, a conscientious objection to the tyranny of a scrap of paper. He has a conscientious objection to all the old religion implied in the old international standards ... If you tell him he is immoral, he will tell you, as the Pacifist does, that he has a higher morality."[40] The objector and the Prussian are alike, to Chesterton, in their lack of respect for the law and traditional values, and in their apparent common belief that they are entitled to exemption from these norms. As he saw it, the war, fought to protect democracy, was opposed to aristocratic privilege and the sense of exceptionalism of leaders such as the kaiser. Recognition of individual conscientious objection to military service was as undemocratic as despotism. An article in the *Manitoba Free Press* made a similar point:

> It seems to me that the conscientious objectors are suffering from the same mental malady that afflicts the Germans. In one case the patients think so highly of their spiritual and mental attainments that they want to force their habit of thought and style of living on the whole world. In the other case the patients consider themselves to be so much finer in sensibility and truer to their ideals than their brothers that they can indulge themselves in those same feelings at the expense of these same brothers who are thinking more of the good of others than of themselves.[41]

This writer was appalled by the "stupendous egoism" of both the Germans and the conscientious objectors. Such irritation at the COs' perceived sense of moral superiority was commonly voiced. One article in the *Canadian Baptist* sarcastically called the CO "the superman of reason and a paragon of virtue."[42] The conscientious objectors' seemingly wilful separation from the activities of the rest of the country implied a certain smugness that the public was determined to quell.

Conscientious objectors, then, struck many Canadians as being selfish, undemocratic, and stubbornly attached to a completely illogical position. Their apparent insistence on what today might be termed "minority rights" also seemed egregiously undemocratic to most of their contemporaries. Their odd ideas were antithetical to the majority opinion on the war. In a neat phrase, G.K. Chesterton said, "We fight for the right of normal people to define normality."[43] This is a fair point, although the country was theoretically also fighting against what was often termed "state worship" in Germany. It could also be argued, in response to the attack on conscientious objection as peculiar and undemocratic, that pacifism was no novelty. And the fact that it had earlier been espoused by wide segments of Canadian and British society now supporting the war itself showed the weakness of a solely democratic morality.

In examining the image of the stereotypical Canadian CO, we see echoes of the British newspapers' derisive comments regarding over-intellectualism and the preference for thought over action. In a signal difference, however, COs in Canada were also frequently maligned for their stupidity. We have seen this in Kellogg's description of the typical Mennonite conscientious objector. A poem in the *London Free Press* likened the CO to a scarecrow:

> There stood a scarecrow in the field
> On guard amid the golden yield
> Firm stood he under heaven's arch:
> He was fixed so he could not march.
> He had no weapon to resist –
> In fact he was a pacifist.
> 'Twas also noticeable that
> He had no brains inside his hat.
> Because some crows retained their greed
> He cried, "Behold, how I succeed."
> Nor did he dream they learned to shun
> Because the farmer kept a gun.[44]

Here, the brainless pacifist is completely ineffectual in his set task, yet full of misplaced pride. He believes he is protecting the crops, doing the right thing, but it is the man with the gun whom the scavengers respect and fear.

The same qualities of illogical stubbornness and selfish superiority come across even in relatively sympathetic treatments. A January 1918 *Maclean's* editorial urged consideration for, and no persecution of, "the man who sincerely believes that taking a rifle in hand and going out to kill his fellow men is

contradictory to the religious principles he has espoused." The editor acknowledged how puzzling and annoying the conscientious objector's stance could
be, especially for those administering the Military Service Act: "His attitude
seems so unfair and illogical and even cowardly that there is a natural tendency
to treat him harshly. He generally gets a severe buffeting when he comes before
a tribunal. His holier-than-thou attitude irritates the officials. He seems priggish,
mulish even, and blandly obtuse to any arguments save Biblical texts." It was
important, though, the editorial suggested, to be fair, because many objectors
were sincerely conscientious, and there was bravery in their stubborn standing
apart. So the editor advocated tolerance towards "these strange, ridiculous and
contradictory creatures." He supplied further reasons for such forbearance: "The
strange part of it is that most conscientious objectors believe the cause of the
Allies is a just one and that God has put it into the hearts of the British people
to fight for the freedom of the world. Only, the stern duty of helping in the
consummation of God's purpose is not for them! They remember a text or two
that Christ spoke and they forget that, when the money changers invaded the
temple, Christ took a scourge in hand and drove them out!"[45] The writer argued
that objectors should not be treated harshly, because their beliefs were not so
different from those of most Canadians. They too supported the war and wanted
the Allies to win. They were held back from physically joining the fighting solely
because of a simple misreading of the Bible and a subsequent misinterpretation
of Christian behaviour as exemplified by Jesus. Well intentioned though it was,
this effort to make the objector more palatable by making his views less foreign
ultimately reduced his objection itself almost to invisibility – certainly nothing
that reference to a good New Testament concordance couldn't resolve.

An editorial in the *Manitoba Free Press* agreed with the picture of the dim-
witted, stubborn, deluded CO, asserting, "No doubt there is, here and there a
'conscientious objector' who has some rational idea of why he is a non-resistant;
but, in the great majority of cases, this attitude is the result of stupidity and
fanaticism."[46] The foppish and fastidious objector, with his artistic leanings,
perhaps most famously epitomized by English biographer and critic Lytton
Strachey, constituted one side of the Canadian stereotype.[47] However, the image
of the Canadian CO as unintelligent, which appeared somewhat more often, is
rather distinctive and worth a closer examination.

That Canadian COs were associated with stupidity, obstinacy, and a refusal
to listen to reason is probably connected to the restriction of exemption to peace
church members and racist ideas about these groups. It may also spring from
a perceived lack of sophistication in rural areas: that objectors were uneducated
hicks and bumpkins. Members of the Anabaptist churches were traditionally

farmers, and many objectors from outside these denominations also came from rural backgrounds. Many were from fundamentalist religious groups, basing their refusal on a literal interpretation of the Bible that frustrated tribunal judges, although they generally responded with similar arguments and evidence. To some extent, the image had a basis in fact: any CO who persisted in his unpopular stance would have needed a certain amount of doggedness.[48] On the other hand, the conscientious objectors who showed flexibility in their acceptance of non-combatant service were treated with more understanding than the absolutists.

DIFFERENTIATING BETWEEN absolutists and those willing to take on some forms of military service was not the only distinction Canadians made between COs. The difference between objectors of various denominations, or between religious and secular objectors, was a very real one in the public mind. Even William Lacey Amy, in the midst of an anti-CO diatribe, took care to mention that he did not intend to disparage "the honest conscientious objector, like the Quaker." The Friends tended to be divided from the rest, mainly as a result of their general willingness to perform non-combatant work, and were exempt from Amy's criticism because they saw "some connection between a tender conscience and the care of the wounded."[49] The fact that, due to their history and social work, they were already familiar to many people also helped. They were not seen as a sect that had sprung up conveniently in wartime. And they were ethnically similar to mainstream society and more integrated into it than the other historic peace churches, making them seem less alien and more "Canadian." Also, they were often excepted from the general derision because they did not seem to be irrationally following a too-literal interpretation of the Bible. In an article for the *North Atlantic Review,* British social reformer and economist Sidney Webb lauded the Quakers for their "informed conscience" and cited them as exemplars of the laborious spiritual examination he advised for those considering conscientious objection.[50]

For many Canadians, then, the key difference between pacifist religious groups was that between absolutist and conditional objection. Quakers tended to be least disparaged, partly because they would generally take on non-combatant work in areas such as the Friends Ambulance Unit. A June 1918 *Toronto Globe* editorial lamented the appearance of objectors belonging to other than the recognized peace churches as those who "mistake their crochets for their conscience": "The Military Service Act made allowance for bona fide objectors, the members of organized religious denominations in existence when the Act was adopted, whose articles of faith forbade combatant service. The provision covered those worthy people, the Quakers, but a surprising number of sects who hid their light under a bushel before conscription became law appeared to claim the same privilege ... With these shirkers conscience is a highly elastic affair, which can be stretched to cover any evasion of duty. The authorities need have no conscientious objections to dealing adequately with freaks of this species."[51]

The sense of a hierarchy of COs was also connected to their ethnicity. Like the majority of Canadians, Quakers and Christadelphians tended to come from an Anglo-Celtic background, but the Mennonites, Amish, and Tunkers were of German origin, which threw suspicion on their motives in refusing to join the CEF. Although he disparaged Mennonite COs, Kellogg celebrated their Quaker counterparts, whom he found both intelligent and sincere. Their spiritual sincerity was reflected in their pleasing appearance, quite different both from the unkempt Mennonite and Amy's physically underdeveloped CO: "I think of the majority of the Quakers that I have seen as pleasant-appearing, clean-limbed young men." They differed from the Mennonites in other ways as well: "They knew and understood the causes of the war, they were well versed in current events, they balked only at actual fighting. A large part of them desired non-combatant service ... They understood the dangers and were willing and anxious to risk all of them ... The spirit of the Friends, though we may attribute it to an inherent narrowness, is yet a brave spirit, prompted by a genuine intelligence and backed by a fine sincerity."[52] Quaker objectors seemed genuinely patriotic and thus were more comprehensible to Canadian society. Their willingness to join non-combatant and reconstruction units seemed to show a shared conception of national duty, and their readiness to risk dangers at the front countered allegations of cowardice.

One group that faced nearly ubiquitous condemnation for the frequent absolutism of its adherents was the International Bible Students Association. Kellogg judged IBSA COs to be brighter than some – "Many were above the average in intelligence" – but was not pleased with them as a group: "Regarded as a class, they impressed one as weak characters, easily molded." The moulders, apparently, were the IBSA leaders. Kellogg described Russell's writing as "rabidly pacifist" and identified Rutherford as one "lately convicted of sedition." If some objectors were dangerous in their ethnic and social insularity, those from the IBSA posed a threat because their faith pervaded "all nationalities ... The immigrant may absorb it in his native tongue before he ever comes to our shores in search of that liberty for which he will not fight."[53]

Saturday Night also saw the Bible Students as easily manipulated, in this case not by their leaders but by Germany. The magazine reported that American spy trials had revealed that "German propagandists have made a deliberate use of floating religious organizations (as distinguished from those churches which have real traditions behind them) to promote the belief that it was God's will that Germany should conquer the world. Probably something of the kind has coloured the literature of the International Bible Students' Association."[54] The relative novelty of the sect was suspicious, and its adherents' willingness to accept such innovation seemed to imply a weakness that could easily be exploited by anyone wishing to do so. This seems a further explanation for the differences between religious conscientious objectors in the eyes of the Canadian public. Sects such as the Quakers, Mennonites, and Christadelphians had some history behind them, a fact that seemed to impart authenticity to their members' claims to non-resistance. Almost on principle, cautious Canadians doubted the integrity of the newer religious groups, especially those with unorthodox beliefs. The Society of Friends, then, was also deemed worthy of exemption because it was well recognized. The smaller, newer, or more isolationist groups were more vulnerable to charges of shirking because their views were less familiar.

HOWEVER, SOME CANADIAN newspapers, magazines, and wartime novels did include sympathetic portrayals of objectors who were not members of the historic peace churches. The few representations that appear in works of fiction focus on men whose scruples were not religiously motivated, presenting them as imaginative, artistic types. Though supportive of the war and publishing a clear condemnation of COs in "The Slacker" in 1918, *Maclean's* tended to be somewhat more sympathetic with those "supersensitive consciences."[55] A *Maclean's* short story touching on the question of moral principles against killing, though published before the enactment of conscription legislation, was "Porteous, V.C.: The Story of a Man Who Went to the Front through Fear." The hero is Arthur Porteous, a motherless and sensitive young artist with a cold and greedy war profiteer of a father. Young Arthur is troubled by the thought of becoming a soldier: "He had ferocious moments in which he thrust himself toward the recruiting office. There were days in which he endeavoured desperately to take hold of a rifle or touch a machine gun. But a uniform was to him the panoply of legalized murder. Deep in his soul he believed that high above the crash of battle brooded beauty and truth, immune from war and butchery – waiting the day when they might again settle serenely on the earth. For their advent he desired above all things to prepare himself. But that he should kill!"[56] Arthur's opposition to killing, though heartfelt, would not have satisfied a Canadian exemption tribunal's restricted definition of conscientious objection. Pushed by his father, he volunteers and is killed. The story ends somewhat ambiguously. His father, still an unlikeable character, brags to his friends about Arthur's death in battle, his son having become a source of pride, a position he had never been able to achieve in life.

More obviously virtuous is Larry Gwynne's progress from pacifism to enlistment in Ralph Connor's *The Major*. In conversation with his Quaker mother, Larry struggles with the issue: "I don't believe I could kill a man, and yet in the Bible they are told to kill." A later discussion with his sister echoes exemption tribunal assessments of CO veracity. Larry remarks,

> "I cannot see myself hitting a man on the bare face, and as for killing a fellow being, I would much rather die myself. Is that being a coward?"
> "But if that man ... mad with lust and rage were about to injure your mother or your sister –"
> "Ah," said Larry, drawing in his breath quickly, "that would be different, eh?"[57]

This response reassures his sister, and the reader, of his courage. By the end of the novel, Larry has perceived the iniquity of the German cause and the propriety of violence to put it down: "I have come to see that there is no possibility of peace or sanity in the world till that race of mad militarists is destroyed. I am still a pacifist, but, thank God, no longer a fool."[58]

A similar questioning of universal military service comes from Walter Blythe, protagonist of Lucy Maud Montgomery's novel *Rilla of Ingleside*. Walter is the second son, the handsome, romantic poet and dreamer. When his brother and friends enlist in a patriotic rush, he declines to join them, saying that fear prevents him from doing so. However, this assertion does not seem entirely believable. What comes across more clearly is that he has a vivid imagination. Walter understands what the war will be, as others seem not to: "Some days I *almost* make up my mind to do it – and then I see myself thrusting a bayonet through another man – some woman's husband or sweetheart or son – perhaps the father of little children – I see myself lying alone torn and mangled, burning with thirst on a cold, wet field, surrounded by dead and dying men – and I know I *never* can."[59] His disinclination is not based solely upon aversion to pain, though that forms a part of it. Like the conscientious objectors, he cannot reconcile himself to the necessity of killing. Nor can he depersonalize the German soldiers as "the enemy," and, without actually experiencing it, he comprehends the suffering entailed in war. Despite the fact that such empathy is generally considered a social virtue, Walter's community actively encourages his perception of his own cowardice. He receives white feathers in the mail and letters calling him a coward. In a letter to his sister Rilla, he despairs of the situation:

"Sometimes I wish I had never been born."[60] When Walter does enlist, the catalyst, as for McClung, that prompts him to do so is the sinking of the *Lusitania*: "When I pictured those dead women and children floating about in that pitiless ice-cold water – well, at first I just felt a kind of nausea with life. I wanted to get out of the world where such a thing could happen – shake its dust from my feet forever. Then I knew I had to go."[61] His decision to enlist seems to be based on a sort of death wish, perhaps the logical conclusion of the desire for self-sacrifice the country saw as the expression of true patriotism. Like Arthur Porteous in the earlier story, Walter is killed in France. The death of these characters is seemingly necessary to prove that, despite their earlier hesitation, they are courageous men.

Fear of condemnation such as that faced by Walter, and the isolation it engendered, led many erstwhile pacifists to accept the war, or at least to refrain from criticizing it. Thomas Socknat discusses the ways in which many people who had been pacifists before the war accommodated the new status quo and attempted to reconcile it with their pacifist beliefs.[62] The natural disinclination to oppose popular morality meant that COs were sometimes portrayed as men who were simply contrary, who objected to conscription because they objected to everything, and who liked the attention garnered by their moralistic stance. This aspect of the stereotype seems to have been one that at least some pacifists fought to dispel.

Aleta Dey, one of the few novels written by a pacifist, found it necessary to adopt this stance. Its author, Francis Marion Beynon, was a journalist for the *Winnipeg Grain Growers Guide* who later fled to the US under pressure for her anti-war views. In *Aleta Dey*, an important pacifist work, Beynon employed the figure of a CO named Ned Grant to argue that the typical objector was not "a jaunty seeker after the limelight of publicity," revelling in the attention given by public denunciation: "Often, as a matter of fact, he is a drab, medium-sized man like Ned, discouraged and saddened by his social isolation, but going doggedly on, impelled by some unknown law to follow the stony path of resistance."[63] A competitor for the affections of Beynon's protagonist Aleta Dey, Ned Grant is a socialist who, though his radical views have always prompted a negative reaction, is profoundly disturbed by the opprobrium aroused by his anti-war stance.

Like Beynon herself, Aleta Dey is a journalist, one whose character and motivations offer a foil for the negative CO stereotype. Although, as a woman, Dey is not subject to conscription (and thus, the public stance of CO is not available to her), her experiences mirror those of many COs: she loses friends, doubts herself, and is imprisoned (for distributing anti-war pamphlets). She even suffers the martyr's fate with which COs were threatened. At the end of the novel, Dey is mobbed while giving a pacifist speech and dies of her injuries. Her death seems to be tied to the perception that suffering and self-sacrifice were the most important indicators of truth and patriotism. In her portrayal of Dey's death and funeral, Beynon emphasizes that pacifism provides an opportunity for heroism and self-sacrifice as great as the soldier's. That Dey's death is imbued with a heroic meaningfulness is acknowledged by her neighbours, who unexpectedly attend her funeral: "McNair was wrong about there being few to follow her. Her death brought hundreds of people with Pacifist leanings, who had said nothing about it, to declare themselves openly."[64] In the novel, the degree of community support desired by the pacifists and objectors finally comes about through individual self-sacrifice; Dey needed only to be strong and consistently true to her beliefs to create it.

Another of the few self-presentations by pacifists is Alice Chown's autobiography *The Stairway*. Like Beynon, Chown argued against the image of the anti-war activist as stubborn, unintelligent, and close-minded. Chown, whose approach to fixed attitudes and all-encompassing ideology resembled that of Beynon, stressed the absence of dogmatism in her own Christianity and pacifism. *The Stairway* details her progression from conventional Christianity to a radical philosophy encompassing rational dress, communal living, and pacifism.[65] Hers was a highly personalized moral philosophy. *The Stairway* is also interesting for its idealism. Chown plays down any popular resentment of her views; in fact, once the characters in the book have the opportunity to speak to her in person, they generally admire her stance. If their reaction corresponds to reality, it implies that disapprobation of pacifists depended upon the degree to which they were seen as individuals: the idiosyncrasies of an acquaintance could be more easily understood and forgiven than those of a faceless group that would not support its country in wartime.

Although it was not published until nearly two decades after the war, Philip Child's *God's Sparrows* merits inclusion here simply because it is the only Canadian novel of the period that features a protagonist who, while performing combat duty, decides to become a conscientious objector and who discusses his motivations for doing so. The first objector introduced by Child's work, however, is the protagonist's father, Pen Thatcher, who is too old to be conscripted. Blocked, like Aleta Dey, from protesting through conscientious objection, he makes another form of pacifist protest, refusing to pay taxes that will fund the war effort.[66] His wife Maud, who generally supports him, secretly despairs of his attitude and the primacy he accords to his own personal sense of right and wrong. Early in the book, contemplating Pen's decision not to have his children christened, she admits that "She could not understand why Pen had to torture himself by thinking differently from other people. It only made one unhappy. When there was a thing to do, something that people *did* – like christening, why could not one simply do it without *worrying?*"[67] Even those who were sympathetic to the objectors seemed to feel that they were causing unwarranted problems for themselves, that they suffered from a kind of spiritual obstinacy, and that they were separating themselves from the majority due to pride or a relish for trouble and difficulties.

The weight of this pressure for democratic unity affected even the most independent-minded individuals. As argued in the previous chapter, many pacifists and conscientious objectors felt the need for some element of community support. Pen's son, Quentin Thatcher, is highly self-reliant. He has, and apparently wants, few friends. However, when the behaviour expected of him in the war goes beyond what he can personally countenance, he reaches out to his cousin and best friend Daniel Thatcher for confirmation of the righteousness of his next step. In England, about to be decorated for his participation in a particularly hard-fought raid in which he had to bayonet surrendering Germans, Quentin writes Daniel a letter: "I'm not physically afraid a bit and never was. But I haven't it in me to do a butchery like that again ... Shall I become a conscientious objector and fight this whole dirty business? What do you advise? If I had one friend who approved I could do it."[68] Although Daniel does not offer him that approval, Quentin informs his battalion commander of his decision not to return to his unit or to take alternative service.

Child describes the subsequent sequence of events as Quentin's "descent into hell." He is insulted, stripped of his medal, and sent back to France where he could be shot for his stance. A concerted effort is made to break his spirit and those of the other objectors with whom he spends time in military detention: "They were put in cells of corrugated iron, so cold that frost rimmed the walls; when they sat down they got so cold and stiff that they could not get up without using their hands. They were fed on army biscuit and water, and sometimes they were ironed with their faces to the wall. They still refused duty. They were knocked about by soldiers wearing boxing gloves for two or three hours, revived with cold water and kicks, knocked about again ... They refused duty."[69] However, Quentin does not make it to Wandsworth military prison, or its fictional equivalent: unable to persevere in his lonely stance, he rejoins his battalion. Later, he meets Daniel in London, who asks him to explain his change of heart. Quentin replies, "I can't really explain. I found I couldn't nourish an intellectual loyalty in an emotional vacuum – if that means anything to you ... I found I depended on people more than I thought." The same explanation comes across in Quentin's dream at the end of the novel. He dreams that he is in a place where souls come after death, to pronounce judgment upon themselves. Quentin, feeling a failure, deliberately chooses the harsh fate of annihilation. "Seeing clearly the greater loyalty, I turned my back upon it and chose the lesser. I knew a man such as I was had to fight against the war, not simply because it brought suffering to the world, but because it destroyed man's love of life and faith in it and by putting despair in its place, destroyed their spirits ... I did not persevere unto the end."[70] When asked why he failed to persevere, Quentin explains that he faltered because he stood alone. Although he was imprisoned with Quakers, absolutists like himself, his experience differed from theirs, and he did not feel one of them. In the end, he returned to those with whom he felt a connection and an owed loyalty – the soldiers at the front.

MANY WARTIME JOURNALISTS would have seen Quentin's decision to end his reliance on his own personal ethics as a sound one. "Downeaster," a columnist for the *Canadian Churchman*, argued that those who fell back on their consciences as the final arbiter of their behaviour were deluded: "Conscience ... does not tell us when we are doing right, but when we mean to do right. That is as far as it can go. Therefore it follows that while the State should always, when expedient, respect a man's conscientious scruples, it cannot be bound by them. Where the conscience of one man clashes with that of another on a point which affects the general welfare, the State must step in and decide. Thus there are manifest limits to the authority of conscience."[71] The individual basis of conscientious objection was a problem partly because it limited the authority of the state. Also, its veracity was difficult to discern, both publicly and even to oneself. Using a Quaker definition of conscience, Sidney Webb offered a "rough and ready test" to help a man determine whether a "stop in the mind" was actually the voice of conscience, rather than fear, reluctance to change, or mere obstinacy: "Is the course of action dictated by Conscience in any way more pleasurable or more advantageous to the Objector than that to which he conscientiously objects?"[72] An article in the *Manitoba Free Press* made a similar point: "How can they be sure that they believe in non-resistance when there are so many brave men between them and danger?"[73] Their conscience needed some sort of a test, and their courage was always at issue. This issue of sacrifice, and the benefits of suffering for some noble goal, permeates war literature. The bravery of the soldiers consisted of their willingness to suffer for their country. COs, it seemed, would always be viewed with a certain degree of suspicion while the course they chose seemed safer or easier than that of the enlisted men.

The dilemma of how to deal justly with the CO problem perplexed some Canadians throughout the war, and not just those in government. One writer to the *Toronto Globe*, Edwin Wyle, reminded the newspaper's readers about the British sense of fair play, arguing that regardless of how odd the objectors' philosophy might seem, they were entitled to a presumption of sincerity. He doubted that any good would ever accrue "from incarcerating men at Burwash and other places for lengthy periods whose only offence is a misplaced fidelity to conscience. Whilst most of us are unable, try as we may, to understand the viewpoint of these conscientious objectors to military service under existing conditions, yet it seems to me that British fair play should at least lead us to believe them to be sincere, and give them exemption from actual fighting accordingly without saddling them with the stigma of 'jailbirds,' a procedure which does no one good and may possibly do much harm." But, to prevent men from taking advantage of such an assumption of legitimacy, a test was required. Wyle proposed that all conscientious objectors be drafted to service on the North Sea minesweepers. This work, which would not involve killing, was in fact "an important life-saving service." The sole objection he could imagine to such a service was that of cowardice.[74] Theodore Roosevelt, on a visit to Toronto, voiced similar thoughts about resolving the dilemma of the CO. On minesweepers, COs "would not kill anyone else, and they would be certain of a chance to go to the blue end of the rim."[75] The vast crowd that cheered his speech evidently agreed with him.

Other Canadians offered different solutions to this knotty problem. Mrs. Margaret Gibson wrote to the *Canadian Churchman*, suggesting that "the temptation to conscientious objection might be diminished if every man who adopts it were to have his name at once and for life blotted out from the registers of voters, Parliamentary and municipal." The editor called this a "clever and original, if somewhat drastic method of dealing with a question difficult enough at any time, but doubly so to-day, when shirkers of every description are sheltering themselves as Quakers and, therefore, conscientious objectors."[76]

These responses to COs conflicted sharply with the Christian tradition in which people who took such a position were counted among its martyrs and saints. A *Manitoba Free Press* editorial attempted to explain why conscientious objection, often seen historically as a courageous and noble response, manifestly could not be perceived as such during this war. The ideal of meeting physical attack with non-resistance, it argued, was laudable only when the courage of the person being attacked was not in question: "Perhaps it is on this point that the balance swings, making non-resistance fine in the man who could not fear the consequences of resistance." The limitations on the acceptability of this stance were unambiguous: "When, however, the blow is directed at, and the wrong done to, others to whom he is obliged, it is another matter. It is the right of the individual to humble himself to the lowest hell, but he is presumptuous beyond man's right whose conscience will say that others must suffer injustice and oppression which he could help to avert. Not all the scriptures that ever were written, however interpreted, can be made to justify a view which, if generally accepted, would loose the hell-hounds of Prussia on the civilized world."[77] In this interpretation, choosing to object conscientiously, however high-minded, was a selfish and self-serving act. Public opinion conceded a CO's right to refuse to fight on his own behalf but saw the implications of that non-resistance as untenable, given that, in theory, Canada was at war not to protect itself, but to defend the women and children in Belgium. In this way, objectors were particularly vulnerable to wartime propaganda that paraded "Hun" atrocities.

These articles share a sense that, regardless of how he expressed them, the values of a conscientious objector could never be as noble as those of the soldier who faced danger at the front. By extension, respect tended to be more readily accorded when a CO was seen to suffer, or to accept a dangerous situation. John Evans, a Christadelphian conscientious objector who was transported overseas and court-martialled, records one conversation that gave him "considerable courage to face the unknown perils of Wandsworth":

> One morning a young man who had landed afoul of the King's orders landed in the guardhouse. As he came through the door, he exclaimed, "I'd like to meet that conscientious objector." My friend the Irish policeman replied, "Well, here he is, meet him." He strode over to shake hands and said, "Evans, I don't suppose you know it, but you are a mighty popular man in this camp." He continued, "Do you know what the CO told us on the parade ground the other morning?" I said, "No." "Well," he said, "He told us that if every man in the British army was as good a man as you are, we would have licked the Germans three years ago."[78]

Evans' stoicism and fortitude had earned their respect. Recording several such incidents in his memoirs, Evans remarked that the soldiers began to support him after they saw him endure punishments without complaining and make principled decisions resulting in punishments that could have been avoided.

Evans was not alone in receiving support from friends and associates outside his pacifist denomination. Arthur Hill, a Christadelphian aged twenty-five, was evidently the only CO who inspired people to write letters to the editor. Unusual in the amount of attention it received, Hill's case offers an opportunity for a more in-depth examination of the variety and breadth of public opinion surrounding a specific instance of conscientious objection. On 14 November 1918, three days after the war ended, Hill was sentenced to ten years' imprisonment for refusing to put on a uniform.[79] The judgment itself is not extant, but he was refused exemption apparently because "the company of which Arthur Hill's father is the President, and the holder of the majority stock, and of which Arthur

Hill was the superintendent was one of the largest contractors in Canada with the Imperial Munitions Board for the manufacture of certain shell parts."[80] By this time, the Christadelphian Church had been granted recognition as an organization, but the appeal court judge deemed that Hill did not meet the proper individual criteria for conscientious objection. This prompted a brief mention in the "Notes and Comments" section of the *Toronto Globe* editorial page: "Are the 'conscientious objectors' worse than the 'defaulters?' Why should a fine type of a citizen like Arthur Hill go to penitentiary for ten years, a prisoner for conscience sake, while thousands of men who sneaked out of military service are free to return home immune from punishment?"[81] This sympathetic language was unusual and did not appear earlier in the war, even in the *Globe*, which tended to be somewhat more tolerant of COs than other newspapers. The editor did not elaborate on what precisely he meant by describing Hill as "a fine type of a citizen," and at least one reader, W.R. Smythe, was irked by this representation. Smythe based his disagreement on the Christadelphian tenets against political participation and fighting: "If a sufficient percentage of the community professed these views or actually held them – taking advantage of the safety and security of society, while casting their share of the obligations of citizenship on others, life on the theories of modern civilisation would be impossible." Smythe asserted that, on two grounds, Hill was quite the antithesis of "a fine type of citizen": his beliefs were untenable for civilization as a whole, and he himself was personally hypocritical in claiming them in the first place.

Hill had his defenders, however. Unlike the *Globe* editor, V.A. Clark had no problem with the gentle treatment of "deserters." He commented that, "in times of victory it has been customary to release criminals from prisons to give them a chance to redeem their past." Clark knew Hill and approved of him on a personal level, having found him to be "an exceptionally fine young man (apart from the shackles of his creed)." He also disagreed with Smythe's characterization of the conscientious objector as a bad citizen. Although the CO did cause difficulties in wartime, he was generally "a fine type in normal civilian times." The war was over now, and civilian values were due for a return. Clark illustrated his point with a sketch of Hill's qualities: "I am sure he found it harder to resist military service than to don the uniform and fight in Flanders as other young men of his acquaintance of different creeds have done. His greatest chum is in the aviation corps. He himself is a quiet, gentlemanly, considerate chap – a favourite both in social and business circles ... He was a foreman in the plate glass factory and highly esteemed by the employees."[82] In defending the objector, Clark found it important to emphasize his normality: that he was popular and probably had the same urge to fight as everyone else. Clark also offered a correction to a story that Hill had worked in a munitions factory, claiming that, though the Toronto plate glass factory that employed him did have a munitions department, he had not worked there.

Another letter defending Hill appeared a couple of days later, signed by "S.J. Rutherford, President of the Toronto Plate Glass Importing Co. Ltd." Rutherford refuted the allegation that Hill had been engaged in the manufacture of munitions: "Arthur Hill was never at any time engaged in or connected with our munitions department, but, on the contrary, at his own request, was left in the glass department, although at a monetary loss to himself." Although Rutherford did not "profess to understand the mind of the conscientious objector," he defended Hill's personal bravery by citing two incidents in which he saved women or children from drowning. Apocryphal or not, these accounts were deemed necessary to prove that Hill's objection did not spring from cowardice.[83]

The last published word on the Arthur Hill case came from T.H. Lister, who thought the public at large was probably more supportive of conscientious objectors than the sentences handed down to them would seem to indicate: "I wish some persons in prominent places would have petitions placed where they could be signed. I am convinced that thousands would avail themselves of a chance to help undo a colossal injustice." Lister's letter mentioned that he had also written to the Department of Justice, urging that "justice [be] done to every conscientious objector."[84] The case of Arthur Hill, especially the story in which he had saved people from drowning, had struck him strongly. In voicing an opinion on Arthur Hill as an individual and on the treatment he had received, the *Toronto Globe* sparked an interesting debate regarding what constituted good citizenship. That Hill merited such attention is probably at least partly attributable to his social standing. As the foreman in a factory in which his father owned the majority stock, he came from a higher economic class than most conscientious objectors who have left records. That Hill, one of the very few objectors of some social standing, excited so much commentary suggests that the lesser attention accorded other COs is at least partly attributable to their lower economic class.

Hill's supporters defended him by comparing him to men who evaded conscription. Although COs were quite obviously not alone in their apparent detachment from the spirit of national self-sacrifice, they were much more visible than men who simply failed to register. Everyone knew that a great many men, whose silent evasion was also a form of opposition to the war, were simply avoiding the draft.[85] But the conscientious objectors were protesting the conscription of their bodies publicly and explicitly, and in terms that threatened the monopoly of religious virtue held by the supporters of the war.

Comparisons between "deserters" and COs became more frequent towards and after the armistice, and attitudes regarding the latter softened somewhat.

COs also began to receive more sympathy due to the harshness of their prison sentences. "Spectator," who wrote for the *Canadian Churchman,* was annoyed by the fact that "We somehow do not hear of the sentences of men who have taken to the woods and the turnip patches, or who boldly challenge the authorities to come and get them. 'Spectator' has no sympathy with so-called conscientious objectors in wartime, but he confesses that he sees nothing nationally heroic in hustling these friendless people off to jail while others who have made public demonstrations and private retreats still roam at large."[86] The enforcement of the Military Service Act presented some problems. Had an objector simply chosen to hide, he would probably have escaped the draft altogether. When groups of "deserters" were rounded up late in the war, they tended to receive fairly lenient punishments. The CO, who was availing himself of a position legally allowed under an act of Parliament, faced ignominy and censure. Near the end of the war, and especially after the armistice, several newspaper editorials decided that this was unfair and that the conscientious objector represented at least a better type of citizen than the deserter. In "The Shirkers' Triumph," the *Toronto Globe* lamented the situation:

> A conscientious objector was sentenced to two years in the Kingston Penitentiary last week for refusing to don the King's uniform, though he had worked for five months without pay. Three men this week were given a year each for refusing to obey an order to report for military duty ... Yesterday in another court one hundred men were fined $5 for evading the Military Service Act, and were restored to full citizenship. The disparities in these sentences require some explanation. Conscientious objectors who stay to take their medicine are less obnoxious than slackers who sneak out of the reach of the law.[87]

Two weeks later, the same newspaper made a stronger appeal, demanding "the immediate release of conscientious objectors unless in flagrant cases of proven fraud or sedition":

> Conscientious objectors who are serving sentences are being pardoned and released in several States of the Union, and the federal authorities are reviewing the whole situation relating to this class. The Canadian Department of Justice might well consider the cases of those conscientious objectors who are still serving terms of imprisonment. Many of them have been given prison or penitentiary sentences of two, three, or five years. There is an outrageous inequality between this punishment and that meted out to defaulters under the Military Service Act. Even supposing that some of the so-called conscientious objectors were shamming, their offence was not so gross as that of men who tried to get out of the reach of the

law – hundreds of whom have since been restored to full civil rights and liberties on payment of nominal fines.[88]

In response to a post-war query about treatment of deserters, defaulters, and conscientious objectors still in military or civilian prisons, the deputy minister of justice did not make the same distinction between them but did advise officers to look at cases individually, if it was feasible:

> We think that enquiry should be made through the Remission Branch in regard to each individual case, and that reports on each case be obtained from the Parole Offices throughout the country, so that it may be ascertained, as far as it is possible to do so, whether the defaulter is a bona fide objector for conscience sake, or whether on the other hand he has been more or less of a "slacker" ... In the case of a bona fide conscientious objector, we think that a minimum term of confinement should be six months, but where a person, who is in reality a "slacker," has posed as a conscientious objector in order to avoid military service, we think that the penalty should be not less than two years.[89]

In instructing officers to determine whether an objection was genuine, this memorandum asked them to make a complicated decision. That COs were in prison at all was partly due to the difficulty of ascertaining whether their objection was bona fide. Interestingly, fairly strict minimum sentences were still being recommended several months after the war ended. This indicates that the imprisonment of COs was connected less to immediate worries that they might discourage recruiting or set an example of non-compliance with conscription than to the intent of punishing behaviour deemed socially unacceptable.

Conscientious objectors, then, were widely seen as unintelligent, unimaginative, and obdurate. The vision of the stubborn, oafish objector differed from the stereotypical over-intellectual and self-important British variant. Predictably, COs faced frequent charges of cowardice and pro-Germanism. In holding religious duty higher than its civic equivalent, or in differing from the vast majority of their compatriots in their definition of political responsibility, they were frequently vilified as having no sense of duty whatsoever. This was a significant insult, given that acceptance of duty was a key virtue in Canadian society at this time and a prime component of both masculinity and citizenship. Most Canadians discerned manifest distinctions between conscientious objectors of differing religious and ethnic backgrounds. The Quakers tended to be more respected than pacifists from other sects, due to the familiarity of their tenets and good works, their willingness to undertake non-combatant service, and their Anglo-Celtic origins. The German background of Mennonites, Tunkers, and the Amish raised many suspicions, and their insularity also proved offensive. This reaction meant that the problem of conscientious objection was closely connected to that of minority education rights for these Anabaptist groups. The case of Arthur Hill also suggests that the treatment of COs depended on how they were viewed as individuals, something largely determined by class and how well they were known. Members of the more established churches, who were good citizens in other respects, were also better tolerated than other conscientious objectors. The treatment accorded objectors, then, seems to have been largely predicated upon the degree to which they were judged "respectable" – participating in the same discourse of duty as their compatriots and otherwise behaving as good citizens.

Conclusion

THE END OF THE First World War did not mean the end of the problem of the conscientious objector. Precisely how many objectors were in prison when the armistice was signed is unclear. Many were still awaiting trial, and several men received long prison sentences after hostilities ended. By the end of the war, the standard sentence had actually increased from two years to life, commuted to ten years, although no one actually spent so long in prison. COs were released piecemeal as the Canadian Expeditionary Force was demobilized. In response to a query in late January 1919 about remission of sentences now that the war was over, E.L. Newcombe, the deputy minister of justice, noted that there were "at present undergoing sentence a total of three hundred sixty two prisoners, of whom one hundred sixty three are conscientious objectors, and that there are thirty six awaiting trial by court-martial."[1] About a week later, in a circular letter of 5 February 1919 advising punishment for various kinds of desertion and conscientious objection, Newcombe stated that "there are now about one hundred thirty two persons in confinement as conscientious objectors."[2] Some COs were discharged, their records citing grounds of misconduct rather than demobilization, on 28 February 1919.[3] On 24 March, Rodolphe Lemieux, MP for Gaspé, Quebec, introduced a motion in the House of Commons "That, in the opinion of this House, amnesty should be granted to religious conscientious objectors to military service." He reminded the House that Great Britain had always led the world in the protection of religious and civil freedom, and urged the government to be "Merciful to these honest and sincere young men, law-abiding citizens in every other respect, who did not default but presented themselves boldly before the tribunals and stated their objections ... I have received many letters on this subject from different parts of the country, and I say that the least we can do now that the war is over ... is to act generously."[4] Lemieux particularly praised the active, non-violent service of Quakers in France and Belgium. He tabled his appeal when told that the objectors were already scheduled to be released by the summer. In May 1919, when a question was asked in Parliament about how many COs were still incarcerated, the Department of Justice made inquiries and found that forty were serving prison terms; thirty-four were in federal penitentiaries and six in provincial jails.[5]

SCHOLARS SUCH AS Thomas Socknat have argued that the First World War in Canada marked a transformation in pacifism, a move from the primarily religious pacifism of the nineteenth century to the primarily political dissent of the twentieth. Canadian conscientious objectors, in general, seem to have subscribed to the older religious variant, at least at the beginning of the war. But even among the quietist groups that received recognition for their conscientious objection, a coming together can be seen. If the shift to a more political objection is difficult to discern among members of these groups, for whom obedience to government strictures was an element of doctrine, an increased post-war activism at least is apparent. Various sects within the historic peace churches began to communicate with each other and organize. Immediately after the war, they took an active role in restoration work overseas. And, by the Second World War, many of their leaders met with members of the government prior to the enactment of conscription legislation, to work out a means of service that would be acceptable to the aims and requirements of war, Canadian public opinion, and the ethical scruples of their adherents.[6]

Although the most obvious aspect of the peace church discourse of dissent during the First World War was its unique combination of obedience and intransigence, the war also marked another change in relations between the non-resistant churches and Ottawa. In *The Story of the Mennonites*, C.H. Smith suggests that, historically, Anabaptist groups preferred to deal with autocratic governments rather than with their democratic counterparts because the latter tended to be less considerate of conscientious scruples and less patient with special privileges granted to minorities than were the former.[7] In "The Politicization of the Mennonite Peace Witness in the Twentieth Century," Joe Mihevc makes a similar argument: "The egalitarian spirit of American society carried with it a greater intolerance of nonconformity and social dissent. The intolerance of the majority toward the minority group was more prevalent in the United States than in Canada where special arrangements with different classes and groups were more acceptable."[8] Although First World War Canada was part of the British Empire, it was also a democracy, whose citizens responded to the war with a rhetoric of individual duty and who had, at least implicitly, voted for conscription. This experience changed the way in which Canadian Anabaptist groups approached war and military service. In *Mennonite Peacemaking: From Quietism to Activism*, Leo Driedger and Donald B. Kraybill discuss the transformation in Mennonite pacifism, noting a shift during the First World War from use of the term *non-resistance* to terms that included *peace*. The semantic change was indicative of the beginnings of a move to a more active, self-conscious service ethic and away from the focus on prohibitions. M.J. Heisey shows that, at least for the Brethren in Christ (Tunker) Church, this change also created tensions that weakened the church's corporate peace stand and "its appreciation of being a unique, small community."[9]

THE EXPERIENCE OF Canadian conscientious objection in the Second World War is much more fully documented. Once again, peace church members comprised the largest group of COs and the dominant force shaping the characteristics of conscientious objection in wartime Canada.[10] Devi Prasad and Tony Smythe, in their world survey of conscription, estimate that during this war, ten thousand conscientious objectors were recognized in Canada, and a further four hundred were given prison sentences. According to their figures, 63 percent of COs, or more than six thousand, were Mennonites, 20 percent were Doukhobors, and 17 percent were what they term "miscellaneous."[11]

In the Second World War, recognized conscientious objectors had the option of undertaking alternative service. One factor that contributed towards making this option acceptable to them was the 1923 immigration of a Mennonite group fleeing a severe famine and oppression in the USSR.[12] Initially, however, a secret Order-in-Council had to be passed to permit their immigration. At the end of the First World War, prompted by public dislike of Mennonite and Hutterite "un-Canadian" doctrines of non-resistance and separate education, Ottawa had prohibited the further immigration of these groups. The new arrivals, dubbed "Russlanders" by Canadian Mennonites, were allowed to immigrate if they fulfilled certain conditions: They were to be placed on the land as farmers and should "find shelter and support among their brethren," so that none would become a public charge. Furthermore, the complete military exemption granted to the earlier group of Russian Mennonite immigrants in 1872 would not apply to them. This last stipulation partly explains their readiness to accept alternative service in the Second World War. They were also probably amenable to the idea because they had performed similar service in Russia during the First World War, where absolute exemption had not been granted.[13]

Conscientious objection was a more frequent subject in parliamentary debates during the Second World War than it had been in the first, where the general readiness of the historic peace churches to find other ways to serve won them support. J.G. Gardiner, minister of national war services, was one minister who promoted civilian national service for conscientious objectors. Walter Tucker, an MP from Rosthern, Saskatchewan, also championed their cause and applauded their efforts:

We find that within the last ten days representatives of the Mennonites of Western Canada, the Mennonites of Ontario, the Quakers in Canada and the Tunkers came to Ottawa to interview the ministry of national war services to say to that department that while they do not believe in bearing arms, they are prepared to go into any branch of the service of the country where they could help to save life, where they could help the wounded, and for other services of that kind. It did not matter to them whether[sic] it was and they have asked too, that their operations should be made under civilian auspices ... They appreciate the rights of citizenship in Canada. They wanted to show their appreciation, and they were not trying to get out of doing their full share. All this was done after the Government had exempted them from military service.[14]

As in the earlier war, duty was a prime component of Mennonite philosophy. Because it accorded well with the rhetoric of sacrifice and responsibility in the rest of wartime Canada, it was well received by the government. The diplomacy with which William Lyon Mackenzie King is credited in enacting conscription legislation with minimal provocation to Quebec was also evident in his willingness to accept the peace church offer to perform work of national importance under civilian auspices.[15]

Not all denominations were able to countenance such a compromise. The IBSA suffered censure during the Second World War beyond that related to the unwillingness of its members to join the military. In July 1940, Ottawa banned the Canadian Watch Tower Bible and Tract Society – the legal entity that owned Bible Students' (known since 1931 as Jehovah's Witnesses) meeting halls and arranged for the printing of their literature. It became an offence to belong to the society, and all the organization's property was placed in the hands of the custodian of enemy property. Police confiscated Jehovah's Witness literature, seized Watch Tower Society property, shut up Witness meeting halls, and prosecuted Witnesses for possessing or distributing banned literature.[16] The Witnesses met repression with intransigence, insisting that all baptized adherents were ministers and thus exempt from military service, and that voluntary alternative service was wrong and unacceptable.[17]

Most other COs were amenable to alternative selective service, which provided employment for them in Canada under civilian auspices. They worked in lumber camps, coal mines, the paper industry, and agriculture, receiving minimal pay, with the balance given as a compulsory donation to the Red Cross.[18] They were often sent far from their home communities, to work hard in uncomfortable conditions. But few seem to have complained. Indeed many COs, at least in retrospect, seem to have perceived the experience as something of an adventure. They knew that conditions for soldiers were equally unpleasant and more hazardous, and welcomed a chance to prove themselves.

First World War objectors aided the creation of an organization to implement alternative service and fostered the willingness of Ottawa and the non-resistant churches to accept it; they also formed links on a more individual level. Either directly or through example, they could often provide the next generation of potential conscripts with the sort of guidance that they themselves had been denied. One member of the Pentecostal Assemblies, Douglas Rudd, recalls the conflict he felt regarding whether to become a conscientious objector during the Second World War:

> When it came time for World War II, of course we were organized. I remember looking to some of the elders for guidance because I was in that age group. I was called out of Bible College and felt very keenly about it. It so happened that my basic training was in Peterborough and George Chambers was the pastor. I remember making a special trip to his home one Saturday to ask him for advice. That is when he told me about Elmor Morrison [a First World War CO], but he would not commit himself. I had been looking forward to some guidance. But I can understand his position now. It had to be my choice ... I joined a non-combatant arm of the service. It was good experience for me, helped me mature and in turn I found the opportunity to help many servicemen spiritually. Many found it hard to take a stand for the Lord.[19]

Faced with conscription, the young Douglas Rudd turned to senior members of his church and was able to speak to people with direct experience who helped him reach his own decision, a course unavailable to a Pentecostal conscript during the First World War. In the Tunker Church, CO Ernest John Swalm helped guide the next generation. He became a minister, and later a bishop, and was a popular evangelist who travelled widely in the Tunker community. In 1938, the church published Swalm's *My Beloved Brethern*, describing his experiences with conscription, court martial, imprisonment, and release.[20]

Other First World War COs also played a more formal role in securing recognition for like-minded men in the next war. John Walter Evans, who had been sent overseas and imprisoned for refusing to obey military orders, became the Hamilton representative of the Canadian Christadelphian Standing Committee when it was revived in 1934. Another committee member, Frederick C. Welshman, was the brother of William R. Welshman, who had suffered imprisonment for his conscientious objection in the First World War.[21]

The experience of the First World War COs probably had some effect in other quarters as well. Of Evans, John Botten writes, "there is little doubt that his faithfulness under extreme pressure helped to bring about the Alternative Service

Act which allowed conscientious objection in the Second World War."[22] This is, of course, a somewhat simplistic reading: the amendments to the National War Service Regulations making provision for alternative service were the result of a great deal of organization and effort on the part of several peace churches and government officials. But it is possible that positive reports about the behaviour of individual COs in the last war coloured the attitudes of some of the officials involved and made them more open to negotiation regarding the alternative service option.

THE MOST IMPORTANT aspect of the experience of conscientious objection in Canada during the First World War, arguably, was the inability of pacifist anti-conscriptionists to come together. A number of factors affected this situation to varying degrees. For instance, writing about Australia, Paul Wilson has surmised that the cost and time associated with travel between states was one factor hindering the formation of an Australia-wide peace movement during the Second World War.[23] A similar inference could be made as a partial explanation for the weakness of the movement in First World War Canada. Communication difficulties, in a country with a relatively small and dispersed population, could also account for the markedly uneven regional distribution of objection.

Also, and more importantly, leadership was notably absent. In Canada, conscientious resistance by the political and intellectual elite was minor in nature. Although the popularity of the war was a key factor here, this silence was also due to the limited categories of exemption, which made secular resistance difficult. The fact that exemption on the grounds of conscience could be gained solely through membership in a recognized pacifist sect seems to have been tremendously effective in isolating objectors and curtailing the organization of dissent. That, under the MSA, the Anabaptist groups were accorded preferential treatment also hindered the formation of a broader-based peace movement along the lines of the No-Conscription Fellowship in Britain. Most members of the pacifist sects preferred to remain outside mainstream society and to avoid the political confrontation that a wider dissent would have required.

In addition, the diversity of the men who objected to military service on conscientious grounds probably contributed to their inability to organize. Those who accepted non-combatant service, such as the Seventh-day Adventists who distanced themselves from other dissenters by describing themselves as "conscientious cooperators," probably did not wish to be too closely associated with the more intransigent types. Nor did it help that the unpopular IBSA tended to provide most of the more prominent instances of absolute objection. Even the Society of Friends, which made efforts for a more inclusive conscientious objection clause, wished, at times, to avoid association with those for whom conscience might be a convenience. Religious differences probably came into play as well. During the Second World War, COs from differing denominations were housed together in work camps; Claude Klassen remembers being called a "darkened heathen" by another objector.[24] First World War COs, not interned in large groups and less secure about their possible fate in the military, seem to have been fairly tolerant of doctrinal differences when they did encounter each other. Nonetheless, similar divisions probably existed for them as well. The paucity of memoirs, however, makes any conclusion tenuous. Further barriers to a unified response arose from the fact that religious objectors tended to emphasize their good citizenship and would probably have avoided any association with anti-war socialists and French Canadians. At any rate, they did not pursue this connection.

Another theme common to the various pacifist sectarian and non-sectarian bodies in Canada is the relative absence of a desire for martyrdom. In Britain, conscientious objector Stephen Hobhouse, who knew that he would fail his medical exam and thus be exempt from conscription, refused to permit his medical board to examine him. Fenner Brockway, editor of the *Labour Leader,* quit his job because editors were exempt from conscription.[25] Neither wanted to take advantage of grounds for exemption that were not open to all. This stubbornness is not evident in Canada. Objectors, especially from the predominantly agrarian peace churches, often applied for exemption on grounds of occupation, as farmers. Others listed a conscientious objection to military service among several grounds for exemption and accepted whatever grounds were available to them. Obviously, this picture is incomplete, and in the preceding chapters we have encountered several men who took a principled public stand and who suffered for it. But the apparent absence in Canada of individuals like NCF president Clifford Allen and Fenner Brockway has several possible causes. It was probably exaggerated by the lack of leaders and organization. Arguing one's right to exemption on conscientious grounds, especially when other means to the same end were available, was difficult without the support of a group of like-minded individuals. Those who were not recognized but who persevered in their objection often came from the IBSA and similar sects, and the support they were able to draw from their co-religionists mitigated the rigours of an otherwise rather lonely and frightening experience.

Not all COs chose the simplest route to exemption. When men such as Vernal Running and Oswald Peacock, who could have avoided military service without undergoing the physical, emotional, and economic suffering and ignominy associated with conscientious objection, chose to go that route; nonetheless, they seem to have gained a degree of respect and sympathy from government and military officials for whom sacrifice and patriotic duty were largely conflated. Men perceived as taking this route do seem to have received lighter sentences when court-martialled overseas, although they are too few in number to yield any definitive conclusions. For refusing an order to go on parade, Vernal Running and Oswald Peacock, both eligible to be considered for exemption on financial grounds, were sentenced to six months' detention, whereas Henry Naish and Robert Clegg, who had refused the same order, were both sentenced to eighteen months, later remitted to twelve. This, however, could also be attributed to bias against the IBSA, to which Naish and Clegg belonged.

Another factor discouraging organization and prompting objectors to pursue other channels of exemption may have been government repression, though this argument is complicated by the fact that constraint sometimes encourages dissidence. Assessing government repression is also problematic, given that none of the extant records cite it as explaining a man's decision not to claim conscientious objection (or, conversely, for seeking out such martyrdom). The death of David Wells brought widespread and generally sympathetic publicity, engendered a flurry of telegrams, was mentioned in the Manitoba Legislature, and roused the Trades and Labor Congress to support objectors. Had there been more instances of such apparent heroic self-sacrifice, the story of conscientious objection in this country might have had a markedly different tone. The Borden administration seems, implicitly at least, to have recognized this danger. Although it did send COs overseas, they were soon returned to Canada. Objectors were sentenced to life imprisonment, even after the end of the war, but all seem to have been quietly released by the end of 1919. The strategy of the Canadian government of a harsh public face combined with a recognition that it was better not to attempt to force the intransigents – acted to limit objection and to avoid making martyrs for the cause.

THE LIST OF conscientious objectors given in Table 1 of the appendix, though as complete as possible, does not purport to be definitive; at the very least, it will serve as a starting point for further research. Most of the men recorded there were named in newspaper accounts of exemption tribunals and courts martial or mentioned in histories of pacifist sects or individual biographies. I located some of them by compiling lists of common Mennonite, Tunker, Doukhobor, and Quaker names, and checking the Canadian Expeditionary Force files for a record of an objection. Since the MSA deemed all men, when their group was called up, to be soldiers, I verified all objectors, where possible, by their CEF records. I have already discussed the problems of definition that plague a project such as this. A further, and rather interesting, variant on these is the fact that nearly all the men listed in the appendix are there because, at some stage in their interaction with legal and military regulation, they were deemed *not* to be true conscientious objectors. The great mass of individuals who did not serve in the CEF for reasons of conscience do not appear. The members of the historic peace churches, who were excepted from the MSA, and the greatest part of those who were exempted from it, left few records of their experience. It was those whom the Borden administration and tribunals did not recognize who tended to be reported in the newspapers, or who generated court martial records.

Despite these limitations, certain trends are nonetheless discernable in the appendix tables. The peace church members show a preponderance of Ontarians, or men born in Ontario – perhaps a reflection of the difficulties and inconsistencies in their exemption. The disproportionate number of farmers probably arises partly from the traditional farming basis of the historic peace churches.[26] Almost without exception, the COs listed in the appendix are working-class men. This is one reason that the British image of the pretentious, overly intellectual, effeminate conscientious objector was not the only stereotype of the conscientious objector in Canada. Why working-class men are so over-represented is difficult to explain. Perhaps upper-class men were better able to receive exemption on other grounds. Perhaps a degree of class bias existed in the tribunals. One interesting point is that, in both Britain and Canada, the conscientious objector was typically perceived as selfish and a poor citizen. However, the British stereotype presented him as something of an unrealistic and avant-garde character, with a wayward and selfish focus on individual freedom. In the Canadian version, CO selfishness revolved around close-mindedness, a stubborn determination to look backward rather than joining the rest of the country in what had been widely agreed was a nationally improving venture.

That most COs appear to have been manual labourers or farmers, as well as members of marginalized religious groups, would seem to have affected their experience in other ways as well. Although the imprisonment of Stephen Hobhouse, who came from a wealthy and politically active family, did much to raise the profile of British conscientious objectors, their Canadian counterparts seem by and large to have come from groups that did not attract government or public attention. Apparently, they had no aggressive defenders in the House of Commons and could not organize themselves to lobby. In Britain, the treatment of a CO tended to depend upon the degree to which he was seen as an individual. And being an individual, especially at the level of the appeal tribunal, was often predicated upon sharing the upper-middle-class background of the tribunal judges. Adrian Stephen reminisces that class was an important element in some of the inconsistencies incurred by the British tribunals: "The frenzied patriotism whipped up by the war lost some of its power for evil when the man to be dealt with was a real live human being whom everybody knew. When the applicant was a nobody he had less chance; the heated fantasies conjured up by war conditions could not be dispelled in a minute by a nervous young man whose business must be dispatched in time for tea."[27] The stance of an individual, the idiosyncrasies of a friend or neighbour, could be understood. It was the CO who was also a stranger who seemed obviously a coward. And significantly British conscientious objectors as a group seemed threatening. The absence of this threat, and of politically or socially prominent Canadian objectors, has contributed to their consequent historical neglect.

One other unifying aspect is a tendency to religious fundamentalism among those who claimed exemption from military service on conscientious grounds. Many groups and individuals who objected relied heavily on biblical support for their stance. This stems from the focus on religion in the MSA conscientious objection clause. It is also, arguably, linked to the support of the mainstream churches for the war. The leaders of the Anglican, Catholic, Methodist, Baptist, and Presbyterian Churches, as well as of many smaller churches, were among the most vigorous proponents of the war effort. Those who disagreed with their ecclesiastical advisors needed an alternative authority for their convictions. It seems either that those who tended to rely more closely on biblical authority were more likely to take the step of conscientious objection, or that those contemplating objection looked to their Bibles for support.

Regional disparities are also evident in the appendix tables, which show a clear preponderance of COs in Ontario, fewer in the West, and hardly any in Quebec and the Maritimes. Conclusions here are necessarily tenuous. That pacifists had little public presence in Quebec could be linked to the anti-conscription support there, which meant that their exemption might not have seemed as newsworthy as in other parts of the country. In addition, Quebec tended to be somewhat more generous with exemptions than was Ontario; thus, even if a man did oppose military service for reasons of pacifism, he had a good chance of receiving exemption on financial or occupational grounds and thus might not have felt compelled to make a stand as a CO. The anti-war atmosphere in Quebec would also have made it easier for him simply to default. The paucity of pacifists in Quebec could also be connected to the dearth of Catholic pacifists in general and the adherence of church leaders to the just-war facet of Catholic doctrine.[28]

The scarcity of objectors in the Maritimes is less easily explained. The most obvious factor is that both the historic peace churches and the newer millenarian sects had a weak presence on the east coast. The 1911 census lists only eighteen Friends and nineteen Mennonites in New Brunswick, Nova Scotia, and Prince

Edward Island combined. Thirty-four people in New Brunswick gave their religion as Christadelphian and none at all in the other Atlantic provinces.
Throughout the Maritimes, there were only sixty-seven Plymouth Brethren,
forty-eight Bible Students, and 108 Pentecostals.[29] The greater numbers of COs
in Ontario, and to a lesser extent the West, were linked to the greater numbers
of members of both the peace churches and the smaller unrecognized non-
resistant sects in these regions. Among the mainstream denominations, the
Methodist Church, which supported the war but had perhaps the strongest
pre-war pacifist voice, was also predominantly Ontario-based.[30]

Conscientious objectors during the First World War constituted a minority
group at a severe disadvantage. Their views were unfamiliar to many Canadians,
and the perceived need for greater unity during wartime also increased the
distrust engendered by their alternative reading of religious obligations. They
were made to discuss often deeply held but difficult-to-express views in a highly
confrontational setting, where they were judged in public by the community's
elite. That many were young, and often members of sects that encouraged reliance on church elders in spiritual matters, added stress to their tribunal experience and diminished the eloquence necessary to convince their judges. This in
turn exacerbated the stereotype of the conscientious objector as obstinate and
uneducated.

Objectors and mainstream Canadian society shared the predominantly
Christian discourse regarding the war but differed in their interpretation of
appropriate Christian behaviour. The negative stereotype of the CO was based
in both the content of the objection itself and the manner of its expression.
Conscientious objectors seem to have been linked, and handicapped, by their
language. Many, appearing before hostile and often abusive tribunal judges,
made earnest statements of their beliefs but generally failed to recognize that,
no matter how convincing, these were secondary to proof of membership in a
recognized and organized denomination with strict non-resistant principles.

CO dissent was also shaped by ethnicity. Members of religious minority
groups, many objectors belonged to ethnic minorities as well. Mennonites and
Tunkers spoke the same language and were of the same ethnic background as
the enemy, the deeply reviled "Hun," who was capable of any atrocity. The need
to prove their good citizenship in a suspicious and antagonistic environment
muted their ability to dissent. In some quarters, they were already distrusted as
unassimilated groups; thus, their pacifism simply increased demands that they
be educated in appropriate Canadian values, a development that caused them
more anxiety than the inconsistent recognition accorded their non-resistant
beliefs. The efforts at assimilation led parts of the Old Colony and Bergthal
Mennonite groups to emigrate after the war.[31]

Doctrinal and social structures that stressed deference also played a role in forging CO dissent. A belief in submission to authority strongly coloured the experience of many religious objectors. Anabaptist tradition emphasized obedience and focused on passive non-resistance in preference to active pacifist dissent. To a significant extent, other forms of dissent were not open to COs. In social terms as well, adherents were generally unfamiliar with traditional avenues of protest. Although the Quakers made an early effort to extend their protection to pacifists outside their denomination, for most of the war the historic peace churches made no effort to universalize their behaviour. Their experiences in the First World War were an important element in changing this approach.

In the face of such attitudes, it is instructive to examine the behaviour of groups that succeeded in gaining some form of recognition for their beliefs. Seventh-day Adventists were eventually recognized, due to their willingness to accept non-combatant service. The Christadelphian Church, unwilling to follow suit, constitutes the only other sect whose non-resistance was not protected by an earlier Order-in-Council but that nonetheless achieved recognition. Success for this group seems to have arisen from its comprehension of what the Canadian government was looking for and its ability to provide it. Instead of focusing on the strength of their belief, individual Christadelphians stressed their membership in the denomination, offering precedents of historical longevity and recognition gained in Britain. A small group, it was also organized: its standing committee was able to append a complete roll of members to its correspondence with the Borden administration. The church emphasized that any slacker who attempted to take advantage of its exemption would encounter major barriers. Also, unlike the IBSA, this denomination was not novel and potentially subversive; nor did it speak a foreign language and live in suspiciously "un-Canadian" group settlements. Its members were ethnically similar to the majority of the Canadian population. And they seem to have been fairly familiar figures in the community, with friends and acquaintances from outside their own church. Recognition of conscientious objection in Canada, then, seems to have been largely predicated on organization, familiarity, and historical longevity: in other words, on respectability.

IN AN EDITORIAL sympathetic to the position of conscientious objectors, *Maclean's* attributed much of the difficulty in dealing fairly with them to the awkwardness of the task confronting exemption tribunals: "If the authorities could only determine in each individual case where a man's conscientiousness ends and his mere objections begin, it would be possible to protect those who honestly object on religious principles and to find those who are working the pretext of a conscience."[32] The author hit upon the key problem in offering exemption from conscription on ethical grounds; and it seems that Ottawa's solution to this problem was to limit exemption on conscientious grounds to members of recognized religious groups. Membership in a pacifist sect was more amenable to proof, and less susceptible to abuse, than the claims of individual conscience. Even with this clarified definition, the exemption tribunals' responsibility of negotiating the conflict between obligations to family and nation remained formidable.

Even when a tribunal accepted the validity of his objection, a CO was commonly obliged to contend with the widespread conviction that he must earn his exemption. The only obvious means of ascertaining the genuineness of his beliefs seemed to be to subject the man himself to some form of test. The notion that suffering could verify authenticity frequently recurred in discussions of how to judge something as private and innate as a person's conscience. As we have seen, public attitudes began to display a certain tolerance of at least some objectors only towards the end of the war, after they had spent time in prison. The *Maclean's* editorial was intended partly as a record of protest against the severe punishments meted out to COs in Britain. "Submitting to the harshest treatment" would indeed prove an objector's sincerity, but he believed a well-appointed tribunal should be able to save the public that trouble. He also counselled against overstating the threat posed by COs: "The number of these conscientious objectors is said to be very small, so that their participation or non-participation in the war can have practically no influence on the efficiency of the army. It is of course easy to frame arguments showing that the objectors are not practical. But it is not a crime to be visionary."[33] Many Canadians were indeed frustrated at the apparent impracticality of the CO stance. There was also an unexpressed conflict in the angry impatience at the "unreasonable" mulishness of COs, and the desire to see sincerity proven, usually by withstanding abuse over a period of time.

If we are to understand the reaction of mainstream Canada to COs, it is important to situate their objection within contemporary society. A key element of historicizing the response to conscientious objectors is the centrality of the discourse of duty and obligation. In a *Canadian Baptist* editorial, the writer promoted conscription for its perceived educational value: "It teaches every man that he is under obligation to defend his country if it needs him."[34] Although there was no "citizenship" as such for Canadians, who were officially subjects of the British monarch, very clear ideas about what citizenship entailed nonetheless existed. In "Uncle Sam Wants You: Political Obligations in World War I America," Christopher Joseph Capozzola examines the relationship between voluntarism, obligation, and coercion in the workings of a democratic state, looking at conscription in the context of a society with a vivid conception of political and moral obligation. Much of his argument can be applied to Canadian society. Regarding voluntarism in the US, Capozzola remarked, "This was a society predicated on obligations yet exercised through voluntary associations – people were obliged to volunteer. In the context of the war, volunteering on behalf of the war effort became not a moral obligation, but a political one, with coercive political consequences for those who failed to volunteer of their own free will."[35] In political discourse, responsibility outweighed rights, a fact simply intensified by presenting participation in the war effort as a duty. In this context, discussion of conscience in relation to military and home-front war service took on predictable hues. One newspaper editorial lamented the apparent emphasis on exemption rather than service and reminded readers that "the national conscience gives no peace to any Canadian whose soul is not enlisted and whose service is not complete":

> But what needs most of all to be said to hundreds of thousands of Canadians, every man saying it to himself, every woman to herself, in the inner chamber of conscience and the moral judgement is this: This war is my most serious personal affair: into it I must go, either in the trenches in Europe, or in trenches of service in Canada as I can best hold: into that service I must put whatever of power or skill or devotion I can command, with the unselfish purpose and the holy passion that make and mark a good soldier on the salient at Ypres.[36]

In examining political obligation as an idea and set of social practices in the United States during the First World War, Capozzola reconstructs elements of a society very similar to its northern neighbour: "a political culture in which political obligations were articulated *as* obligations, in which concepts like duty, sacrifice, and responsibility were core elements of the rhetorics and realities of ... citizenship."[37] Capozzola's discussion is a reminder that the wartime focus on duty and sacrifice was not wholly a product of the war itself: even before the war, American and Canadian understandings of citizenship tended to concentrate on responsibilities over rights. This is an important consideration in trying to situate the conscientious objector in his social environment.

Military service in the First World War was understood to be a duty, possibly the prime duty, of citizenship. The threat posed by conscientious objectors lay in their refusal to accept that duty outright. In failing to share this concept of duty, or in according primacy to other, non-military duties, COs appeared especially foreign, at a time when unity of belief and behaviour seemed the highest and most necessary good. Although, of themselves, few objectors could be described as radicals, what they requested from Canadian society was implicitly radical in nature. They articulated a different kind of citizenship, one grounded in "a rights-based individualism or an alternative vision of political obligation."[38] Whether they knew it or not, objectors, especially those from outside the historic peace churches, were demanding a sea change in the relations between citizens and the state in treating conscientious objection as a right.

Although, by its very nature, conscientious objection is an individual reaction, during the First World War the Canadian government chose to treat it as a corporate response. This worked to limit the potential number of COs with whom the tribunal system would have to deal. In the Canadian experience, then, the individual basis of conscientious objection was almost negated. One interesting aspect of this is that the Canadian attitude, to a degree, accorded with the pacifist churches' own tendency to discount individualism. The process towards recognizing conscientious objection on individual grounds was complicated in this country, partly because many of the objectors argued for exemption in terms that agreed with the Borden administration's vision of conscientious objection as a corporate response, one based on certifiable religious doctrine.

The exemption from military service granted to the historic peace churches in this country was more conservative than that granted in Britain or the United States because, in the explicit narrowness of its focus, it understood conscientious objection as a privilege. However, that the MSA's conscientious objection clause existed at all, even though its intent was largely to restrict exemption to Doukhobors and some Mennonites, nonetheless opened the door for a wider individual objection. Those whose conscience forbade them from undertaking military service in the First World War helped to create a more modern, flexible, and individual understanding of conscientious objection and, as such, marked a significant change in the relationship between Canadians and those who govern them.

Canada has a distinctive history of pacifism, one that is largely founded in separational religious pacifism.[39] In the First World War, this had important implications for the experience of conscientious objection. Although this study has tended to focus on the difficulties encountered by COs – the isolation, fear, and sometimes serious physical maltreatment – Canada's record is commendable in some ways. The historic peace churches' expressions of thanks for tolerance of their non-resistant beliefs are profuse and recognize the harsher treatment faced by their brethren in the United States. Post-war emigrations of Hutterites and Mennonites to this country also speak to the greater toleration for religious pacifism in Canada. The decision to grant indefinite leaves of absence to the Ontario Mennonites who had not been excepted from the MSA also shows a degree of government flexibility that perhaps presaged the wider ground for allowable objection during the next war. Such evolution in provisions for conscientious objection were an important part of the changing relations between Canadians and those who governed them.

A discussion of the phenomenon of conscientious objection raises funda-mental questions concerning individual and corporate identity in First World War Canada. The Borden government was obliged to balance its promises to certain religious groups with the tradition of liberal individualism inherited from Britain and its need to provide troops for the war in Europe. Individual Canadians also had to balance the competing claims of their various respon-sibilities. Even though the national obligation to join the war in Europe was apparently agreed upon, the fact that the overwhelming majority of conscripted Canadians requested exemption shows that COs were not alone in their sense of the precedence of other duties. With their discourse of obedience in all except spiritual matters, conscientious objectors were the reluctant and well-mannered vanguard of individual rights in Canada.

Appendix:
Lists of Conscientious Objectors

ALTHOUGH THEY ARE as complete as possible, the lists in the tables that follow are in no way comprehensive. Almost none of the men who were actually recognized as conscientious objectors appear in them, as only those who claimed that privilege but were not recognized as such generated paperwork in records such as newspapers and courts martial. The destruction of registration cards and tribunal records has hampered the search. Nonetheless, the names I have found do constitute a useful sample group from which to draw conclusions about the nature, extent, and image of the conscientious objector to compulsory military service in First World War Canada.

Most of the information presented here comes from the Canadian Expeditionary Force files. However, in some cases no CEF file is extant, and those few men I have found who were exempted would have no military file at all. In those instances, I have taken what information I could from other sources.

For clarity, I have corrected any spelling mistakes in CO statements of place of residence. The objector's religious affiliation and occupation, however, have been recorded exactly as he wrote them on his attestation paper. Evidence of a different religious affiliation taken from another source has been entered in the category "Other." This category also includes other information from the CEF file – for instance, inclusion in a minority group. It also notes when objection on conscientious grounds was coupled with an exemption claim on some other basis, whether the appellant's case was taken to the Central Appeal Tribunal (thus setting the precedent for his denomination) or he was among those objectors sent overseas.

Table 1

Claims of conscientious objection to military service

Name and number	Religious affiliation	Residence	Age	Born	Occupation	Prison	Other
Adams, Joseph 3057735	Christian	Peterborough, ON	24	UK	newspaper man	various 6-month sentences	did not sign attestation paper, overseas
Anderson, James 3035288	Methodist	Waterford, ON	24	ON	druggist		also physical, support
Babcock, Sherman 3108684	Free Methodist	Hamilton, ON	22	ON	harness maker	31/7/18, 10 yrs.	
Bagnall, William 2381474	Christian	Regina, SK	23	MB	driver		overseas, Plymouth Brethren
Bailey, Norman 3110831	Plymouth Brethren	Lemsford, SK	21	ON	upholsterer	16/7/18, life (commuted to 10 yrs.)	did not sign attestation paper
Baker, Isaac 3315160	Tunker	Maple, ON	21		farmer	conscientious objection recognized, struck off service 25/8/18	erroneously ordered to report
Basharst, Ezra	Mennonite	Milverton, ON				exempted 18/9/18	
Bates, Nelson 3037670	Gospel Hall	Toronto, ON	21		salesman	23/5/18, 2 yrs. (less 1 day)	
Bauman, Jeremiah 3139991	Mennonite	Waterloo, ON					
Bell, William 3337686	Christians Gathered unto the Name of the Lord Jesus	Tillsonburg, ON	35	ON	carpenter	26/6/18, 2 yrs.	

▼ *Table 1*

Name and number	Religious affiliation	Residence	Age	Born	Occupation	Prison	Other
Bender, Daniel 3135074	Evangelist	Gowanstown, ON	21	ON	farmer	conscientious objection recognized, struck off service 21/8/18	
Bender, William 3135076	Evangelist	Gowanstown, ON	20	ON	farmer	conscientious objection recognized, struck off service 30/8/18	
Benson, Frederick	Church of England	Norwood, MB	30	UK	streetcar motorman	17/6/18, 2 yrs. (less 1 day)	CO relatives in UK
Bourgeois, Arthur 3036074	International B.S. Ass.	Toronto, ON	24	NB	labourer/mail filler	2 yrs., Kingston Pen.	did not sign attestation paper, marked "CO"
Boutillier, William	I.B.S.A.	Montreal, QC					
Bradley, Ferguson 3107424	Christian	New Liskeard, ON	23	ON	farmer	4/7/18, 10 yrs.	
Brennan, R.		Calgary, AB				5 yrs.	
Brenneman, Daniel 3135154	Mennonite	Tavistock, ON	23	ON	farmer	conscientious objection recognized, struck off service 26/9/18	
Brenneman, William 3135155	Mennonite	Tavistock, ON	24	ON	farmer	conscientious objection recognized, struck off service 26/9/18	

Name / Number	Affiliation	Place	Age	Origin	Occupation	Sentence	Notes
Brotherston, George 3110384	Christian Brethren	Foxmead, ON	23	ON	farmer		did not sign attestation paper
Brotherston, Stephen 3035701	Brethren	Foxmead, ON	22	ON	farmer		did not sign attestation paper
Brown, Claudius 2381450	International Bible Student	Winnipeg, MB	27	Grenada	porter	27/5/18, 2 yrs. (less 1 day)	did not sign attestation paper, "Negro," overseas
Brown, Levi 3235739	Quaker	Kettleby, ON	32	ON	thresher		later accepted service
Bubolz, Charles 3207702	Member of International Bible Students Association	Calgary, AB	21	ON	salesman		did not sign attestation paper, later accepted service
Burgess, Herbert 269146	Seventh Day Adventist	Warmley, SK	21	SK	farmer		
Burrows, Mitchell 3230893	C of E	Brampton, ON	26	ON	bookbinder		
Calma, Harold 3040250	Methodist	Housey's Rapids, ON	19	ON	painter	life, Kingston Pen.	
Calma, Wilson 3040251	Methodist	Housey's Rapids, ON	25	ON	storekeeper	life, Kingston Pen.	
Carnegie, Amos 3036079		Toronto, ON	32		minister	23/5/18, 2 yrs., Burwash Prison Farm	refuses particulars
Carrick, David 3235270	Christadelphian	Hamilton, ON			auto livery	27/6/18, 2 yrs., Burwash Prison Farm	refuses particulars

▼ *Table 1*

Name and number	Religious affiliation	Residence	Age	Born	Occupation	Prison	Other
Carver, John 3109415	Dunker	Stevensville, ON	21	ON	farmer	conscientious objection recognized, struck off service 30/9/18	
Cassidy, William 4100811	R.C.	Barons, AB	29	ON	steam engineer	5 yrs., Alberta Pen.	
Charlton, William 3235409	Tunker	Perry Stn., ON	21	UK	farmer		did not sign attestation paper
Chase, Winsor 3035982	Tunker	St. Catharines, ON	29	ON	preacher/ confectionary		did not sign attestation paper
Clay, Edward 3035776	IBSA	Toronto, ON					
Clegg, Robert 2380155	International Bible Student	Winnipeg, MN	32	UK	clerk	Stony Mountain Pen.	overseas
Cody, Joseph 3236010	Quaker	Newmarket, ON	20	ON	farmer	conscientious objection recognized, struck off service 14/7/18	
Cooke, David 2380622	Protestant	Winnipeg, MB	36	UK	wood machinist	Stony Mountain Pen.	case taken to Central Appeal Tribunal, IBSA
Copeland, Donald	IBSA	Winnipeg, MB			clerk		
Cotton, Louis 2023853	Christadelphian	Rossland, BC	34		miner	several 6-month sentences	overseas

Name	Religion	Place	Age		Occupation	Sentence/Service	Notes
Coverdale, John 2139787	Christadelphian	Victoria, BC	31	ON	machinist	30/4/19, 1 yr., Oakalla Prison Farm	did not sign attestation paper
Crawford, George 3311446	Methodist	Toronto, ON	27	ON	salesman		did not sign attestation paper
Crawford, Walter 3207497	Christadelphian	Onoway, AB	29	UK	farmer	Lethbridge Jail	
Cressman, Hillard 3354650	Mennonite	Regina, SK	20	ON	farmer	conscientious objection recognized, struck off service 19/8/18	
Culp, Raymond 3110398	Disciple	Beamsville, ON	26	ON	farmer		died of disease 6/9/18
Currie, James 3135576	Church of Christ	Rockwood, ON	23	ON	farmer		
Curry, Sydney 3107843	Christadelphian	Swansea, ON	30	UK	motorman	16/5/18, 2 yrs. (less 1 day), Burwash Prison Farm	
Cuthbertson, Andrew	I.B.S.A.	Montreal, QC					
Darlington, Charles 2378391	Church of England	several given		UK	machinist		labelled "CO" in newspaper or military papers but appears to have made no personal claim as such
Davies, Arthur 3317391	International Bible Student	Toronto, ON	23	UK	glasscutter		joined after war

▲

▼ *Table 1*

Name and number	Religious affiliation	Residence	Age	Born	Occupation	Prison	Other
Detwiler, Benjamin	I.B.S.A.	Montreal, QC					
Doerksen, Harry 2771760	Mennonite	Calgary, AB	25	MB	dining car employee		
Draper, Charles	non-denominational					17/5/18, 2 yrs. (less 1 day)	
Driedger, Henry 3355493	Mennonite	Carlton, SK	33	Germany	farmer	conscientious objection recognized, struck off service 9/9/18	
Driedger, Jacob 4099034						conscientious objection recognized, struck off service 4/11/18	incomplete file
Duckett, Carl 3209606		?, AB				10/6/18–20/3/19	incomplete file
Dyck, Abraham 4070640	Mennonite	Lowe Farm, MB	21	MB	farmer	conscientious objection recognized, struck off service 15/6/18	
Dyck, Barney 204740	Mennonite	Warman, SK	21	MB	farmer	conscientious objection recognized, struck off service 30/9/18	

Name / Number	Religion	Place	Age	Country	Occupation	Date / Term	Notes
Eaton, Otto 3135779	Methodist	Blythe, ON	22	ON	farmer		
Edwards, Charles 640062	IBSA	Winnipeg, MB			teamster		
Edwards, Thomas 3107472	International Bible Student	Haileybury, ON	27	UK	carpenter	31/5/18, 2 yrs.	
Egger, Frederick 3035989	Christian	South River, ON	29	ON	farmer	17/5/18, 2 yrs. (less 1 day)	did not sign attestation paper
Elliott, Earl 3135799	Christadelphian	Wingham, ON	23	ON	farmer		
Elliott, Robert 3207730	Plymouth Brethren	Calgary, AB	31	ON	minister		case taken to Central Appeal Tribunal
Ellis, Harry 3110582	Brethren	Brantford, ON	35	UK	labourer	conscientious objection recognized	did not sign attestation paper
Ernst, Noah 3110412	Evangelical	Toronto, ON	25	ON	farmer		
Evans, John 3314545	Christadelphian	Hamilton, ON	23	ON	sewer constructor	12 months	overseas
Fast, Isaac 258753	Mennonite	Rosthern, SK	32		fisherman	conscientious objection recognized 19/3/18	erroneously ordered to report
Fisher, Clarence 3109093	Tunker	Batteau, ON	22	ON	farmer		
Fletcher, Clifford 2023856	Adventist	Nelson, BC	20	USA	student		

▼ *Table 1*

Name and number	Religious affiliation	Residence	Age	Born	Occupation	Prison	Other
Frey, Clarence 3203818	Mennonite	Carstairs, AB	23	ON	farmer	conscientious objection recognized, struck off service 7/6/18	did not sign attestation paper
Frey, Leonard 3212837	Moravian	Bruderheim, AB	22	Austria	farmer	conscientious objection recognized, struck off service 9/9/18	
Friesen, Cornelius 1069662	Church of England	Gull Lake, SK	18	MB	teamster	conscientious objection recognized, struck off service 20/5/17	volunteered
Friesen, John 3355581	Mennonite	Rosthern, SK	19	USA	telegraph operator	conscientious objection recognized, struck off service 30/9/18	
Frisson, P.K.	Mennonite	Vancouver, BC					
Fukier, D.S.							
Fuller, Stanley 3036869	Brethren	Forest, ON	23	ON	farmer/student	23/5/18, 2 yrs. (less 1 day)	
Garvin, James 3110417	Christian Brethren	Toronto, ON	27	UK	railroad worker	13/6/18, 2 yrs. (less 1 day)	did not sign attestation paper
Ghent, George 3352580	Christadelphian	Battleford, SK	20	ON	farmer		did not sign attestation paper
Gibb, Andrew 3033895	Plymouth Brethren		33			18/4/18, 2 yrs. (less 1 day), Burwash Prison Farm	

Name	Religion	Residence	Age	Origin	Occupation	Sentence	Remarks
Gillespie, John 2380926	International Bible Student	Winnipeg, MB	34	ON	car checker		did not sign attestation paper, overseas
Goding, George 3033984				Barbados			refuses particulars, West Indian
Gray, George					farmer	18/4/18, 2 yrs., Burwash Prison Farm	
Greenfield, Clifford 3036142	C of E	Toronto, ON	31	UK	carpenter	life (commuted to 10 yrs.), Kingston Pen.	did not sign attestation paper
Grigsby, George 3031707	Christian	Humber Bay, ON	21	ON	mechanic	18/6/18, 2 yrs.	Latter Day Saints
Grimsley, Alfred 3110634	Christian	Simcoe, ON	21	UK	farmer	life (commuted to 10 yrs.), Kingston Pen.	
Grove, Oscar 3110421	Mennonite	Toronto, ON	23	ON	clerk		
Guest, Arthur 3036876	International Bible Student	Toronto, ON	20	ON	canvasser	9/5/18, 2 yrs., Kingston Pen.	
Guinn, William 260299	7th Day Adventist	Forget, SK	22	MB	farmer		
Hager, Benjamin 3207307	Baptist	Edmonton, AB	26	USA	student/teacher		German descent, father minister
Hamacher, Gordon 3136184	Mennonite	Petersburg, ON	22	ON	farmer	conscientious objection recognized 11/12/18	
Hamacher, Roy 3136187	Evangelical	Petersburg, ON	22	ON	farmer	11/7/18, 2 yrs.	
Hangen, Edwin		Calgary, AB				5 yrs.	

▼ *Table 1*

Name and number	Religious affiliation	Residence	Age	Born	Occupation	Prison	Other
Hawkins, Russell 313238	Christadelphian	Guelph, ON	22	ON	grocer	4/5/18, 2 yrs., Kingston Pen.	
Heath, Cyril	I.B.S.A.	Montreal, QC					
Heels, James 3035950	No denomination	Wabaushene, ON	25	ON	clerk/timekeeper	13/5/18, 2 yrs. (less 1 day)	
Heise, John 325130	Tunkerd	Richmond Hill, ON	23	ON	labourer	2 yrs. (less 1 day)	
Hil(l)ey, Frederick 2382290	Christadelphian	Norwood, MB	21	UK	farmer		later accepted service
Hill, Alfred Thomas 311118	Christadelphian	Toronto, ON	27	ON	hardware clerk		did not sign attestation paper
Hill, Arthur Ernest 331515O	Christadelphian	Toronto, ON	25		factory supt.	14/11/18, 10 yrs.	
Holoboff, Michael 260990	Doukhobor	Canora, SK	22	Russia	farmer	conscientious objection recognized 22/5/18	erroneously ordered to report
Hultgren, Albert 3208451	Doctrine of Christ	Crossfield, AB	22	USA	farmer		did not sign attestation paper, later accepted service, joined non-combatant unit
Hultgren, Levin 3209037	Christian	Crossfield, AB	21	USA	farmer	20/6/18, 2 yrs. (less 1 day)	

Name	Religion	Place	Age	Origin	Occupation	Sentence	Notes
Jeffrey, David 3109603	Christian	Toronto, ON	34	ON	drover/farmer	5/6/18, 2 yrs. (less 1 day), Burwash Prison Farm	
Jess, Robert J. 3110437	Christian Brethren	Toronto, ON	27	UK	fireman	13/6/18, 2 yrs. (less 1 day), Burwash Prison Farm	did not sign attestation paper
Jones, Floyd 3207839	7th Day Adventist	Strathcona, AB	21	USA	farmer	conscientious objection recognized, struck off service 24/8/18	
Jordan, James							
Joyce, A.W. 3036323	Christian	Toronto, ON	21	UK	bank clerk	18/6/18, 1 yr., Burwash Prison Farm	did not sign attestation paper
Joyce, John 3311603	Plymouth Brethren	Toronto, ON	24	UK	carpenter	25/6/18, 2 yrs., Kingston Pen.	did not sign attestation paper
Kerrison, Roy 3212150	International Bible Student	Lac la Nonne, AB	23	USA	farmer	2/7/18, 2 yrs. (less 1 day), Lethbridge Jail	
King, Cuthbert 2023940	Plymouth Brethren	Vancouver, BC	25	UK	dry goods traveller		
Kitcher, Edward	Plymouth Brethren	Toronto, ON					
Kitcher, Eric 3039476	Christian	Toronto, ON	21	UK	signwriter	4/7/18 life (commuted to 10 yrs.)	did not sign attestation paper, Plymouth Brethren
Laporte, Armand 4035400	Mission of the Holy Ghost	Montreal, QC	24	QC	labourer	15/4/18, 2 yrs.	did not sign attestation paper

▼ *Table 1*

Name and number	Religious affiliation	Residence	Age	Born	Occupation	Prison	Other
Leader, Frederick 3310966	Pentecostal	Caledonia, ON	22	UK	farmer		later accepted service
Lee, Alfred John 3108707	Mennonite	Humberstone, ON	21	ON	farmer		
Loewen, Abe 3356077	Mennonite	Hepburn, SK	21	USA	farmer	conscientious objection recognized, struck off service 20/9/18	
Loewen, David 2380279	Mennonite	Haochstadt, MB	21	MB	farmer		
Loewen, Peter 335578	Mennonite	Morse, SK	26	MB	farmer		
Luard, George 3201758	Christadelphian	Hardisty, AB	22	ON	fireman		
Mabley, George 3137105	Quaker	Ilderton, ON	23	UK	farmer	9 months, Kingston Pen.	did not sign attestation paper
Macdonald, Charles							
MacLennon, John	non-denominational						
MacSwiney, John 3033945	R.C.	Iroquois Falls, ON	31		pipefitter	Kingston Pen.	labelled "CO" in newspaper or military papers but appears to have made no personal claim as such

Name	Religion	Location	Age	Origin	Occupation	Notes	
Marks, Johnston 3311971	Christians gathered unto the Name of the Lord Jesus	Toronto, ON	30	UK	carpenter	19/8/18, 10 yrs., Kingston Pen.	Tunker
Marshall, Dudley 3034003	IBSA	Toronto, ON	22		shoe shine parlour		
Marshall, Franklin 3311786	Christadelphian	Toronto, ON	27	ON	grocer		
Martens, Jacob 3354324	Mennonite	Aberdeen, SK	23	MB	farm labourer	conscientious objection recognized, struck off service 21/8/18	
Martin, John 3137152	Mennonite	Waterloo, ON	21	ON	farmer		
Martin, Peter 3137160	Mennonite	Waterloo, ON	21	ON	farmer		
Matheson, Charles 2380116	Pentecostal						
Matthews, Herbert 3112524	7th Day Adventist	Tomston, ON	30	ON	farmer	conscientious objection recognized, struck off service 12/15/18	
Maxwell, John	Christadelphian	St. Catharines, ON	25		plumber		
McAulay, E.W.	Plymouth Brethren						overseas
McCartney, William 3037075	Christian Brethren	Port Credit, ON	30	UK	farmer		did not sign attestation paper

Name and number	Religious affiliation	Residence	Age	Born	Occupation	Prison	Other
McMullen, Isaac 3042030	Plymouth Brethren	Toronto, ON	27	UK	retail shoe business		did not sign attestation paper
McPherson, Alick 269102	Christadelphian	Richard, SK	23	UK	farmer		
Merkel, Norman 3109624	Christian	Hamilton, ON	21	ON	student	31/5/18, 2 yrs.	
Merritt, Fred 3311341	Disciple of Christ	Beamsville, ON	22	ON	farmer		
Mitchell, Sydney 3132063	Plymouth Brethren	Forest, ON	21	UK	farmer	12/4/18, 2 yrs., Kingston Pen.	
Moore, John 3035974	Anglican	Toronto, ON	24	UK	carpenter	17/5/18, 2 yrs. (less 1 day)	
Morris, Harold		Montreal, QC			civil servant		
Morrison, Allan 3311125	Christian Brethren	Lyndoch, ON	21	ON	blacksmith	31/5/18, 2 yrs. (less 1 day)	
Morrison, Elmor 3138859	Pentecostal	Moorefield, ON	21	MB	farmer	Kingston Pen.	
Morton, Clarence 3311126	Pentecostal	Brantford, ON	20	ON	labourer	16/9/18, Kingston Pen.	"Negro"
Murray, Jonas 3234415	R.C.	Sheguindah, ON	21	ON	farmer		
Murray, Joseph		Winnipeg, MB					also Socialist

Name	Affiliation	Place	Age	Origin	Occupation	Sentence	Notes
Naish, George 3355899	International Bible Student	Winnipeg, MB	23	UK	clerk	Prince Albert Jail	did not sign attestation paper, overseas
Naish, Henry 2380174	I.B.S.A.	Winnipeg, MB	21	UK	railway clerk	1 yr.	
Nettleton, Sidney	I.B.S.A.	Montreal, QC					
Nichols, David 3107963	Protestant	Toronto, ON	34	UK	grocer	31/5/18, 2 yrs., Kingston Pen.	also physical
Nichotia, D.H.							
Noakes, Edward 3137381	Brethren	Windsor, ON	22	UK	farmer	conscientious objection recognized, leave without pay 13/6/18	
Noakes, John 3315164	Mennonite	Markham, ON	22	UK	farmer	struck off service, "deserter" 18/11/18	discharge demob 28/6/18
Noonan, W.J.		Regina, SK				life (commuted to 10 yrs.)	
Nugent, Frederick	Presbyterian	Toronto, ON			steamfitter		later accepted service
Olton, A.J. (Alton) 3036910	Plymouth Brethren	Toronto, ON	21	ON	brickmaker	23/5/18, 2 yrs. (less 1 day), Burwash Prison Farm	
O'Neal, Ebenezer 3346052	Methodist	Winnipeg, MB	30	Barbados	chauffeur		later accepted service
Orr, James	I.B.S.A.	Montreal, QC					
Orr, Nelson 3311350	Plymouth Brethren	Bracebridge, ON	21	ON	farmer		

▼ *Table 1*

Name and number	Religious affiliation	Residence	Age	Born	Occupation	Prison	Other
Payne, James 3036913	Christians known as Brother	Toronto, ON	21	UK	farmer	23/5/18, 2 yrs. (less 1 day)	
Peacock, Oswald 3037082	Christian Brethren	South River, ON	31	ON	farmer	23/5/18, 2 yrs. (less 1 day)	incomplete file
Penner, Henry 3356015			21				
Penner, John 3354056	Mennonite	Herbert, SK	22	MB	farmer	conscientious objection recognized, struck off service 16/8/18	
Pennington, Harry		Toronto, ON					
Peters, Peter	Mennonite	Emerson, MB	21		telegraph operator		also occupation
Phillips, Alfred 3234414	Methodist	Laurel, ON	22	ON	farmer		enlists
Phillips, John 3169642	Pentecostal	White Hall, ON	22	ON	farmer	16/7/18, life (commuted to 10 yrs.)	
Pimlott, Oliver 3058078	IBSA	Belleville, ON	22		salesman	various 6-month sentences	overseas
Plant, John 3236338	Roman Catholic	Toronto, ON	24	UK	fireman	death (commuted to 15 yrs.), Kingston Pen.	labelled "CO" in newspaper or military papers but appears to have made no personal claim as such

Name, Number	Denomination	Place	Age	Country	Occupation	Disposition	Notes
Popow, Max 3207838	7th Day Adventist	Lacombe, AB	25	Russia	farmer	conscientious objection recognized, struck off service 10/9/18	
Radford, Francis 331361	Christian Brethren	Toronto, ON	21	UK	sheet metal worker	13/6/18, 2 yrs. (less 1 day), Burwash Prison Farm	did not sign attestation paper
Rawstron, James	I.B.S.A.	Montreal, QC					
Raymer, Eli 3235185	Mennonite	Markham, ON	22	ON	farmer		
Raymer, Elmer 315143	Mennonite	Ringwood, ON	21	ON	farmer	conscientious objection recognized, struck off service 17/10/18	
Reid, John							
Reimer, Otto 3212493	Mennonite	Dudsbury, AB	20	MB	farmer	conscientious objection recognized, struck off service 11/12/18	
Rempel, Diedrich 259382	Bible Student	Hague, SK	34	MB	farmer		Mennonite?
Renshaw, Alan 3033956	Christadelphian	Toronto, ON	30	ON	bank clerk	29/5/18, 2 yrs., Burwash Prison Farm	
Ricketson, Percy 4060986	Christadelphian	Hatsfield Point, NB	21	NB	farmer		
Roberts, Hugh 3035990	Christian	Toronto, ON	34	UK	clothing salesman	10/5/18, 2 yrs., Kingston Pen.	

▼ Table 1

Name and number	Religious affiliation	Residence	Age	Born	Occupation	Prison	Other
Robertson, Peter	IBSA		22				non-combatant unit
Robinson, Charles 3291057	Presbyterian	Windsor Mills, QC	21	QC	farmer		"mentally deficient"
Rodman, Percy 331438	International Bible Student	Port Perry, ON	26	ON	decorator	18/6/18, 2 yrs. (less 1 day), Burwash Prison Farm	
Rose, Sydney						2 yrs.	
Roth, Alvin 318074	Mennonite	Gadshill Stn., ON	23	ON	farmer	conscientious objection recognized, leave without pay 24/8/18	
Roth, Henry 4005076	Mennonite	Woodstock, ON	23	ON	farmer	conscientious objection recognized, struck off service 26/9/18	
Roth, William 3133768	Mennonite	New Hamburg, ON	22	ON	cheesemaker	struck off service, "deserter" 17/6/18	discharge demob 2/4/19
Roulston, E.J.L.	I.B.S.A.	Montreal, QC					
Running, Vernal 3059035	Pentecostal	Lansdowne, ON	21	ON	farmer	112 days	overseas
Sanders, Alva 3035692	No Denomination	Toronto, ON	30	ON	salesman	7/5/18, 2 yrs. (less 1 day)	
Saword, Sidney 2381480	Plymouth Brethren	Winnipeg, MB	23	UK	rate clerk		later accepted service

Name / Number	Religion	Location	Age	Country	Occupation	Sentence	Notes
Scott, Albert E. 3110348	Methodist	Schomberg, ON	21	ON	farmer	life (commuted to 10 yrs.), Kingston Pen.	
Seeley, H.D.							
Seeley, W.E.							
Sheldrake, Frank 3311553	Christian	Hamilton, ON	31	UK	clerk	13/6/18, 2 yrs. (less 1 day)	
Sheriffs, Alexander 3035975	Plymouth Brethren	Toronto, ON	29	UK	machinist	13/5/18, 2 yrs. (less 1 day)	did not sign attestation paper
Shields, Frank 3232170	Roman Catholic	Toronto, ON	24	ON	gardener	9/7/18, Kingston Pen.	
Shuttleworth, Nicholas 2129542	Baptist-IBSA	Brandon, MB	23	ON	bookkeeper		overseas, prison convert
Sider, Albert 303309	Tunker	Perry Stn., ON	23	ON	farmer		
Sider, Earl 3235413	Tunker	Perry Stn., ON	21	ON	farmer		
Sider, Gordon 3108584	Tunker	Marshville, ON	23	ON	electric craneman		
Simons, P.G. 2380184	Christian	Winnipeg, MB	24	UK	drug clerk		
Smallwood, Harold 3110287	Christadelphian	Hamilton, ON	23	ON	draftsman		
Smith, Joseph 3235665	Mennonite	Unionville, ON	21	ON	farmer		
Snow, John H.G.	I.B.S.A.	Montreal, QC					

▼ *Table 1*

Name and number	Religious affiliation	Residence	Age	Born	Occupation	Prison	Other
Sparham, William 3235230	Christadelphian	Hamilton, ON	21	ON	farmer		did not sign attestation paper
Starr, Stuart 3036758	Quaker	Newmarket, ON	23	ON	salesman		
Steckley, Elmer 3235131	Tunker	Gormley, ON	21	ON	farmer	conscientious objection recognized, struck off service 23/7/18	
Steele, Samuel 3133459	Faith in the Lord	Sarnia, ON	28	UK	shoe repairer	23/5/18, 2 yrs.	did not sign attestation paper
Steinburg, William 3034250	Pentecostal	Seguin Falls, ON	21	ON	labourer	11/7/18, 2 yrs. (less 1 day)	
Stewart, Harold						2 yrs., Stony Mountain Pen.	
Sullivan, Samuel	IBSA				farmer (dual exem)		
Swain, H.J.							
Swalm, Ernest 3109171	Tunker	Duntroon, ON	20	ON	farmer		case taken to Central Appeal Tribunal
Tait, Henry 2700269	IBSA	Winnipeg, MB	21	USA	farmer		
Taylor, Walter 277315	Seventh Day Advent.	Sonningdale, SK	21	USA	farmer		

Name / Number	Denomination	Location	Age	Province	Occupation	Sentence / Status	Notes
Telfer, Thomas 3035318	Plymouth Brethren	Toronto, ON	23	ON	bookkeeper	2/5/18, 2 yrs. (less 1 day), Burwash Prison Farm	did not sign attestation paper
Thomas, Sydney 3056944	Bible Student	Haliburton, ON	27	ON	stonemason/farmer		did not sign attestation paper, overseas
Thompson, C.A.							
Thompson, Comford 3234438	Pres.	Duncan, ON	21	ON	farmer (dual exem)	4/7/18, 10 yrs., Burwash Prison Farm	nondenominational
Toole, Howard 3038453	Quaker	Mount Albert, ON	23	ON	farmer	31/5/18, 10 yrs., Kingston Pen.	
Toorish, Joseph 3110505	R.C.	Toronto, ON	29	UK	clerk	17/7/18, 10 yrs., Kingston Pen.	labelled "CO" in newspaper or military papers but appears to have made no personal claim as such
Unger, Abram 4090159	Mennonite	Lanigan, SK	23	MB	farmer	conscientious objection recognized struck off service 17/4/18	erroneously arrested
Unger, Arthur 4097105	Mennonite	Borden, SK	20	USA	teamster		"deserter"
VanLoon, George 3310831	Baptist	Brantford, ON	20	ON	farmer	14/8/18, 10 yrs., Kingston Pen.	
Wagner, James 3207837	7th Day Adventist	Lacombe, AB	26	NS	student mission work	conscientious objection recognized, struck off service 1/10/18	

▼ *Table 1*

Name and number	Religious affiliation	Residence	Age	Born	Occupation	Prison	Other
Wallace, Robert 3057651	Plymouth Brethren	Kingston, ON	21	ON	student		
Ward, Wilfred 2380434	Brethren	Winnipeg, MB	30	ON	credit manager	13/6/18, 2 yrs., Stony Mountain Pen.	
Watts, Jeffrey 4082576	Baptist	Fernie, BC	26	USA	edgerman	13/6/18, 2 yrs., leave without pay	
Weber, Gordon 3208987	Mennonite	Didsbury, AB			farmer	conscientious objection recognized, struck off service 20/7/18	
Weeks, Gordon 3108848	Christian	Sault Ste. Marie, ON	29	ON	salesman	20/2/18, 2 yrs., Burwash Prison Farm	
Weller, David 3039211	Protestant	Zephyr, ON	20	ON	farmer		later accepted service
Wells, David	Pentecostal	Tugaske, SK	24		teamster	Stony Mountain Pen.	
Wells, Frank	Seventh Day Adventist					exempted	insane, dies
Welshman, William 3132187	Christadelphian	Guelph, ON	26	ON	gardener		
White, D.A.		Toronto, ON					"coloured"
Wick, Frederick 3235186	Christian Brethren	Swansea, ON	23	UK	bookkeeper	4/6/18, 2 yrs. (less 1 day), Burwash Prison Farm	

Name/No.	Religion	Place	Age	Origin	Occupation	Outcome	Notes
Wideman, Roy 3315165	Mennonite	Unionville, ON	20	ON	farmer	conscientious objection recognized, struck off service 13/8/18	
Wigmore, George 2139688	Plymouth Brethren	Victoria, BC	21	UK	bookkeeper		later accepted service
Wilkie, Thomas 3108846	Christian	Hamilton, ON	27		clerk	life (commuted to 10 yrs.), Kingston Pen.	
Williams, Albert 3235271	Christadelphian	Hamilton, ON	22	ON	clerk	4/6/18, 2 yrs. (less 1 day), Burwash Prison Farm	
Williams, Joseph 3317466	Christadelphian	Toronto, ON	28	ON	farmer	Kingston Pen.	had served with RCMP
Willis, William 3036935	Protestant	Toronto, ON	23	UK	driver	23/5/18, 2 yrs. (less 1 day), Burwash Prison Farm	Plymouth Brethren
Wilson, Robert	Presbyterian						
Winger, Cyrus 3354698	Tunker	Deslisle, SK	20	ON	farmer	conscientious objection recognized, struck off service 12/12/18	
Winger, Norman 3109707	Tunker	Stevensville, ON	20	ON	farmer	conscientious objection recognized, struck off service 29/8/18	

▲ *Table 1*

Name and number	Religious affiliation	Residence	Age	Born	Occupation	Prison	Other
Wood, Frederick 3039537	Brethren	Creemore, ON	23	ON	harnessmaker		
Woods, Robert		Toronto, ON					later accepted service
Woolner, Wesley	Mennonite	Kitchener, ON	22	ON	farmer	conscientious objection recognized, struck off service 11/12/18	
Work, James	I.B.S.A.	Montreal, QC					
Wright, Charles 3039061	Tunker	Wellandport, ON	22	UK	farmer	2yrs. (less 1 day)	did not sign attestation paper
Zoerb, Lee 3356041	Tunker	Unity, SK	22	USA	farmer		

Table 2

Members of historic peace churches who enlisted voluntarily or accepted service when conscripted

Name and number	Church	Residence	Age	Born	Occupation	Attested	Status	Other
Augustine, Charles 3314255	Mennonite	Port Colborne, ON	30	ON	toolmaker	05/10/2018	conscript	
Beach, Robert 3109206	Dunkers	Brookfield, ON	21	ON	farmer	05/08/2018	conscript	died of disease 26/10/18
Bearinger, Norman 3135008	Mennonite	Waterloo, ON	22	ON	farmer	13/05/2018	conscript	non-combatant unit
Bricker, Washington 3234834	Mennonite	Elmira, ON	27	ON	garageman	15/05/2018	conscript	struck off service, epilepsy
Brown, Claude 3039973	Quaker	Traverse City, MI	19	QC	shipping clerk	13/06/2018	volunteer	
Brown, Robert 474092	Baptist	Harris, SK	19	ON	baker	03/02/2016	volunteer	left Tunker Church, died of disease
Buck, Alonzo 1036172	Christadelphian	Providence Bay, ON	38	ON	mason	06/04/2016	volunteer	
Cooley, Welby 3107149	7th Day Adventist	Hamilton, ON	27	ON	chauffeur	02/12/2017	conscript	became sgt.
Cressman, Aulton 751243	Mennonite	Breslau, ON	23	ON	labourer	23/12/2015	volunteer	
Detweiler, Clara	United Brethren	Kitchener, ON	24	ON	graduate nurse	04/06/2017	volunteer	
Dyck, George	Mennonite	Gretna, MB	32	USA	doctor	15/04/2018	volunteer	
Eby, Glenn 334771	Mennonite	Kitchener, ON	20	ON	drug clerk	19/04/2018	volunteer	

▼ Table 2

Name and number	Church	Residence	Age	Born	Occupation	Attested	Status	Other
Eby, Gordon 126368	Mennonite	Berlin, ON	24	ON	gardener	09/06/2016	volunteer	
Eby, Milton 255485	Mennonite	Alsask, SK	21	ON	mechanic	26/05/2018	volunteer	killed in action 8/8/18
Elliot(t), Clyde 106211	Wesleyan	Collingwood, ON	21	ON	farmer	29/12/2014	volunteer	left Tunker Church
Ernst, Herbert 3353052	Mennonite	Plunkett, SK	22	ON	farmer	22/06/2018	conscript	had volunteered 27/3/16, later accepted service
Ewert, William 2476380	Mennonite	Gretna, MB	22	MB	student	13/06/2017	volunteer	
Fast, Alexander 258364	Mennonite	Rosthern, SK	27	Russia	labourer/ farmhand	16/02/2018	conscript	non-combatant unit
Fast, Ernest	Mennonite	Waterloo, ON					volunteer	
Fast, Nicholas	Mennonite	Waterloo, ON		Russia			volunteer	died of wounds 19/5/17
Fretz, Daniel 3209465	Mennonite	Didsbury, AB	20	ON	farmer	05/09/2018		died of wounds 29/10/18
Fretz, Franklin 231620	Mennonite	Didsbury, AB	20	ON	farmer	20/05/2016	volunteer	
Friesen, Abraham 288945	Mennonite	Plum Coulee, MB	22	MB	chauffeur	13/12/2016	volunteer	
Friesen, John 523235	Mennonite	Eunice, MB	23	MB	farmer	06/07/2016	volunteer	

Name	Religion	Place	Age	Occupation	Date	Status	Notes
Funk, Abram 288151	Mennonite	Rosenfeld, MB	19	MB	merchant	21/03/2016	volunteer	delusional insanity
Funk, Peter Carl 269411	Mennonite	Prelate, SK	19	MB	bookkeeper	27/05/2018	volunteer	
Gascho, Moses 267285	Mennonite	Quill Lake, SK	18	ON	grocery clerk	03/06/2016	volunteer	
Gingrich, Oscar 751580	Mennonite	Preston, ON		USA	farmer	29/03/2016	volunteer	non-combatant unit
Gregory, Goldwyn	Quaker	Toronto, ON	20					Friends Ambulance Unit
Hilts, Charles 300065	Dunkerd	Newmarket, ON	35	ON	chauffeur	09/08/2015	volunteer	
Hoff (Hopf), George 525530	7th Day Adventist	Edmonton, AB	19	USA	farmer	13/07/2015	volunteer	non-combatant unit
Janz(s)en, Peter 1069439	Mennonite	Prelate, SK	24	MB	clerk	02/12/2017	volunteer	became cpl.
Long, Walter 260997	Dunkard Church	Estevan, SK	21	USA	farmer	16/05/2018	conscript	
Muirhead, David 3314172	Quaker	Pelham Corners, ON	30	ON	labourer	01/10/2018	conscript	killed in action 27/9/18
Neufeld, John 472160	Adventist	Rosthern, SK	24	USA	farmer	08/02/2015	volunteer	combatant unit, wounded
Neufeld, Peter 288140	Mennonite	Rosenfeld, MB	18	Russia	thresher	21/03/2016	volunteer	combatant unit
Noyes, Albert 3311680	Tunker	Stevensville, ON	19	ON	railroad sectionman	28/06/2018	conscript	died of disease 23/10/18

▼ Table 2

Name and number	Church	Residence	Age	Born	Occupation	Attested	Status	Other
Penner, John 3215549	Mennonite	Edmonton, AB	21	Russia	restaurant employee	09/03/2018	volunteer	Siberia
Penner, Peter 874559	Mennonite	Morden, MB	22	Russia	labourer	27/12/2015	volunteer	wounded
Posnikoff, James 887358	Doukhobour	Arran, SK		Russia	farmer	11/12/2015	volunteer	
Raymer, Arthur 2011211	Mennonite	Ringwood, ON		ON	driver	06/11/2018	conscript	non-combatant unit, became cpl.
Rempel, Abraham 2205008	Mennonite	Los Angeles, CA	36	MB	machinist		volunteer	
Rogers, David	Quaker	Toronto, ON	23					Friends Ambulance Unit
Rogers, Ellsworth	Quaker	Toronto, ON	20					Friends Ambulance Unit
Saylor, Gordon 3314622	Tunker	Stevensville, ON	32	ON	farmer	19/02/2018	conscript	wounded
Stanton, James 3138273	Friends	Denfield, ON	22	UK	farmer	06/12/2018	conscript	
Starr, Edgar 778113	Quaker	Newmarket, ON	32	ON	farmer	20/12/2015	volunteer	
Stauffer, Herbert 2528467	United Brethren	Enola, PA	23	USA	horse jockey	20/09/2017	volunteer	
Strelioff, Peter 887433	Doukhobour	Canora, SK	20	SK	farmer's help	02/10/2016	volunteer	struck off service, underage

Name / Service no.	Denomination	Place	Age	Province/Country	Occupation	Date	Status	Notes
Wall, Abraham 875358	Mennonite	Marden, MB	31	MB	barber	13/03/2016	volunteer	
Warkentin, Bernard	Mennonite	Gretna, MB	18	MB			volunteer	British Army (later accepted service)
Weber, Rufus 3211983	Mennonite	Lethbridge, AB	28	ON	farmer	22/05/2018	conscript	
Wenger, Christian 2650841	United Brethren	Houghton, MN		USA	teacher	30/04/2018	volunteer	
Wideman, Ernest 228102	Mennonite	Toronto, ON	32	ON	student	21/02/2016	volunteer	killed in action 26/10/17
Willis, Howard 3040031	Quaker	Chicago, IL	26	ON	med student	18/06/2018	volunteer	
Wright, Ewart	Quaker	Pickering, ON						Friends Ambulance Unit
Young, Alexander 3110490	Brethren	Toronto, ON		UK	druggist	06/06/2018	conscript	
Zavitz, Edwin	Quaker							
Zimmerman, Vernon 3108859	Dunkard	Humberstone, ON		ON	barber	29/04/2018	conscript	Friends Ambulance Unit

Notes

Introduction

1 Military Service Act, 1917, SC 1917, c. 19, s. 11(1)(f). The full text of the act is at "Military History: First World War: Homefront, 1917," The Loyal Edmonton Regiment Museum, http://www.lermuseum.org/ler/mh/wwi/homefront1917.html.

2 Conscientious objector J.F. Moore to his exemption tribunal. "Has Sensitive Nature, Doesn't Like to Kill," *Toronto Daily Star*, 17 May 1918, 2. Moore's objection was not recognized, and he was sentenced to two years less a day in prison for his refusal to serve.

3 See Michael F. Noone Jr., ed., *Selective Conscientious Objection: Accommodating Conscience and Security* (Boulder: Westview Press, 1989); James Finn ed., *A Conflict of Loyalties: The Case for Selective Conscientious Objection* (New York: Pegasus, 1969).

4 See, for instance, William Janzen and Frances Greaser, *Sam Martin Went to Prison: The Story of Conscientious Objection and Canadian Military Service* (Winnipeg: Kindred Press, 1990); Lawrence Klipperstein, ed., *That There Be Peace: Mennonites in Canada and World War II* (Winnipeg: Manitoba CO Reunion Committee, 1979); Peter Lorenz Neufeld, *Mennonites at War, a Double-Edged Sword: Canadian Mennonites in World War Two* (Deloraine, MB: DTS, 1997); David P. Reimer, *Experience of Mennonites in Canada during World War II* (Altona, MB: D.A. Friesen, [1945?]); and John Aron Toews, ed., *Alternative Service in Canada during World War II* (Winnipeg: Publication Committee, Canadian Conference of the MBC, 1959).

5 Elizabeth H. Armstrong, *The Crisis of Quebec, 1914-1918* (New York: Columbia University Press, 1937); Jean-Yves Gravel, *Le Québec et la guerre, 1914-1918* (Montreal: Éditions du Boréal Exprès, 1974). See also Gerard Filteau, *Le Québec, le Canada et la guerre, 1914-1918* (Montreal: Éditions de l'Aurore, 1977); and Roch Legault and Jean Lamarre, eds., *La Première Guerre Mondiale et le Canada: Contributions sociomilitaires Québécoises* (Montreal: Meridien, 1999).

6 A. Ross McCormack, *Reformers, Rebels, and Revolutionaries: The Western Canadian Radical Movement, 1899-1919* (Toronto: University of Toronto Press, 1977). See also Mary Veronica Jordan, *Survival: Labour's Trials and Tribulations in Canada* (Toronto: McDonald House, 1975); and Paul Arthur Phillips, *No Power Greater: A Century of Labour in British Columbia* (Vancouver: Federation of Labour and Boag Foundation, 1977).

7 Frank H. Epp, *Mennonites in Canada, 1786-1920: The History of a Separate People* (Toronto: Macmillan, 1974); Arthur Garratt Dorland, *The Quakers in Canada: A History* (Toronto: Ryerson Press, 1968); E. Morris Sider, *The Brethren in Christ in Canada: Two Hundred Years of Tradition and Change* (Nappanee, IN: Evangel Press, 1988).

8 Thomas Socknat, *Witness against War: Pacifism in Canada, 1900-1945* (Toronto: University of Toronto Press, 1987); Kenneth McNaught, *A Prophet in Politics: A Biography of J.S. Woodsworth* (Toronto: University of Toronto Press, 1959); for more on Woodsworth, see Allen George Mills, *Fool for Christ: The Political Thought of J.S. Woodsworth* (Toronto: University of Toronto Press, 1991); Barbara Roberts, *"Why Do Women Do Nothing to End the War?" Canadian Feminist-Pacifists and the Great War* (Ottawa: Canadian Research Institute for the Advancement of Women, 1985); and Barbara Roberts, "Women against

War, 1914-1918: Francis Beynon and Laura Hughes," in *Up and Doing: Canadian Women and Peace*, eds. Janice Williamson and Deborah Gorham (Toronto: Women's Press, 1989, (48-65).

9 Margaret Levi, *Consent, Dissent, and Patriotism* (Cambridge: Cambridge University Press, 1997); Charles C. Moskos and John Whiteclay Chambers III, eds., *The New Conscientious Objection: From Sacred to Secular Resistance* (New York: Oxford University Press, 1993); James F. Childress, *Moral Responsibility in Conflicts: Essays on Nonviolence, War, and Conscience* (Baton Rouge: Louisiana State University Press, 1982); Nigel James Young, "The Nation State and War Resistance" (PhD diss., University of California Berkeley, 1976).

10 Moskos and Chambers, *The New Conscientious Objection*, 1.

11 Socknat, *Witness against War*, 111.

12 Levi, *Consent, Dissent, and Patriotism*, 12.

13 Michael Ignatieff's Massey Lecture, *The Rights Revolution* (Toronto: Anansi, 2000), discusses this development in the Canadian context, with a focus on language rights and Native land claims. His work examines the "double-sided" relationship between rights and democracy, and the effort towards "enhancing equality while safeguarding difference" (2). See also Luan-Vu N. Tran, *Human Rights and Federalism: A Comparative Study on Freedom, Democracy, and Cultural Diversity* (Boston: Kluwer Law International, 2000); Gary Brent Madison, *Is There a Canadian Philosophy? Reflections on the Canadian Identity* (Ottawa: University of Ottawa Press, 2000); Don Carmichael, Tom Pocklington, and Greg Pyrcz, eds., *Democracy, Rights, and Well-Being in Canada* (Toronto: Harcourt Brace Canada, 2000).

14 John Rae, *Conscience and Politics: The British Government and the Conscientious Objector to Military Service, 1916-1919* (London: Oxford University Press, 1970), 207.

15 Thomas C. Kennedy, *The Hound of Conscience: A History of the No-Conscription Fellowship, 1914-1919* (Fayetteville: University of Arkansas Press, 1981), 225. Ghost-written by Bertrand Russell, Margaret Hobhouse's *I Appeal unto Caesar* (London: George Allen and Unwin, [1918?] was an eloquent and influential appeal for her son's release that included statements from prominent religious, political, and literary figures.

16 Margaret R. Higonnet et al., eds., *Behind the Lines: Gender and the Two World Wars* (New Haven: Yale University Press, 1987).

17 Estimates vary, but Rae offers probably the most reliable statistics. As is the case for all studies of conscientious objection, there are problems of definition. Some men, for instance, later renounced their objection and accepted combatant service. Others, such as the novelist E.M. Forster, developed a conscientious objection during the war. Forster was meant to have faced a tribunal but the war ended before he could be sent back to face it. Rae, *Conscience and Politics*, 70, 71.

18 "Table 1: Religions of the People by Provinces for 1911 and Totals for 1901 and 1911," *Fifth Census of Canada, 1911*. Vol. 2 (Ottawa: C.H. Parmelee, 1913), 2-3. Chris Sharpe, "Enlistment in the Canadian Expeditionary Force, 1914-1918: A Regional Analysis," *Journal of Canadian Studies* 18, 4 (Winter 1983-84): 15-29, has offered a workable means for calculating the percentage of a population that would be subject to the draft. I have followed his formula, which suggests that about a quarter of the population was made up of men of conscription age.

19 A man giving his religious affiliation as such might be a member of the Plymouth Brethren or the Brethren in Christ Church. The latter, an offshoot of the Mennonites, were sometimes called Tunkers or Dunkers in Canada. Furthermore, Plymouth Brethren and members of some of the smallest sects repudiated denominational labels altogether, referring to themselves simply as Christians. They apparently had little thought for the needs of later historians.

20 Exceptions include E.R. Evans' biography of his father's experience, *Test Case for Canada '3314545': The Experiences of a Christadelphian Conscientious Objector in World War I, 1914-1918* (Hamilton, ON: privately published, 1972). Ernest John Swalm's memoirs also contain a chapter on his time as a CO. Swalm, *My Beloved Brethren: Personal Memoirs and Recollections of the Canadian Brethren in Christ Church* (Nappanee, IN: Evangel Press, 1969).

21 For Britain, see especially John W. Graham, *Conscription and Conscience: A History, 1916-1919* (1922; repr., New York: Garland Publishing, 1971); along with Kennedy, *Hound of Conscience;* and Rae, *Conscience and Politics.*

22 Susan Schultz Huxman, "Mennonite Rhetoric in World War One: Lobbying the Government for Freedom of Conscience," *Mennonite Quarterly Review* 67 (July 1993): 283-303.

23 Here, I am referring to the absence of prominent objectors themselves. There were, of course, political figures who supported them, such as Fred J. Dixon, MLA in the Manitoba Legislature, and Reverend William Ivens, who later started the Labour Church. Pacifists Alice Chown and Laura Hughes were also from prominent families. See Roberts, "Women against War"; and Diana Chown's Introduction to Alice Chown's autobiography *The Stairway* (1921; repr., Toronto: University of Toronto Press, 1988). Objectors were also supported by J.S. Woodsworth, who left the Methodist Church partly because of a dispute about the church's recruiting for the war. He later became an MP and the leader of the Canadian Commonwealth Federation (CCF); he cast one of the few dissenting votes against Canada's participation in the Second World War.

24 See Kennedy, *Hound of Conscience,* 190-94; Stephen Hobhouse, *The Autobiography of Stephen Hobhouse: Reformer, Pacifist, Christian* (Boston: Beacon Press, 1951), especially 106-8.

25 Quoted in Epp, *Mennonites in Canada,* 370.

26 Peter Brock and Malcolm Saunders, "Pacifists as Conscientious Objectors in Australia," in *Challenge to Mars: Essays on Pacifism from 1918-1945,* ed. Peter Brock and Thomas Socknat (Toronto: University of Toronto Press, 1999), 217.

27 To clarify names and roles briefly, the Military Service Council was the body appointed to assist the Minister of Justice in implementing the Military Service Act. Newcombe, as Deputy Minister of Justice, headed the Council. In June 1918, it was replaced with the Military Service Branch of the Department of Justice, directed by H.A.C. Machin, which ran the show for Justice for the rest of the war. The interests of the Department of Militia and Defence were represented by the Military Service Sub-Committee headed by Willoughby Gwatkin. See David Ricardo Williams, *Duff: A Life in the Law* (Vancouver: University of British Columbia Press, 1984), 95, for a discussion of Duff's time at the Central Appeal Tribunal.

28 E.L. Newcombe, from R.H. Picher, 23 February 1922, Library and Archives Canada (LAC), Ottawa, Department of Justice Records, RG13, vol. 266, file 2311-2326/1921.

29 "Go to Prison with a Song," *Toronto Globe,* 21 May 1918, 6. "Conscientious Objectors Sing a Hymn When Officers Read Sentence," *Toronto Globe,* 16 December 1918, 3; "Heavy Penalties Will Face Seven Mil. Objectors," *Toronto Daily Star,* 4 July 1918, 1.

30 "Decision of Judges on Exemption Appeals," *Toronto Globe,* 24 December 1917, 6.

31 My list in Table 1 of the appendix does include one man, John Plant, who was a political objector. He refused to fight until Ireland was independent from England but was fairly consistently referred to in newspaper headlines as a conscientious objector and therefore was part of the image of the CO for Canadians. See "Take Any Punishment Rather than Fight," *Toronto Globe,* 24 August 1918, 11. Charles Darlington was also identified several times as a CO while court-martialled in England, but transcripts of his court martial reveal

that he did not identify himself as such. See Advocate-General Canadian Militia to Secretary, Overseas Military Forces of Canada, 7 June 1918, LAC, Department of Militia and Defence Records, RG9, ser. 3, vol. 95, file 10-12-70, listing Charles Darlington as among the conscientious objectors sent overseas.

32 J.S. Woodsworth is a convenient Canadian example of such a mixture of the moral doctrines of religious pacifism with the pragmatic tenets of socialism. See McNaught, *A Prophet in Politics,* 67.

33 McCormack, *Reformers, Rebels, and Revolutionaries,* 118.

34 "Objector Sent to Jail," *Montreal Gazette,* 24 November 1917, 9.

35 Service record for #49460 Alpine Augustine Grant McGregor, LAC, Canadian Expeditionary Force Service Records, RG150 accession 92/93, box 6858-40; and service record for #751415 Menno Gingrich, box 3562-21.

Chapter 1: The Responsibilities of Citizenship

1 J.L. Granatstein and J.M. Hitsman, *Broken Promises: A History of Conscription in Canada* (Toronto: Copp, Clark, Pitman, 1985), 10.

2 For Canada's participation in the South African War, see Carman Miller, *Painting the Map Red: Canada and the South African War, 1899-1902* (Ottawa: Canadian War Museum, 1998); Miller, *Canada's Little War* (Toronto: Lorimer, 2003); and Brian A. Reid, *Our Little Army in the Field: The Canadians in South Africa, 1899-1902* (St. Catharines, ON: Vanwell, 1996).

3 Leaflet in LAC John Taylor Fotheringham Fonds, R2421-0-0-E. Cited in Granatstein and Hitsman, *Broken Promises,* 16.

4 Granatstein and Hitsman, *Broken Promises,* 16.

5 See, for example, "A Citizen," *For All We Have and Are* (N.p.: Imperial Press, [19?]); John Henry Collinson, *The Recruiting League of Hamilton* (N.p., [1918?]); "Pleasant Speeches Useless to Recruit," *Toronto Globe,* 19 January 1919, 6; J. Castell Hopkins, ed., *The Canadian Annual Review of Public Affairs, 1916,* and *1917* (Toronto: Canadian Review, 1917 and 1918). For secondary examinations of the slowdown of voluntary recruiting and growing calls for conscription, see Granatstein and Hitsman, *Broken Promises;* William Magney, "The Methodist Church and the Conscription Crisis of 1917," Paper for Dr. D.G. Creighton, University of Toronto, 1968; and G.W.L. Nicholson, *Canadian Expeditionary Force, 1914-1919* (Ottawa: Queen's Printer, 1964).

6 Canada, *House of Commons Debates* (22 January 1917), 15.

7 Quoted in Hopkins, *Canadian Annual Review 1917,* 520. Currie had been promoted partly in support of a proposed conscription bill. Upon his appointment, Borden had signalled Canadian High Commissioner G.H. Perley, "I shall send a message of congratulations to him. It would be well if in his reply he would make clear the need for reinforcements to maintain Canadian Army Corps at full strength." R.B. Borden to G.H. Perley, 21 June 1917, Library and Archives Canada (LAC), Ottawa, Robert Borden Papers, MG26, H1(a), vol. 136, p. 71768. See also Nicholson, *Canadian Expeditionary Force,* 284; and A.M.J. Hyatt, "Sir Arthur Currie and Conscription: A Soldier's View," *Canadian Historical Review* 13 (September 1969): 285.

8 J. Murray Clark, letter to the editor, "Conscription Always Law," *Toronto Globe,* 31 July 1917, 4.

9 Despite his views, Oliver stayed with his party as a Laurier Liberal when many members joined Borden's Union Party due to the conscription issue. Canada, *House of Commons Debates* (19 January 1916), 104.

10 Editorial, *Toronto Globe,* 27 March 1917, 4.

11 Military Service Council, *For the Defence of Canada* (Ottawa: Military Service Council, 1917), 5.

12 Clark, "Conscription Always Law," *Toronto Globe,* 31 July 1917, 4.

13 Quoted in "Conscription Has to Come," *Toronto Globe,* 7 May 1917, 3.

14 "Winning the War the Supreme Issue Confronting the Nation," *Ottawa Citizen,* 10 November 1917, 12, 13.

15 Editorial, "Compulsory Service," *Toronto Globe,* 31 May 1917, 6. Talk of "citizenship" was rife in discussions of conscription and conscientious objection, in spite of the fact that Canadians were British subjects. It seems that the term "subject" did not lend itself as well to discussion of civic obligations. Interestingly, the historic peace churches tended to use the term "subjects" rather than "citizens" in their own discourse and correspondence with the government.

16 Editorial, "Selective Draft," *Canadian Baptist,* 21 June 1917, 1. *Ottawa Citizen,* "The Military Service Act," 14 June 1917, 4.

17 For English studies of the conscription crisis in Quebec and its implications, see especially Elizabeth H. Armstrong, *The Crisis of Quebec, 1914-1918* (New York: Columbia University Press, 1937). Histories of the war from a French Canadian perspective tend to give more attention to the conflict than do their English Canadian counterparts. See Jean Provencher, *Québec sous la Loi des Mesures de Guerre, 1918* (Trois Rivières: Éditions du Boréal Exprès, 1971); Jean-Yves Gravel, *Le Québec et la guerre, 1914-1918* (Montreal: Éditions du Boréal Exprès, 1974); Gerard Filteau, *Le Québec, le Canada et la guerre, 1914-1918* (Montreal: Éditions de l'Aurore, 1977); and Roch Legault and Jean Lamarre, eds., *La Première Guerre Mondiale et le Canada: Contributions sociomilitaires Québécoises* (Montreal: Meridien, 1999). Hugh MacLennan addresses the conflict in his novel *Two Solitudes* (Toronto: Collins, 1945).

18 S.D. Chown, letter to the editor, "Voluntary Service a Failure?" *Toronto Globe,* 20 September 1917, 6.

19 Robert Borden, *Canada at War: A Speech Delivered by Rt. Hon. Sir Robert Laird Borden in the House of Commons Introducing the Military Service Bill* ([Galt, ON?] [1917?]), 20.

20 Military Service Council, *For the Defence of Canada,* 28.

21 Canada, *House of Commons Debates* (27 June 1917), 2715.

22 Robert Craig Brown and Ramsay Cook, *Canada, 1896-1921: A Nation Transformed* (Toronto: McClelland and Stewart, 1974), 220.

23 Editorial, "The Duty of Canada," *Toronto Globe,* 2 July 1917, 6.

24 Letter to the editor, *Toronto Globe,* 15 December 1915, 6.

25 T.G. Mathers, "The Voluntary System," letter to the editor, *Christian Guardian,* 15 November 1916.

26 Mrs. C. Robertson to Robert Borden, 15 July 1917, LAC, Robert Borden Papers, MG26, H1(a), vol. 26, p. 44249. Worrell is quoted in Hopkins, *Canadian Annual Review 1917,* 414.

27 E. Beveridge, letter to the editor, "Calls Objectors Undemocratic," *Manitoba Free Press,* 5 January 1917, 9. The 1917 *Canadian Annual Review* includes a partial list of petitions received by Borden from various groups along with their opinions of what conscription ought to entail. Hopkins, *Canadian Annual Review 1917,* 348.

28 Editorial, "Canada, Despite the Ottawa Mess," *Toronto Globe,* 9 June 1917, 6.

29 Editorial, "Compulsory Service," *Toronto Star,* 31 May 1917, 6.

30 Canada, *House of Commons Debates* (21 January 1916), 180.

31 Editorial, "Compulsory Service Not Practicable," *Toronto Globe,* 15 June 1916, 6. J.A. Macdonald, the editor of the *Toronto Globe,* was an advocate of pacifism and liberal

internationalism at the start of the First World War, yet became an ardent advocate of its prosecution, first on a solely voluntary basis and later through conscription. The transformation of his viewpoint was not unusual in wartime Canada, as is discussed more fully in Chapter 5. See Thomas Socknat, *Witness against War: Pacifism in Canada, 1900-1945* (Toronto: University of Toronto Press, 1987), 45-48.

32 Canada, *House of Commons Debates* (17 January 1916), 19. For Laurier's efforts for political unity between French and English Canada, see Roderick Stewart, *Wilfrid Laurier: A Pledge for Canada* (Montreal: XYZ Publishing, 2002); Laurier L. LaPierre, *Wilfrid Laurier and the Romance of Canada* (Toronto: Stoddart, 1996); and Barbara Robertson, *Wilfrid Laurier, the Great Conciliator* (Toronto: Oxford University Press, 1971).

33 McClung describes *The Next of Kin* as a collection of other women's experiences. One excerpt, presented as a conversation, deals with conscription. When a woman asks why the government does not "drag out the slackers," her pro-voluntarism sister-in-law protests, saying that calling for the draft is a form of treason because conscription is a form of slavery. But this defender of the voluntary system promptly weakens her argument by adding that her own boy is too weak for combat and that common people should go out to fight before – and preferably instead of – others. Nellie L. McClung, *The Next of Kin: Those Who Wait and Wonder* (Toronto: T. Allen, 1917), 136.

34 Editorial, "Compulsory Service Not Practicable," *Toronto Globe*, 15 June 1916, 6. S.D. Chown, "Voluntary Service a Failure?" *Toronto Globe*, 20 September 1917, 6.

35 For a discussion of socialist anti-conscription reaction, see A. Ross McCormack, *Reformers, Rebels, and Revolutionaries: The Western Canadian Radical Movement, 1899-1919* (Toronto: University of Toronto Press, 1977); John Edward Hart, "William Irvine and Radical Politics in Canada" (PhD diss., University of Guelph, 1972); and Donald Avery, *Dangerous Foreigners: European Immigrant Workers and Labour Radicalism in Canada, 1896-1932* (Toronto: McClelland and Stewart, 1979).

36 "One Interested," "The Voice of the People," *Toronto Globe*, 28 May 1917, 6; "Local Labour Leaders against Conscription," *Toronto Globe*, 8 January 1916, 8.

37 See, for example, J.F. Gadsby, "Fixing the War Horse," *Saturday Night*, 2 June 1917, 4.

38 James Shaver Woodsworth, "Suspicious of Registration," *Manitoba Free Press*, 28 December 1916, 7; and Kenneth McNaught, *A Prophet in Politics: A Biography of J.S. Woodsworth* (Toronto: University of Toronto Press, 1959), 75.

39 Editorial, "National Service," *Manitoba Free Press*, 2 January 1917, 9.

40 The leaders of the unions advised not filling in registration cards, but most workers, like the rest of the country, did so. McCormack, *Reformers, Rebels, and Revolutionaries*, 51-56.

41 "R.N.W.M.P., Rosthern Detach. 5/4/17. Report re distribution of National Service Cards," LAC, Robert Borden Papers, MG26 H1(a),vol. 214, 121098.

42 Granatstein and Hitsman, *Broken Promises*, 46.

43 The minister of Militia and Defence, Sir Edward Kemp, kept Borden apprised of the results. A telegram of 30 April 1917 concluded that "any further effort for voluntary enlistment would provide ... wholly inadequate results." Quoted in Robert Borden, *Robert Laird Borden: His Memoirs* (Toronto: Macmillan, 1938), 2:698; Nicholson, *Canadian Expeditionary Force*, 342.

44 Procès-Verbale of First Meeting, Imperial War Cabinet, 20 March 1917, Public Record Office (London), Cabinet Records, Cab 23/43, quoted in Granatstein and Hitsman, *Broken Promises*, 62.

45 Borden, *Canada at War*, 3.

46 Borden to Monsignor Bruchési, Archbishop of Montreal, 31 May 1917, quoted in Nicholson, *Canadian Expeditionary Force*, 342 43.

47   Borden, *Canada at War,* 9.
48   W. Lambert to Robert Borden, 21 May 1917, LAC, Robert Borden Papers, MG26, H1(a), vol. 26, 43992.
49   Edwin Hill to Robert Borden, 21 May 1917, LAC, Robert Borden Papers, MG26, H1(a), vol. 26, 43996.
50   For an important collection of documents relating to conscientious objection in the American Civil War, see Peter Brock, ed., *Liberty and Conscience: A Documentary History of the Experience of Conscientious Objectors in America through the Civil War* (New York: Oxford University Press, 2002). Also valuable in this context is Lillian Schlissel, ed., *Conscience in America: A Documentary History of Conscientious Objection in America, 1757-1967* (New York: Dutton, 1968). For the American Civil War, see Samuel Horst, *Mennonites in the Confederacy: A Study in Civil War Pacifism* (Scottdale, PA: Herald Press, 1967); and S.F. Sanger and D. Hays, *The Olive Branch of Peace and Good Will to Men: Anti-war History of the Brethren and Mennonites, the Peace People of the South, during the Civil War, 1861-1875* (Elgin, IL: Brethren, 1907).
51   Canada, *House of Commons Debates* (12 July 1917), 3303-5.
52   Military Service Act, 1917, SC 1917, c. 19, s. 11(1)(f), "Military History: First World War: Homefront, 1917," The Loyal Edmonton Regiment Museum, http://www.lermuseum. org/ler/mh/wwi/homefront1917.html.
53   Military Service Act (No. 2), 1916, s. 2(3), quoted in John Rae, *Conscience and Politics: The British Government and the Conscientious Objector to Military Service, 1916-1919* (London: Oxford University Press, 1970), 48.
54   LAC, Robert Borden Papers, MG26 H1(a), reel C4321 consists almost entirely of clippings from British newspapers with stories about conscientious objectors in Britain.
55   Military Service Council, *For the Defence of Canada,* 26-27.
56   Military Service Act (No. 2), 1916, s. 2(3).
57   Rae, *Conscience and Politics,* 50-51. Like Britain and Canada, the United States and New Zealand had provision for exemption from military service on conscientious grounds during the First World War.
58   New Zealand Military Service Act, 7 Geo. 5, No. 8 (1 August 1916), s. 18(I)(e), quoted in ibid., 48. New Zealand was the first country in the empire to institute conscription, before Britain itself.
59   Ibid., s. 18(4), quoted in Rae, *Conscience and Politics,* 49.
60   The ambiguity was intentional. The American secretary of war Newton D. Baker purposely kept definitions of conscientious objection vague, hoping to thin pacifist ranks. M.J. Heisey, *Peace and Persistence: Tracing the Brethren in Christ Peace Witness through Three Generations* (Kent, OH: Kent State University Press, 2003).
61   Selective Service System, *Conscientious Objection,* Special Monograph No. 11, 2 vols. (Washington DC: USGPO, 1950), 1:41, cited in George Q. Flynn, *Conscription and Democracy: The Draft in France, Great Britain, and the United States* (Westport, CT: Greenwood Press, 2002), 190.
62   United States Selective Service Act 1917, 65th Cong., 1st sess., c. 15 (18 May 1917), cited in Schlissel, *Conscience in America,* 130. See also H.C. Peterson and Gilbert Fite, *Opponents of War, 1917-1918* (Seattle: University of Washington Press, 1971), 124-25. By June 1918, the United States made provisions for conscientious objectors to be furloughed into agricultural and relief work under civilian control.
63   Quoted in Bobbie Oliver, *Peacemongers: Conscientious Objection to Military Service in Australia, 1911-1945* (Perth: Freemantle Arts Centre Press, 1997), 44. The first referendum asked, "Are you in favour of the Government having in this grave emergency, the same

compulsory powers over citizens in regard to requiring their military service, for the term of the war, outside the Commonwealth, as it now has in regard to military service within the Commonwealth."

64 Hugh Smith, "Conscience, Law and the State: Australia's Approach to Conscientious Objection since 1906," *Australian Journal of Politics and History*, 35, 1 (April 1989): 13-28.

65 Hugh Smith, *Conscientious Objection to Particular Wars: The Australian Approach* (Canberra: Strategic and Defence Studies Centre, Australian National University, 1986), 5-6. Smith also sees the Australian tradition of voluntarism, suspicion of authority and militarism, and veneration of the "citizen-soldier" as lying behind the plebiscites' rejection.

66 Military Service Act, 1917, SC 1917, c. 19, s. 11(1)(f). The full text of the act is at "Military History: First World War: Homefront, 1917," The Loyal Edmonton Regiment Museum, http://www.lermuseum.org/ler/mh/wwi/homefront1917.html.

67 Borden, *Canada at War*, 16.

68 Nicholson, *Canadian Expeditionary Force*, 343; Borden to Governor General, 7 June 1917, LAC, Robert Borden Papers, MG26 H1(a), vol. 77 2160-01.

69 For a fuller review of these events, see Granatstein and Hitsman, *Broken Promises;* and Brown and Cook, *Canada 1896-1921*. John Herd Thompson discusses Western Canadian dissatisfaction with party politics and the calls for a Union Government in *The Harvests of War: The Prairie West, 1914-1928* (Toronto: McClelland and Stewart, 1978). Laurier felt that, were he to support conscription, he would alienate his French Canadian supporters and increase the popularity of nationalist Henri Bourassa. Armstrong, *Crisis of Quebec*, 176.

70 The Union Party won 153 seats and 57 percent of the popular vote. The Liberals won 82 seats and 39.9 percent of the popular vote. Liberal conscriptionists and Unionists did not run against each other. There were huge Liberal victories in Quebec and a Unionist landslide in the rest of the country. Liberals, for instance, won only 2 out of 57 seats in the West. See John Duffy, *Fights of Our Lives: Elections, Leadership, and the Making of Canada* (Toronto: Harper Collins, 2002); and J. Murray Beck, *Pendulum of Power: Canada's Federal Elections* (Scarborough, ON: Prentice-Hall, 1968).

71 Quoted in Liberal Party of Canada, *Two Dark Blots of Shame: The Conservative Franchise Act of 1885 and the War-Time Elections Act of 1917* ([Ottawa?]: Liberal Party of Canada, [1917?]), 11. See also Edward Harper Wade, *Autocracy and Democracy* ([Montreal?], [1917?]). Quebec saw the MSA, with justification, as aimed chiefly at itself. See, for example, Henri Bourassa, *Conscription* (Montreal: Le Devoir, 1917); Joseph Charlebois, *La conscription: Tristes dessins et légends triste* (Montreal: Éditions de Devoir, 1917); Anon., *Une page d'histoire: Prenez, lisez et jugez d'après des faits irréfutables, tous les députés libéraux de la province de Québec ont* [sic] *le 5 juillet 1917, voté le principe de la conscription: Farceurs, hableurs et comédiens: La lettre de Laurier* (Quebec City, [1917?]).

72 Desmond Morton, *Marching to Armageddon: Canadians and the Great War, 1914-1919* (Toronto: Lester and Orpen Dennys, 1989), 109.

73 Granatstein and Hitsman, *Broken Promises*, 78.

74 Thomas T. Shields, letter to the editor, "Why Support Union Government," *Canadian Baptist*, 10 December 1917, 8.

75 "Loading Dice for Election," *Toronto Globe*, 7 September 1917, 3.

76 Sidney Webb, "Conscience and the Conscientious Objector," *North Atlantic Review* 205 (March 1917): 411.

77 A.W. Keeton, letter to the editor, "The Higher Law: A Cecil Champions Liberty of Conscience," *Christian Guardian*, 6 March 1918, 13-14. The Latin actually translates to "the safety of the people (populi) is the highest law." Keeton seems to have followed Cecil's

translation. It is unclear whether the mistranslation was on the part of Cecil or of the Kaiser.

78 James E. Lawrence, "Prussianism," *Christian Guardian,* 12 December 1917, 28. See also Charles Bishop, "Unmitigated Prussianism," *Christian Guardian,* 24 October 1917, 21.

79 "Platform of Union Government 1917," LAC, Robert Borden Papers, MG26 H1(a), vol. 96, 373.

80 S.J. Moore, "The Real Issue," *Canadian Baptist,* 13 December 1917, 8.

81 "A Sergeant-Major at the Front," Gordon M. Philpott to his mother from No. 14 Stationary Hospital France, *The Chancellor's Correspondence,* Canadian Baptist Archives (CBA), McMaster University, Hamilton, ON. Box 57 "War." Philpott's letter also appears in abridged form in *McMaster University Monthly* 27 (1917-18): 284-87.

82 The official history of the CEF, Nicholson, *Canadian Expeditionary Force,* 142, gives "well over 90% of the soldiers on active service" as casting their votes for the Union Government. Desmond Morton concurs: "In all the civilian margin for the Unionists was a mere 97,065 of 1,650,958 votes cast; the CEF gave 215,849 votes to the government and only 18,522 to Laurier." Morton, *Marching to Armageddon,* 110. However, in "Polling the Soldier Vote: The Overseas Campaign in the Canadian General Election of 1917," *Journal of Canadian Studies* 31 (1975): 39-58, Morton makes a more equivocal argument. In one place, he says that the act affected the outcome in only a couple of seats, but elsewhere, he asserts that it swung the balance in as many as fourteen.

83 Borden, *Canada at War,* 16.

84 Nicholson, *Canadian Expeditionary Force,* 346.

85 "Exemption Tribunals Men Conscripted by Country," *Toronto Globe,* 7 September 1917, 8.

86 "'Military Service Act 1917,' Explanatory Announcement by the Minister of Justice," *Montreal Star,* 11 September 1917, 1; advertisement in *Toronto Daily Star,* 18 October 1917, 18.

87 Editorial, "The Conscientious Objector," *Toronto Daily Star,* 26 October 1916, 10.

88 This situation was not unique. The British tribunal system was also rife with inconsistent judgments. See "How Conscription Works in Britain," *Maclean's,* May 1917, 48.

89 Captain Gibson to Captain Van Norman, n.d., LAC, Department of Militia and Defence Records, file MD: 2-34-4-105, vol. 2, quoted in Granatstein and Hitsman, *Broken Promises,* 85-86.

90 Reynolds to Crerar, 21 November 1917, Queen's University Archives, Kingston, ON, T.A. Crerar Papers, 1968-023; editorial, *La Presse,* 12 November 1917, 5; Memoir Notes, LAC, Robert Borden Papers, MG26 H1(a), vol. 5, 2114.

91 "Tribunal Floored Religious One," *Toronto Daily Star,* 12 November 1917, 2.

92 Ibid.

93 Ibid. This probably referred to Edward H. Clay. His CEF file is incomplete, although its very existence is evidence that he did not receive exemption. Service record for #3035776 Edward H. Clay, LAC, Canadian Expeditionary Force Service Records (CEFS Records), RG150 accession 92/93, box 1777-10.

94 "Tribunal Floored Religious One," *Toronto Daily Star,* 12 November 1917, 2. Bourgeois' French name aroused no comment; there seems to have been no fear of collaboration between the pacifists and the anti-conscription forces in Quebec. Of more concern, apparently, was the fact that Bourgeois had recently converted from Catholicism to the IBSA, raising suspicion about the reliability of his espousal of a pacifist faith.

95 The earliest published history of the NCF is John W. Graham's *Conscription and Conscience: A History, 1916-1919* (1922; repr., New York: A.M. Kelley, 1971), a useful but somewhat hagiographic source. A more complete and unbiased account of NCF efforts is Thomas C. Kennedy, *The Hound of Conscience: A History of the No-Conscription Fellowship, 1914-*

1919 (Fayetteville: University of Arkansas Press, 1981). Rae's *Conscience and Politics* approaches the NCF from the viewpoint of the government. For individual accounts, see Julian Bell, ed., *We Did Not Fight, 1914-1918: Experiences of War Resisters* (London: Cobden-Sanderson, 1935). A number of biographies are also valuable, including Fenner Brockway, *Towards Tomorrow* (London: Hart-Davis, MacGibbon, 1977); and Arthur Marwick, *Clifford Allen: The Open Conspirator* (London: Oliver and Boyd, 1964).

96 "Wouldn't Wear Khaki," *Toronto Daily Star,* 20 March 1918, 19.

97 "Belongs to God, So Can't Fight," *Toronto Daily Star,* 10 November 1917, 4. On his attestation paper for the CEF, Nichols gave his religion as "Protestant."

98 "Peace with All Men Christian Asks Exemption," *Toronto Daily Star,* 12 November 1917, 12.

99 *Toronto Daily Star,* 23 November 1917, 5.

100 "Wouldn't Wear Khaki," *Toronto Daily Star,* 20 March 1918, 19.

101 Canadian Christadelphian Standing Committee, *A summary of the work of the Canadian Christadelphian Standing Committee, 1917, 1918, 1919: shewing the Christadelphian Church's experience under the Canadian Military Service Act 1917, during the Great War with Germany and the success of the committee's efforts in obtaining recognition by the government of Canada for the Christadelphian body to be entitled to claim exemption from all forms of military and naval service for its bonafide members: with an appendix consisting of copies of the Christadelphian constitution and articles of faith, also the official ecclesial rolls of membership, and other evidences the committee filed at Ottawa* (Toronto: Canadian Christadelphian Standing Committee, 1919), 49. See Chapter 3 for further discussion of the Christadelphian Church.

102 "Is Citizen of Heaven," *Toronto Daily Star,* 10 November 1917, 4. See also service record for #3036876 Arthur Clarence Guest, LAC, CEFS Records, RG150 accession 92/93, box 3873-74.

103 "He Refuses to Fight," *Toronto Daily Star,* 16 October 1917, 19. Service record for #3033951 James Patterson, LAC, CEFS Records, RG150 accession 92/93, box 7642-36.

104 "Peace with All Men Christian Asks Exemption," *Toronto Daily Star,* 12 November 1917, 12.

105 Socknat, *Witness against War,* 79. Heisey, *Peace and Persistence,* 43, also mentions the inability of non-pacifists to understand the non-resistant position.

106 C.L. Fletcher, interview with J. Ernest Monteith, 1956, quoted in Monteith, *The Lord Is My Shepherd: A History of the Seventh-day Adventist Church in Canada* (Oshawa, ON: Canadian Union Conference of the Seventh-day Adventist Church, 1983), 165. The term "conscientious objector" appeared in quotation marks in newspaper accounts until fairly late in 1918, clear evidence of its unfamiliarity.

107 *Montreal Star,* "The Military Service Act," 18 October 1917, 8; Granatstein and Hitsman, *Broken Promises,* 85.

108 David Ricardo Williams, *Duff: A Life in the Law* (Vancouver: University of British Columbia Press, 1984), 94. No records exist specifying how many of these applied for exemption as conscientious objectors.

109 On 28 June 1918, the Alberta Supreme Court ruled that a conscript named Lewis, represented by R.B. Bennett, was being illegally held by the army; it ordered his release and ruled that the Order-in-Council cancelling exemptions was invalid. The Canadian government appealed the ruling to the Supreme Court of Canada and passed a new Order-in-Council so that it could continue to act as before, "notwithstanding the said judgement and notwithstanding any judgement or any Order that may be made by any Court." Quoted in *Broken Promises,* 95. Granatstein and Hitsman call this "a simply astonishing course of conduct." On 20 July 1918, in a four-to-two decision, the Supreme Court ruled that the

Order-in-Council was valid. See Granatstein and Hitsman for a more detailed discussion of this incident.

Chapter 2: Days of Anxiety

1 Although, in literal terms, exemption on conscientious grounds in Britain was open to any individual, widespread interpretation of the act saw it as closer to the Canadian clause. As one newspaper wrote of the British legislation, "It would appear that the clause was introduced in the bill primarily as a concession to the Society of Friends rather than with a view to meeting general religious scruples." "Loophole of Escape for Slacker on Conscientious Grounds" *London Free Press*, 6 January 1916, 1.

2 The Quakers tended increasingly to be an exception to this rule. They were well-known philanthropists, and their work towards prison reform and the abolition of slavery had already contributed to breaking down the barriers between them and political affairs. The spread of evangelism and growth of Quaker business interests also prompted their closer interaction with mainstream society. Brian John Fell, "A Question of Conscience: British and Canadian Socialist Quakers and Their Parliamentary Allies in the First World War" (Master's thesis, University of Manitoba, 1972).

3 Thomas Socknat, *Witness against War: Pacifism in Canada, 1900-1945* (Toronto: University of Toronto Press, 1987), 41, 8-9. Socknat focuses on the radicalization of liberal pacifist thought, rather than the role of sectarian groups.

4 Susan Schultz Huxman, "Mennonite Rhetoric in World War One: Lobbying the Government for Freedom of Conscience," *Mennonite Quarterly Review* 67 (July 1993): 288.

5 See, for instance, J.S. Hartzler, *Mennonites in the World War, or, Nonresistance under Test* (Scottdale, PA: Mennonite Publishing House, 1922); and Frank H. Epp, *Mennonites in Canada, 1786-1920: The History of a Separate People* (Toronto: Macmillan, 1974).

6 Gerlof D. Homan, *American Mennonites and the Great War, 1914-1918* (Waterloo, ON: Herald Press, 1994), 33.

7 Epp, *Mennonites in Canada*, 51. Donald F. Durnbaugh, "The Brethren and Non-resistance," in *The Pacifist Impulse in Historical Perspective*, ed. Harvey L. Dyck (Toronto: University of Toronto Press, 1996), 130, makes a similar point about the Tunkers' support for authority and the Loyalists during the American Revolution. See also Adolf Ens, *Subjects or Citizens? The Mennonite Experience in Canada, 1870-1925* (Ottawa: University of Ottawa Press, 1994).

8 Ens, *Subjects or Citizens?* 11.

9 Most groups chose the United States because of its republican government, proximity to commercial centres, and because its climate was milder than that of Canada. Epp, *Mennonites in Canada*, 191.

10 Quoted in Ens, *Subjects or Citizens?* 20. Ens argues that the Russian Canadian Mennonites felt that their rights would be better protected as subjects of the queen, rather than as citizens of the American republic.

11 The Mennonites were willing to pay fines for the commutation of military service, though the Quakers saw payment as equivalent to fighting, and members were ordered not to pay. For a good history of government responses to non-resistant churches, see William Janzen, *Limits on Liberty: The Experience of Mennonite, Hutterite, and Doukhobor Communities in Canada* (Toronto: University of Toronto Press, 1990).

12 W.H. Breithaupt, "First Settlements of Pennsylvania Mennonites in Upper Canada," Ontario Historical Society, *Papers and Records*, 11 (1906), 103, United Church of Canada Archives, Victoria University, University of Toronto.

13 31 Victoria, C.4, S.17, and Revised Statues of Canada 1868, C.1, S.26.

14 Although one group did arrive in Canada in 1899 and stayed for five years, the Hutterites did not actually emigrate until 1918. Because they were in the country for the last year of the war only, with their pacifism already protected upon arrival, the Hutterites had little interaction with the Canadian authorities over conscription. It is interesting that the wording in the 1868 Militia Act offered more expansive grounds for conscientious exemption than did the later Military Service Act.

15 Robert Kreider found, in the United States during the Second World War, that "Congregations at a great distance from the areas of concentration of their branch [and] ... Mennonites of urban communities produce fewer conscientious objectors." Kreider, "Environmental Influences Affecting the Decisions of Mennonite Boys of Draft Age," *Mennonite Quarterly Review* 16 (October 1942): 249, 254.

16 John A. Hostetler and Gertrude Enders Huntington, *The Hutterites in North America* (New York: Holt, Rinehart and Winston, 1967), vi.

17 The Hutterites were a triple minority in that they were an unassimilated group, their social, economic, and ideological structure differed radically from that of mainstream Canada, and they were conscientious objectors during wartime. Theron Schlabach, ed., "An Account, by Jakob Waldner: Diary of a Conscientious Objector in World War I," trans. Ilse Reist and Elizabeth Bender, *Mennonite Quarterly Review* 48 (January 1974): 73.

18 Homan, *American Mennonites*, 43. See also *Mennonite*, 6 December 1917; and 18 April 1918.

19 See, for example, J.A. Ressler, "What the Bible Teaches," *Scottdale (PA) Gospel Herald,* 9 May 1912, 82; John Horsch, "A Popular Objection to Nonresistance," *Scottdale (PA) Gospel Herald,* 27 March 1913, 819-20; and W.I. Powell, "Nonresistance," *Scottdale (PA) Gospel Herald,* 29 May 1913, 130-31, 133.

20 Ernest John Swalm, *My Beloved Brethren: Personal Memoirs and Recollections of the Canadian Brethren in Christ Church* (Nappanee, IN: Evangel Press, 1969).

21 Abraham Rempel entered the railway construction corps. Service record of #2205008 Abraham Rempel, Library and Archives Canada (LAC), Canadian Expeditionary Force Service Records (CEFS Records), RG150 accession 92/93, box 8189-34; service record for #523235 John F. Friesen, box 3315-34; service record for #288945 Abraham Friesen, box 3315-30; service record for #288151 Abram Funk, box 3339-1; service record for #269411 Peter Funk, box 3339-9. Abram Funk was discharged as medically unfit by reason of "delusional insanity." After eighteen months' service, he had episodes of hallucinations of angels that his doctors deemed were "caused by active service." I have compiled a very provisional list of volunteers from the historic peace churches (see Table 2 in the appendix). There is no official figure on the number of men from these groups who enlisted. Religious affiliation other than Church of England, Roman Catholic, Methodist, Presbyterian, Baptist, or Jewish was listed as "Other" on a soldier's attestation paper. In 1972, S.F. Wise of the Directorate of History and Heritage commented that "There are no records covering Mennonite enlistments in either war." Wise, Director, to Frank H. Epp, 29 February 1972, Directorate of History and Heritage, Department of National Defence, Ottawa, "Conscientious Objectors" file, S13350-5-/E.

22 Epp, *Mennonites in Canada*, 368.

23 "Mennonites Fighting Despite Their Rule," *Ottawa Journal Press,* 9 January 1917, 6. Although this article dates from relatively early in the war, it was printed after the rush of volunteers had ended, and it is unlikely that many Mennonites would have enlisted voluntarily after this time.

24 S. Mabor, Superintendent of the Department of the Interior, to the deputy minister of that department, 18 October 1917, LAC, RG15, vol. 758, file 494483(14), cited in Janzen,

Limits on Liberty, 339. This seems to be quite a high estimate. My search through the CEF files in areas of Doukhobor settlement and for common Doukhobor names yielded only two recruits. See Table 2 in the appendix.

25 Arthur Garratt Dorland, *The Quakers in Canada: A History* (Toronto: Ryerson Press, 1968), 331-32. He does not name any of the volunteers. I have found the record of Claude Otwell Brown, who, in June 1918, at nineteen years of age, volunteered for the CEF, though for which branch is not clear. Service record for #3039973 Claude Otwell Brown, LAC, CEFS Records, RG150 accession 92/93, box 1130-33. Edgar Douglas Starr, from Newmarket, Ontario, volunteered. See service record for #778113 Edgar Douglas Starr, box 9244-57. Some Quakers were conscripted and accepted some form of military service. See service record for #3314172 David Secord Muirhead, box 6463-36; and service record for #3138273 James W. Stanton, box 9237-16.

26 Kyle Jolliffe, *Seeking the Blessed Community: A History of Canadian Young Friends, 1875-1996* (Guelph, ON: Ampersand Printing, 1997), 27. The FAU was under British civilian control.

27 It is likely that not all those identifying themselves as "Brethren" were Tunkers. Newspaper accounts of exemption tribunals show several men belonging to small communities called "The Brethren" or some variant thereof. The anti-war movement in Quebec was not pacifist, and the presence of all the historic peace churches in that province was weak. The 1911 census found only twenty-four Friends, fifty-one Mennonites, and 496 Brethren living in Quebec. "Table 1: Religions of the People by Provinces for 1911 and Totals for 1901 and 1911," *Fifth Census of Canada, 1911* (Ottawa: C.H. Parmelee, 1913), 2-3.

28 See Fell, "A Question of Conscience," 177.

29 Chris Sharpe, "Enlistment in the Canadian Expeditionary Force, 1914-1918: A Regional Analysis," *Journal of Canadian Studies* 18, 4 (Winter 1983-84): 15-29.

30 See Howard Brinton, *Friends for 300 Years: The History and Beliefs of the Society of Friends since George Fox Started the Quaker Movement* (Wallingford, PA: Pendle Hill, 1965).

31 Peter Brock, *Twentieth-Century Pacifism* (New York: Van Nostrand Reinhold, 1970), 6.

32 Ibid., 292.

33 See Thomas C. Kennedy, *British Quakerism, 1860-1920: The Transformation of a Religious Community* (New York: Oxford University Press, 2001).

34 Peter Brock, *The Quaker Peace Testimony, 1660-1914* (York, UK: Sessions Book Trust, 1990), 212.

35 Other groups also sent petitions reaffirming their pacifist position at this time. See E. Morris Sider, *The Brethren in Christ in Canada: Two Hundred Years of Tradition and Change* (Nappanee, IN: Evangel Press, 1988). However, the Quaker response is unusual in its effort to include non-members.

36 *Canadian Friend,* October 1917, 6-7; Socknat, *Witness against War,* 74.

37 Fell, "A Question of Conscience," 224, states that "Most Quakers with whom the author has had conversations also insist that most young Quakers they knew at that time were either just too young or too old for the draft." The research in Dorland, *Quakers in Canada,* 343, found the same thing.

38 Fell, "A Question of Conscience," 221.

39 Dorland, *Quakers in Canada,* 130.

40 John W. Graham, *Conscription and Conscience: A History, 1916-1919* (1922; repr., New York: A.M. Kelley, 1971), 222. Graham estimates that 32 percent of British Quakers enlisted in some branch of the army.

41 Between 1882 and 1901, the Barnardo scheme, named after British philanthropist Dr. Thomas Barnardo, saw thousands of young British orphans brought to Canada to be

fostered with Canadian families. See Gail H. Corbett, *Barnardo Children in Canada* (Peterborough, ON: Woodland, 1981); and Gillian Wagner, *Barnardo* (London: Weidenfield and Nicholson, 1979). That Mabley came to the Zavitz family from Britain and was not born into the Society of Friends probably explains the non-recognition of his objection.

42 From conversations between Mabley and Brian John Fell, in "A Question of Conscience," especially 201-6; service record for #3137105 George Mabley, LAC, CEFS Records, RG150 accession 92/93, box 5825-24. After Mabley completed his term in prison, he was adopted by his employer, Howard Zavitz, and took the surname Zavitz.

43 Information given by E.M. Starr, Newmarket, Ontario, in letter to Brian John Fell, 14 December 1968, in Fell, "A Question of Conscience," 206. See also service record for #3038453 Howard Lewis Toole, LAC, CEFS Records, RG150 accession 92/93, box 9733-9. At the time, the Society of Friends was divided into Conservative, Hicksite, and Progressive Branches.

44 Jolliffe, *Young Friends,* 27.

45 Quoted in Brock Millman, *Managing Domestic Dissent in First World War Britain* (London: Frank Cass, 2000), 23. The letter was signed by Edward Grubb, Joan Mary Fry, and Robert O. Mennell.

46 Charles A. Zavitz to Robert Borden, 21 May 1917, LAC, Robert Borden Papers, MG26, H1(a), vol. 86, 43991.

47 Albert S. Rogers to David D. Priestman, 23 September 1918, Society of Friends Archives, Pickering College, Newmarket, ON, "Military Service Act" folder.

48 Editorial (Ladies' Page), Quoted in "No Friends to Slackers," *Saturday Night,* 7 July 1917, 24.

49 Thomas C. Kennedy, "Public Opinion and the Conscientious Objector, 1915-1919," *Journal of British Studies* 12, 2 (May 1973): 105-19. Labour representatives Ramsay MacDonald, J. R. Clynes, W.C. Anderson, and, most vociferously, Philip Snowden also kept the subject in frequent debate.

50 Canada, *House of Commons Debates* (30 April 1919), 1929-30. The "cattle" comparison was made in other forums as well. The *Calgary Eye-Opener* asked of the Mennonite and Hutterite immigrations, "Why Do They Want to Impose Such a Bunch of Cattle on Us?" 14 February 1919, 1. Fell, "A Question of Conscience," 195, has argued that the absence of Quakers in Canada's Parliament partially explains their comparative silence in regard to conscientious exemption. He appears to have overlooked Pedlow, who was an opposition Laurier Liberal elected 17 December 1917.

51 Isaac Pedlow later initiated the bill that created Armistice Day. Canada, *House of Commons Debates* (9 April 1919), 1305.

52 S.F. Coffman to John R. Ebersol, Milverton, 22 April 1918, Mennonite Archives, Conrad Grebel College (CGC), University of Waterloo, Waterloo, ON, Samuel Coffman Papers, XV 11.4.7.

53 Fell, "A Question of Conscience," 224, 226.

54 Hans Hillerbrand, "The Anabaptist View of the State," *Mennonite Quarterly Review* 32 (April 1958): 84-85. See also Ens, *Subjects or Citizens?* 3.

55 "Petition of the Tunker Church to the Exemption Boards," September 1917, Brethren in Christ Archives, Messiah College, Grantham, PA, USA, quoted in Sider, *The Brethren in Christ,* 226.

56 David Toews, Chairman, and N.W. Bankman, Secretary, to Borden, 15 July 1916, LAC, Robert Borden Papers, RLB 994, MG26, H1(c), vol. 208, 116319.

57 Hartzler, *Mennonites in the World War,* 83.

58 A.L. Haining to David Toews, 16 May 1918, quoted in Ens, *Subjects or Citizens?* 179.

59 S.F. Coffman to L.J. Burkholder, 7 November 1917, CGC, Samuel Coffman Papers, XV 11.4.7.

60 See, for instance, Peter Brock, *Pioneers of the Peaceable Kingdom* (Princeton: Princeton University Press, 1968). The German term for non-resistance is also sometimes translated as "defenceless." James F. Childress, *Moral Responsibility in Conflicts: Essays on Nonviolence, War, and Conscience* (Baton Rouge: Louisiana State University Press, 1982), offers an interesting discussion of trust as the central idea in arguments for non-resistance.

61 Instead of protesting the unfairness of the charges directed at him, Coffman remarked that "we will only have to live a life that disproves any such adverse criticisms" – a convenient illustration of this passivity. S.F. Coffman to L.J. Burkholder, 7 November 1917, CGC, Samuel Coffman Papers, XV 11.4.7.

62 Epp, *Mennonites in Canada*, 213. Janzen, *Limits on Liberty*, also discusses this lack of organization. It is notable that the Mennonites, at least in the first years after the war, seem to recall their own actions as more united and organized than they actually were. See Hartzler, *Mennonites in the World War*, 76. Mark G. McGowan makes a similar point about the effect of the First World War on Toronto's English-speaking Catholics: "If the Great War had alienated Quebec and some immigrant Catholics from the mainstream of Canadian society, it had a centripetal effect on English-speaking members of the Church, allying them more closely with other English Canadians." McGowan, *The Waning of the Green: Catholics, the Irish, and Identity in Toronto, 1887-1922* (Montreal and Kingston: McGill-Queen's University Press, 1999), 284.

63 Huxman, "Mennonite Rhetoric," 286.

64 Swalm, *My Beloved Brethern*, 384.

65 Epp, *Mennonites in Canada*, 366.

66 Ebersol to Coffman, 4 February 1918, CGC, Samuel Coffman Papers, "Military Problems Committee" folder XV-11 4. 7.

67 Orland Gingerich, *The Amish of Canada* (Waterloo, ON: Conrad Press, 1972), 91-92.

68 Swalm, *My Beloved Brethren*, 122.

69 Socknat, *Witness against War*, 8-9.

70 John S. Weber's dissertation on Coffman credits his extensive correspondence and personal contacts in government circles with the more significant exemptions achieved by Mennonites in Canada as compared with their brethren in the United States. Weber, "History of S.F. Coffman, 1872-1954" (PhD diss., University of Waterloo, 1975).

71 Huxman, "Mennonite Rhetoric," 287.

72 Hartzler, *Mennonites in the World War*, 77. This incident is fairly widely recounted: see also Epp, *Mennonites in Canada*, 372.

73 S.F. Coffman to L.J. Burkholder, Moderator, 23 October 1917, CGC, Samuel Coffman Papers, XV 11.4.7.

74 Robert Craig Brown and Ramsay Cook, *Canada, 1896-1921: A Nation Transformed* (Toronto: McClelland and Stewart, 1974), 220. Margaret Levi discusses conscription as a means of equalizing perceptions of sacrifice, in *Consent, Dissent, and Patriotism* (Cambridge: Cambridge University Press, 1997).

75 S.F. Coffman to Aaron Loucks, 17 November 1917, CGC, Samuel Coffman Papers, XV 13.5.5

76 S.F. Coffman and Aaron Loucks to Robert Borden, 30 November 1917, CGC, Samuel Coffman Papers, XV 13.5.5

77 L.J. Burkholder to Borden, 20 November 1917, CGC, Samuel Coffman Papers, XV 11.4.7.

78 For a discussion of ideas about citizenship and voluntarism in the United States during the First World War, see Christopher Joseph Capozzola, "Uncle Sam Wants You: Political Obligations in World War I America" (PhD diss., Columbia University, 2002).

79 S.F. Coffman to L.J. Burkholder, 7 November 1917, CGC, Samuel Coffman Papers, XV 11.4.7.

80 *Mitarbeiter*, March 1917, 7-8, quoted in Ens, *Subjects or Citizens?* 175.

81 *Ottawa Citizen*, "Doukhobors meet with Government," 15 January 1917, 6.

82 *Regina Leader*, 1 March 1917, 3; "A Contribution from the Doukhobors," see also "Doukhobor Settlement in Canada," LAC, Department of the Interior Records, RG15, vol. 758, file 494483(14).

83 J. Castell Hopkins, ed., *The Canadian Annual Review of Public Affairs 1917* (Toronto: Canadian Review, 1918), 581.

84 S.F. Coffman to Aaron Loucks, 19 November 1917, CGC, Samuel Coffman Papers, XV 13.5.5

85 S.F. Coffman to L.J. Burkholder, 7 November 1917, CGC, Samuel Coffman Papers, XV 11.4.7.

86 S.F. Coffman to J.L. Byer, 28 May 1918, CGC, Samuel Coffman Papers.

87 J.M. Bliss, "The Methodist Church and World War I," *Canadian Historical Review* 49, 3 (September 1968): 231-33.

88 Mason Wade, *The French Canadians, 1760-1967* (Toronto: Macmillan, 1968), 2:738, referring to Henri Bourassa's position in the 1916 conscription debate. This irritation, however, does not seem to have been frequently voiced.

89 Henri Bourassa, *Conscription* (Montreal: Le Devoir, 1917), 6 (emphasis in original).

90 S.F. Coffman to L.J. Burkholder, 5 November 1917, CGC, Samuel Coffman Papers, XV 11.4.7.

91 Epp, *Mennonites in Canada*, 365-86, chronicles much of the confusion and vagaries of interaction between various Mennonite groups, local and appeal tribunals, and government officials.

92 This attitude was common to all of the peace churches and millenarian sects. Only Gingerich, *The Amish of Canada*, 129, asserts that "All Amish young men applied for exemption on the basis of their religious convictions."

93 Letter to the editor, *Canadian Friend*, October 1917, 4.

94 Dorland, *Quakers in Canada*, 332; Sider, *The Brethren in Christ*, 227. The non-rural meeting referred to by Dorland was probably the Yonge Street Meeting.

95 While the newspaper article gives his occupation as a farmer, in his attestation paper Starr describes himself as a salesman. "Tribunal No. 362, YMCA College Street," *Toronto Daily Star*, 10 November 1917, 15. Starr's brother was Edgar Douglas Starr, also a farmer from Newmarket, who attested 20 December 1915, at thirty-two years of age. Service record for #778113 Edgar Douglas Starr, LAC, CEFS Records, RG150 accession 92/93, box 9244-57.

96 The issue of names was a constant source of anxiety to this group. Generally called Tunkers in Canada, they had also at various times and places been known as Dunkers, Tunkerts, Dunkarts, and River Brethren. In 1904, they were chartered in Canada as the Brethren in Christ, as they were known in the United States, and members worried about the effect of this on their recognized status as a pacifist church.

97 That these tenets were not elaborated upon in the Tunker "Confession of Faith" does not seem to have been much of a problem. The confession's single sentence "Therefore it is also completely forbidden to bear the sword for revenge or defense" is unequivocal. Sider, *The Brethren in Christ*, 24, explains the lack of detail: "the doctrine was so well accepted

among the early Brethren in Christ that it did not need elaboration." He also suggests that, because the Tunkers were an outgrowth of Mennonitism, they wrote about the aspects of their faith that differed from those of the parent church. For topics upon which the two groups agreed, such as non-resistance, they felt little need to clarify.

98 Sider, *The Brethren in Christ,* 227-29.

99 Swalm, *My Beloved Brethren,* 23. The incidents Swalm mentions here are unproven. It seems likely that they are a conflation of the cases of Robert Clegg and Henry Ralph Naish, as well as the death of David Wells, as discussed in the next chapter.

100 Ibid., 24.

101 Ibid., 25-26.

102 Ibid., 30. Epp, *Mennonites in Canada,* 384. Swalm also thanks Coffman, who lived nearby, for visiting him frequently in prison.

103 Sider, *The Brethren in Christ,* 228-29, also mentions the experience of William Charlton (#3235409), Earl Sider (#3235413), and Frank (John Franklin) Carver (#3109415), who faced imprisonment for their convictions. See also service record for #3109171 Ernest Swalm, LAC, CEFS Records, RG150 accession 92/93, box 9450-5; service record for #3235130 John Henry Heise, accession 92/93, box 42235-53; and service record for #3039061 Charles Henry Wright, accession 92/93, box 10594-27.

104 D.W. Heise, Gormley, Ontario, to Hon. J.A. Calder, 10 May 1918, CGC, Military Problems Committee RG13-A-2; and Epp, *Mennonites in Canada,* 384.

105 *Winnipeg Tribune,* 26 January 1918, 6.

106 Ens, *Subjects or Citizens?* 178-80; service record for #4070640 Abraham Dyck, LAC, CEFS Records, RG150 accession 92/93, box 2791-37.

107 Donald Martin, *Old Order Mennonites of Ontario: Gelassenheit, Discipleship, Brotherhood* (Kitchener, ON: Pandora Press, 2003), 192-94.

108 Epp, *Mennonites in Canada,* 173.

109 During the war, the Doukhobors received little attention in the press. When they were mentioned, the idea that Ottawa needed to keep its word to them was generally accepted, although, as with the Hutterites, their "un-Canadian" ways were seen as suspicious. See "Doukhobors Not to Be Asked to Fight," *Manitoba Free Press,* 15 January 1917, 7; and "Doukhobors and Military Service," *Manitoba Free Press,* 12 October 1917, 2.

110 Allan Teichroew, "World War One and Mennonite Migrations to Canada to Avoid the Draft," *Mennonite Quarterly Review* 45 (July 1971): 229.

111 Benjamin Ewert, Gretna, to David Toews, Rosthern, 25 March 1918; Klaas Peters, Waldeck, to B. Ewert, 23 January 1918, Mennonite Heritage Centre Archives, vol. 542, no. 4, cited in Ens, *Subjects or Citizens?* 176. Ens cites Benjamin Ewert, Gretna, to David Toews, Rosthern, 25 March 1918, Mennonite Heritage Centre Archives, vol. 542, no. 4; and Klaas Peters, Waldeck, to B. Ewert, 23 January 1918, MHCA, vol. 542, no. 4.

112 David Toews to B. Ewert, 21 March 1918, MHCA, vol. 542, no. 4; Ben P. Jantz, "Drake," *Mitarbeiter,* February 1918, 4; March 1918, 7, both cited in Ens, *Subjects or Citizens?* 176. The Herbert and Drake communities and some areas north of Saskatoon had considerable difficulties.

113 Martin, *Old Order Mennonites,* 196.

114 Socknat, *Witness against War,* 77

115 Canadian Expeditionary Force Routine Orders, 773 Military Service Act, 6 July 1918 LAC, Department of National Defence Records, RG24, vol. 1, file 60-1-1, 4498.

116 Hartzler, *Mennonites in the World War,* 83; Janzen, *Limits on Liberty,* 197.

117 Editorial, "Mennonite Slacker Pastors on the Job," *Manitoba Free Press,* 26 October 1918, 1.

118 Although in almost all cases this hysteria appears to have been groundless, ex-Mennonite Klaas Peters was fined three days after the armistice for issuing Mennonite identity cards. Teichroew, "Mennonite Migrations," 244.

119 Janzen, *Limits on Liberty,* 174. My examination of conflict within the Doukhobor Church relies closely on his discussion.

120 Quoted in the *Regina Post,* 12 October 1917, 14 in LAC RG15, Department of the Interior files, vol. 758, "Doukhobor Lands," file 494483.

121 Ibid., 5.

122 It is interesting that, to some degree, this lack of attention recurs in their own histories. For instance, Fred Lichti, *A History of the East Zorra (Amish) Mennonite Church, 1837-1977* (Tavistock, ON: East Zorra Mennonite Church, 1977); and Gingerich, *The Amish of Canada,* are typically terse and matter-of-fact in the single paragraph they each devote to conscription.

123 These were not the only American Mennonites to come to Canada during the war. Teichroew's "Mennonite Migrations" also discusses young men fleeing north individually and larger family groups making a less clandestine journey to Canada to avoid conscription.

124 James C. Juhnke, *Vision, Doctrine, War: Mennonite Identity and Organization in America, 1890-1930* (Scottdale, PA: Herald Press, 1989), 233. This number includes Hutterites.

125 Teichroew, "Mennonite Migrations," 222-23. Teichroew further notes that, whereas the denomination's histories honour Mennonites who abandoned Europe for America so as to preserve their non-resistant lifestyle, they pay little attention to those who went to Canada for the sake of the same principles. Mennonite memory tends to focus on the experiences and difficulties of conscientious objectors within the United States. Huxman, "Mennonite Rhetoric," 287.

126 "More Slackers Coming Our Way," *Manitoba Free Press,* 21 September 1918, 1.

127 "More of This Mennonite Invasion," *Manitoba Free Press,* 5 October 1918, 1.

128 The deficiencies of the educational system were a target in discussions of the failure of non-resistant groups to assimilate, an interesting parallel to the dispute over French-language education. See, for example, F.W. Pickwell, "Mennonite Menace in the West," *Saturday Night,* 2 October 1918, 7.

129 Little seems to link these men directly, beyond their apparent beliefs in civil liberties or the value of historic peace church members as Canadians. Arthur Meighen, a Conservative barrister and solicitor from Ottawa, served as Borden's solicitor general and drafted the MSA. James Alexander Calder, from Moose Jaw, Saskatchewan, was a Liberal member of the Union Government. Frank Stewart Scott was a businessman from Galt, Ontario, and the Conservative MP for South Waterloo, an area with a high concentration of Mennonite Canadians. Edmund Leslie Newcombe, a lawyer from Halifax, served as deputy minister of justice, under whose purview the tribunals fell. Richard Bedford Bennett was a Calgary lawyer and MP with New Brunswick roots. *Who's Who in Canada 1917-1918* (Toronto: International Press, 1920).

130 Janzen, *Limits on Liberty,* 237. See also Martin, *Old Order Mennonites,* 197.

131 Levi, *Consent, Dissent, and Patriotism,* 2.

Chapter 3: An Insidious Enemy within the Gates

1 However, the IBSA did fare better than in the Second World War, when a July 1940 Order-in-Council banned it as an organization, an action William Kaplan calls "the single most serious interference with religious liberties by the state in all of modern Canada's history."

Kaplan, *State and Salvation: The Jehovah's Witnesses and Their Fight for Civil Rights* (Toronto: University of Toronto Press, 1989), xi.

2   M. James Penton, *Jehovah's Witnesses in Canada: Champions of Freedom of Speech and Worship* (Toronto: Macmillan of Canada, 1976), 12.

3   Ibid., 7. My discussion of Jehovah's Witness beliefs relies substantially on both this work and Kaplan, *State and Salvation.*

4   Kaplan, *State and Salvation*, 4.

5   Ibid., 5. According to this view, "Simply put, Roman Catholics are not Christians."

6   The Bible Students were not the only group whose publications were banned during the First World War. Communist and socialist newspapers, along with many foreign-language publications, suffered the same fate. See Jeffrey Keshen, *Propaganda and Censorship during Canada's Great War* (Edmonton: University of Alberta Press, 1996).

7   Penton, *Jehovah's Witnesses in Canada*, 20. Russell was refused entry into Canada on 5 April 1916 for his apparent preaching against participation in the war. After Russell's death on 31 October 1916, Joseph Franklin Rutherford became the leader of the denomination and was also refused entry to Canada for the duration of the war. See "International Bible Students," Library and Archives Canada (LAC), Ottawa, Robert Borden Papers, MG26, vol. 152, 81495-81497.

8   "Table 33: Religions in 1921, 1911 and 1901 with Proportion Per 100,000 Which Each Denomination Forms of the Total Population," *Sixth Census of Canada, 1921* (Ottawa: F.A. Acland, King's Printer, 1924-29), 571. "Conscientious Objectors, International Bible Students Association, the Case of David Cooke #548250," Canada, *Unpublished Sessional Papers*, 2d sess., 13th Parliament (20 February 1919-7 July 1919), no. 140, 77, LAC RG14, D2, vol. 45.

9   Quoted in "Conscience Dictates Claim for Exemption," *Toronto Globe*, 1 March 1916, 8.

10 C.T. Russell, *The New Creation* (Brooklyn, NY: International Bible Students, 1904), 594, 595, cited in Kaplan *State and Salvation*, 39-40.

11 Penton, *Jehovah's Witnesses in Canada*, 21. Rutherford is sometimes referred to as "Judge" Rutherford.

12 W.H. Chittick to Albert Kemp, 7 March 1916, LAC, Department of National Defence Records, RG24, vol. 4498, file 54-21-10-21.

13 H.J. Ross to Brig.-Gen. Wilson, 4 March 1916, LAC, Department of National Defence Records, RG24, vol. 4498, "Jehovah's Witnesses and Conscientious Objectors" file 60-1-2.

14 Brig.-Gen. Wilson to H.J. Ross, 6 March 1916, LAC, Department of National Defence Records, RG24, vol. 4498, file 60-1-2.

15 The file on "Jehovah's Witnesses and Conscientious Objectors" includes affidavits submitted by William W. Boutilier, Andrew Cuthbertson, Benjamin Detwiler, Cyril Heath, William McFeteridge, Sidney Nettleton, James Orr, James Garfield Rawstron, E.J.L. Roulston, John H.G. Snow, and James Work. On the affidavits, their names are signed rather than printed, so the versions given here may be misspelled.

16 "Report on the Administration of the Military Service Act in Military District No. Four (Montreal)," 16 December 1918, LAC RG24, vol. 4498, file 60-1-1. Note the use of the disease metaphor, which is discussed more fully in Chapter 5.

17 *Toronto Globe*, 1 March 1916, 4.

18 "Suspect Hun Plot," *London Free Press*, 1 March 1916, 12.

19 "Conscience Dictates Claim for Exemption," *London Free Press*, 1 March 1916, 9.

20 L.S. Ward, letter to the editor, *Toronto Daily Star*, 16 November 1917, 19. Bourgeois' trial is discussed in Chapter 1.

21 Ibid.

22 This was not an absolute position: many members of non-resistant religious groups expressed sympathy for COs from churches that endorsed the war. See Chapter 4.

23 "Two Years for Conscientious Objector," *Manitoba Free Press,* 26 February 1918, 5. See also service record for #2380622 David Cooke, LAC, Canadian Expeditionary Force Service Records (CEFS Records), RG150 accession 92/93, box 1939-58.

24 "First Ruling on Objectors," *Toronto Globe,* 12 January 1917, 7.

25 "Conscientious Objectors, International Bible Students Association, the Case of David Cooke #548250," Canada, *Unpublished Sessional Papers,* 2d sess., 13th Parliament (20 February 1919-7 July 1919), no. 140, 75-97, LAC, RG14, D2, vol. 45.

26 The Church of Christ, Disciples of Christ, and Pentecostal Assemblies were similarly not recognized. In *Two Worlds: The Protestant Culture of Nineteenth-Century Ontario* (Montreal and Kingston: McGill-Queen's University Press, 1989), 122, William Westfall presents religion in nineteenth-century Ontario as "largely organized institutionally around hierarchies, infrastructure and bricks and mortar." This seems to have held true for at least the first part of the next century as well.

27 Nigel James Young, "The Nation State and War Resistance" (PhD diss., University of California Berkeley, 1976). 495.

28 The Pentecostal Assemblies of Canada does have an archive and a most helpful archivist in James Craig. However, since the denomination was not organized until 1919, it has very few records dating from the First World War.

29 "Tribunals Are Working Steadily," *Manitoba Free Press,* 15 November 1917, 1.

30 "Resent View of Military," *Toronto Globe,* 31 May 1918, 8. The article mentioned a discussion that followed the drafting of the letter: during it, church members complained that, when enlisting, their co-religionists had been put down as Anglicans by military recorders, a fact that further impedes the search for objectors from this denomination. The reference to the "fancy churches" is an interesting phrase; it seems to imply a certain effeminacy on the part of these churches and the objectors within them.

31 J.M. Bliss discusses this rivalry in "The Methodist Church and World War I," *Canadian Historical Review* 49, 3 (September 1968): 213-33. The rejection of MacKenzie as a chaplain probably had almost nothing to do with the perceived number of conscientious objectors within the Church of Christ. There were far more applications for chaplaincies in all the churches than the CEF was able to fill. See Duff Crerar, *Padres in No Man's Land: Canadian Chaplains in the Great War* (Montreal and Kingston: McGill-Queen's University Press, 1995).

32 Edward Crawley, *The Plymouth Brethren (So-Called): Who They Are – Their Mode of Worship Etc., Explained in a Letter to His Friends and Relatives* (Ottawa: Joseph Loveday, 1871), 12.

33 Ibid., 9-10.

34 "Table 33: Religions in 1921, 1911 and 1901 with Proportion Per 100,000 Which Each Denomination Forms of the Total Population," *Sixth Census of Canada, 1921,* 571.

35 David D. Priestman and George Arthur Wigmore to Robert Borden, 5 October 1916, LAC, Robert Borden Papers, MG26, H1(c), vol. 208, 116599.

36 Service record for #2139688 George Arthur Wigmore, LAC, CEFS Records, RG150 accession 92/93, box 10347-47. Wigmore did not serve long overseas, catching a bad case of tonsillitis in Siberia and being invalided home 5 May 1919. David Priestman seems to have escaped being drafted and is possibly the same David Priestman who, as mentioned in the last chapter, inquired into visiting imprisoned Quaker objectors.

37 "The Military Service Act, 1917, Report of Cases Decided by the Central Appeal Judge, March 23rd, 1918," Canada, *Unpublished Sessional Papers,* 1st sess., 13th Parliament (18 March

1918-24 May 1918), no. 97, 29-30, LAC, RG14, D2, vol. 36. A circular letter written later in the war provides a hint at least that the government was moving towards a more flexible response for Plymouth Brethren. It noted that, though the denomination itself was not exempt from the MSA, "In individual cases, however, an opportunity may be given to men of this Brotherhood at the discretion of their Commanding Officer, to be employed in a non-combatant capacity in the combatant unit to which they are attached." See Circular Letter: Adjutant-General to All Districts, 16 February 1918, "Military Service Act 1917," LAC, RG24, vol. 4615, file IG 206-6.

38 One Pentecostal later explained the denomination's position: "We have never taken an official stand on this matter, so individuals have responded according to their understanding of Bible references. Some have taken the commandment, 'Thou shalt not kill,' to include war. Others have curtailed their military service to a non-combatant stance. Since the Old Testament records several 'Just Wars' with God's approval, it is obvious that 'to kill' would have two distinct meanings. The New Testament clearly shows not only killing, but also 'ill will' is forbidden." Reverend W.H. Moody to the author, 13 October 2003.

39 "Objector to M.S. Gets Two Years," *Toronto Globe*, 16 April 1918, 3.

40 Ernest John Swalm, *My Beloved Brethren: Personal Memoirs and Recollections of the Canadian Brethren in Christ Church* (Nappanee, IN: Evangel Press, 1969), 26.

41 Davis Roger Guion, "Conscientious Cooperators: The Seventh-day Adventists and Military Service, 1860-1945" (PhD diss., George Washington University, 1970), 1-3.

42 General Conference Executive Committee, Statement to the Governor of the State of Michigan, 2 August 1864, quoted in J. Ernest Monteith, *The Lord Is My Shepherd: A History of the Seventh-day Adventist Church in Canada* (Oshawa, ON: Canadian Union Conference of the Seventh-day Adventist Church, 1983), 162.

43 Ibid.

44 H.M.J. Richards, President, Ontario Conference, to Borden, 28 May 1917, LAC, Robert Borden Papers, MG26, H1(a), vol. 208, 44088.

45 "The Military Service Act 1917. Report of Cases Decided by the Central Appeal Judge," Canada, *Unpublished Sessional Papers*, 1st sess., 13th Parliament (18 March 1918-24 May 1918), no. 97, LAC, RG14, D2, vol. 36.

46 James Wagner to J. Ernest Monteith, n.d., quoted in *The Lord Is My Shepherd*, 163-64. Service record for #3207837 James Bennett Wagner, LAC, CEFS Records, RG150 accession 92/93, box 9983-21; service record for #3207838 Max Popow, box 7904-10; and service record for #3207839 Floyd Edwin Jones, box 49933-11.

47 Wagner to Monteith, n.d., quoted in *The Lord Is My Shepherd*, 164. The incidents were precipitated because Wagner and Jones had been deleted from a list of those eligible for a draft to Siberia.

48 Dr. John Thomas to unnamed correspondent, 1860, quoted in John Botten, *The Captive Conscience: An Historical Perspective of the Christadelphian Stand against Military Service* (Birmingham, UK: Christadelphian Military Service Committee, 2002), 1. When tracing their history, Christadelphians generally go back farther than the nineteenth century, seeing their own views as the true outgrowth of the non-resistance of the early Christian Church.

49 Quoted in Botten, *The Captive Conscience*, 4.

50 The provision in the North for conscientious objection for members of pacifist denominations also prompted the Brethren in Christ Church (Tunkers) to give their group an official name. E. Morris Sider, *The Brethren in Christ in Canada: Two Hundred Years of Tradition and Change* (Nappanee, IN: Evangel Press, 1988), 26.

51 E.R. Evans, *"Ye Are Strangers and Sojourners with Me": A Study of the Christadelphian Teaching Concerning a Christian's Relationship to the State* (Hamilton, ON: privately published, 1990), 19.

52 E.R. Evans, *Test Case for Canada '3314545': The Experiences of a Christadelphian Conscientious Objector in World War I, 1914-1918* (Hamilton, ON: privately published, 1972), 28.

53 Ibid., 28-29. Forty-six Christadelphian baptisms took place in 1914, sixty-two in 1915, fifty-six in 1916, seventy-five in 1917, and thirty-one in 1918.

54 Evans, *"Ye Are Strangers,"* 1.

55 Quoted in Canadian Christadelphian Standing Committee, *A summary of the work of the Canadian Christadelphian Standing Committee, 1917, 1918, 1919: shewing the Christadelphian Church's experience under the Canadian Military Service Act 1917, during the Great War with Germany and the success of the committee's efforts in obtaining recognition by the government of Canada for the Christadelphian body to be entitled to claim exemption from all forms of military and naval service for its bonafide members: with an appendix consisting of copies of the Christadelphian constitution and articles of faith, also the official ecclesial rolls of membership, and other evidences the committee filed at Ottawa* [CCSC Report] (Toronto: Canadian Christadelphian Standing Committee, 1919), 7.

56 Ibid., 5 (emphasis in original).

57 Ibid., Appendix 3: "Membership Roll of the Christadelphian Church." By the time of the 1921 census, there were 1,810 Christadelphians in Canada.

58 The report states that, of the 73 Christadelphians eligible for service, 49 were exempt from combat. This would seem to leave 24 subject to conscription. However, the report's enumeration of those who enlisted, were excommunicated, or jailed totals 23, not 24. Someone seems to be missing. In my search of the CEF records I discovered 26 men who identified themselves as Christadelphians. Alonzo Valence Buck, a thirty-eight-year-old mason and widower with four children, joined a Forestry Battalion. Service record for #1036172 Alonzo Valence Buck, LAC, CEFS Records, RG150 accession 92/93, box 1233-56. It is interesting that, as the sole supporter of his children, he probably would have been exempted under the MSA. I was unable to locate further details for Allen F. Smith.

59 Somewhat confusingly, Frederick Hiley, whom the roll of Christadelphians notes as "withdrawn [from church membership], owing to having joined up with the army or being called to the colours," is also recorded as having been sent overseas as a conscientious objector. See Appendix 3: "Membership Roll of the Christadelphian Church," CCSC Report, 36; and service record for #2382290 Frederick Hiley, LAC, CEFS Records, RG150 accession 92/93, box 4341-4.

60 I have not found names for the individuals who were excommunicated or who died. For information regarding imprisoned Christadelphian COs, see Table 1 in the appendix. See also service record for #3314545 John Evans, LAC, CEFS Records, RG150 accession 92/93, box 2947-43; and service record for #2023853 Louis Cotton, box 2036-54.

61 CCSC Report, 6, 9.

62 Edwin Hill to Robert Borden, 21 May 1917, LAC, Robert Borden Papers, MG26, H1(a), vol. 86, 43996-43997.

63 CCSC Report, 11, 16. Harold Arthur Machin might be seen as rather an unlikely ally. A Conservative MP for Kenora and the son of an Anglican minister, he had served in the Boer War. A CEF lieutenant-colonel during the First World War, he spent much of it overseas. *Who's Who in Canada 1917-1918* (Toronto: International Press, 1920).

64 Canada, *House of Commons Debates* (12 July 1917), 3305.

65 CCSC Report, 47.

66 See Botten, *The Captive Conscience,* 42-45. Botten asserts that there were fourteen hundred Christadelphian COs in Britain.

67 CCSC Report, 9-10.

68 It stated that "the name 'Christadelphian' was adopted in 1863 as a distinctive appellation for a body of believers who for religious reasons were seeking exemption from military service during the American Civil War." Petition presented through Sir George Foster to the clerk of the Canadian House of Commons [1917?], quoted in CCSC Report, 4-5.

69 See, for instance, the case of Franklin Joseph Marshall, no. 829371, Mennonite Archives, Conrad Grebel College (CGC), University of Waterloo, Waterloo, ON, Samuel Coffman Papers, Military Problems Committee Folder, XV-11.47; and service record for #3311786 Franklin Marshall, LAC, CEFS Records, RG150 accession 92/93, box 5950-50. Marshall was a young Toronto grocer who, though recognized as a bona fide Christadelphian, was refused exemption because he failed to convince his tribunal judge of his personal scruples against fighting.

70 "Willing to Go to Ends of the Earth," *Toronto Daily Star,* 14 November 1917, 12.

71 "Have Scruples of Conscience," *Toronto Globe,* 3 April 1918, 10.

72 Evans, *Test Case for Canada,* especially 34, 42, 43-57, 71. Evans' ordeal is also chronicled in Peter Brock, ed., *"These Strange Criminals": An Anthology of Prison Memoirs by Conscientious Objectors from the Great War to the Cold War* (Toronto: University of Toronto Press, 2004).

73 "Proceedings of a Regimental Court of Enquiry Assembled at Winnipeg, Manitoba, 24 January 1918," LAC RG24, vol. 2028, HQ 1064-30-67, 35. See also service record for #2380155 Robert Clegg, LAC, CEFS Records, RG150 accession 92/93, box 1784-25; and service record for #2380174 Henry Naish, box 7230-52.

74 "Conscientious Objectors Said to Have Been Roughly Handled," *Manitoba Free Press,* 25 January 1918, 5.

75 Ibid. See also service record for #2380116 Charles Matheson (Mathison), LAC, CEFS Records, RG150 accession 92/93, box 6038-86.

76 Fred Dixon was a member of the Independent Labour Party of Manitoba but had won his seat in the Legislature in 1914 as an independent. He supported the strikers in the Winnipeg General Strike of 1919 and later helped found the CCF.

77 T.A. Crerar to Maj.-Gen. S.C. Mewburn, 28 January 1918, LAC, RG24, vol. 2028, HQ 1064-30-67. Thomas Alexander Crerar was the Liberal-Unionist MP for Marquette, Brandon, and Churchill, Manitoba. He served as minister of agriculture from 12 October 1917 to 11 June 1918. A strong advocate for farmers, he was one of the framers and first leader of the Progressive Party in Parliament in 1921.

78 Editorial, "Stop It!" *Manitoba Free Press,* 25 January 1918, 9.

79 "Court-Martial on Hazing Case," *Manitoba Free Press,* 7 February 1918, 8; "Simpson Is Not Guilty of Hazing," *Manitoba Free Press,* 19 February 1918, 3.

80 Penton, *Jehovah's Witnesses in Canada,* 59.

81 Mewburn to Borden, 9 February 1918, LAC, Robert Borden Papers, MG26, vol. 86, 44308.

82 "Objectors Given Two Years by Military," *Manitoba Free Press,* 18 March 1918, 5; service record for #4070189 Francis Wainwright, LAC, CEFS Records, RG150 accession 92/93, box 9986-22.

83 Quoted in "E.R. Chapman's View," *Manitoba Free Press,* 26 January 1918, 5.

84 Quoted in "Two Years for Draft Evaders," *Manitoba Free Press,* 24 January 1918, 5. Charles Edwards' CEF file is incomplete. See service record for #640062 Charles Edwards, LAC, CEFS Records, RG150 accession 92/93, box 2834-35.

85 "'Objector' Dies Raving Maniac," *Manitoba Free Press*, 27 February 1918, 5. The CEF records at LAC do not include those of David Wells.
86 He was described as weighing approximately 220 pounds and, perhaps somewhat conversely, being in "superb physical condition." See E. Robinson, Secretary, Winnipeg Trades and Labor Council, to Robert Borden, n.d., LAC RLB, MG26, vol. 238, 132799; and William Ivens to T.A. Crerar, 25 February 1918, RLB MG26 vol. 238, 132781, 132782.
87 Quoted in "Minto Barracks Cruelty Charges," *Manitoba Free Press*, 26 January 1918, 5.
88 J.P.M. Millar, "A Socialist in Wartime," in *We Did Not Fight, 1914-1918: Experiences of War Resisters*, ed. Julian Bell (London: Cobden-Sanderson, 1935), 176.
89 Quoted in "Pentecostal Missionites Would Not Take Action," *Manitoba Free Press*, 26 January 1918, 5.
90 William Ivens to T.A. Crerar, 25 February 1918, LAC, RLB MG26 vol. 238, 132782.
91 E. Robinson, Secretary, Winnipeg Trades and Labor Council, to Borden, 8 April 1918, LAC RLB MG26 vol. 309, 132799.
92 None of the Canadian COs sent overseas received the death sentence. For those who were not so lucky, see Desmond Morton, "The Supreme Penalty: Canadian Deaths by Firing Squad in the First World War," *Queen's Quarterly* 79, 3 (Winter 1972): 345-52. For an examination of why certain death sentences were carried out whereas others were commuted, see Teresa Iacobelli, "Arbitrary Justice? A Comparative Analysis of Death Sentences Passed and Death Sentences Commuted during the First World War" (Master's thesis, Wilfrid Laurier University, 2003).
93 Service record for #2380926 John Gillespie, LAC, CEFS Records, RG150 accession 92/93, box 3541-18; service record for #2381450 Claudius Brown, box 1130-34; service record for #2129542 Nicholas Shuttleworth, box 8890-9; service record for #504030 Albert Edward Bagnall, box 336-54. I have found no CEF file for McAulay. Service record for #3058078 Oliver Pimlott, box 7839-21; service record for #3056944 Sydney Thomas, box 9614-18; service record for #3314545 John Evans, box 2947-43; interview with Wainwright by Penton, in *Jehovah's Witnesses in Canada*, 62; CCSC Report, 38. See also AG Canadian Militia to Secretary, Headquarters, Overseas Military Force of Canada, 7 June 1918, LAC, Department of Militia and Defence Records, RG9 III A1, vol. 95, and ibid. Mewburn to Kemp, 7 August 1918.
94 Service record for #3057735 Joseph Adams, LAC, CEFS Records, RG150 accession 92/93, box 32-40; and service record for #3059035 Vernal Running, box 8545-10; ADCANEF, London, to Militia, Ottawa, 22 August 1918, LAC, RG24, vol. 2029, HQ 1064-30-67. See also Thomas Socknat, *Witness against War: Pacifism in Canada, 1900-1945* (Toronto: University of Toronto Press, 1987), 85. Socknat's list of objectors sent overseas, however, omits the names of the Christadelphians. John W. Graham puts the number of Canadians sent overseas at twenty-five. Graham, *Conscription and Conscience: A History, 1916-1919* (1922; repr., New York: A.M. Kelley, 1971), 116.
95 Pimlott's experience is also recorded in Graham, *Conscription and Conscience*, 117.
96 *Golden Age*, 29 September 1920, 710.
97 A.N. Shuttleworth to R.L. Borden, 31 May 1918, LAC, RLB, MG26, H1(a), vol. 96, 51402. See also A.N. Shuttleworth to Borden, received 4 June 1918, LAC, RG9 Militia and Defence, series II-F-10, vol. 239, 16738-R-15. While overseas, Shuttleworth converted to the faith of the IBSA COs imprisoned with him.
98 No. 3314545 John Henry Walter Evans, LAC, Courts Martial of the First World War Records RG150, ser. 8, file 1064-30-56-146, reel T-8695.
99 No. 2023853 Louis Alexander Colton [Cotton], LAC, Ministry of the Overseas Military Forces of Canada Records, RG150, ser. 8, file 55-C-161, reel T-8691.
100 Botten, *The Captive Conscience*, 89.
101 Quoted in Evans, *Test Case for Canada*, 54.

102 Ibid., 57. Cotton received the same twelve-month sentence as Evans. No. 2023853 Louis Alexander Colton [Cotton], LAC, Ministry of the Overseas Military Forces of Canada Records, RG150, ser. 8, file 55-C-161, reel T-8691.

103 LAC RG150 Courts Martial of the First World War, Series 8, File 55-C-139, Reel T-8691 R.L. Clegg; and RG150, ser. 8, file 55-N-13, reel T-8691, H. R. Neish [Naish].

104 Calling other COs as witnesses at one's court martial does not appear to have been uncommon. Naish called Francis Cedric Wainwright, another IBSA objector who had been sent overseas. See also service record for #4070189 Francis Wainwright, LAC, CEFS Records, RG150 accession 92/93, box 9986-22.

105 No. 2380155 Robert Litler Clegg, LAC, Courts Martial of the First World War Records RG150, ser. 8, file 55-C-139, reel T-869; and #2380174 Henry Ralph Neish [Naish], file 55-N-13, reel T-8691.

106 Evans, *Test Case for Canada,* especially 60.

107 Ibid., 68, 73.

108 "New Ruling for C.O.s," *Manitoba Free Press,* 24 April 1918, 1.

109 Penton, *Jehovah's Witnesses in Canada,* 62.

110 Evans, *Test Case for Canada,* 94-103.

Chapter 4: Exemption from Religion on Religious Grounds

1 Peter Brock, *The Quaker Peace Testimony, 1660-1914* (York, UK: Sessions Book Trust, 1990) 375. See also Thomas Socknat, "Canada's Liberal Pacifists and the Great War," *Journal of Canadian Studies* 18, 4 (1983-84): 30-44.

2 Canadian Christadelphian Standing Committee, *A summary of the work of the Canadian Christadelphian Standing Committee 1917, 1918, 1919: shewing the Christadelphian Church's experience under The Canadian Military Service Act 1917, during the Great War with Germany and the success of the committee's efforts in obtaining recognition by the government of Canada for the Christadelphian body to be entitled to claim exemption from all forms of military and naval service for its bonafide members: with an appendix consisting of copies of the Christadelphian constitution and articles of faith, also the official ecclesial rolls of membership, and other evidences the committee filed at Ottawa* (Toronto: Canadian Christadelphian Standing Committee, 1919), 16-17. Machin's sympathies were somewhat complex, as he at one point also advocated disenfranchising all eligible men who did not volunteer for the CEF.

3 Brock Millman, *Managing Domestic Dissent in First World War Britain* (London: Frank Cass, 2000), 21.

4 J. Castell Hopkins, ed., *The Canadian Annual Review of Public Affairs 1914* (Toronto: Canadian Review, 1915), 133.

5 "Minutes of the Toronto Baptist Association," 1914, 7, Canadian Baptist Archives (CBA), McMaster University, Hamilton, ON.

6 Quoted in Hopkins, *Canadian Annual Review 1914,* 135.

7 Hopkins, *Canadian Annual Review 1914,* 133.

8 Socknat, "Canada's Liberal Pacifists." 30. See also Michael Eliot Howard, *War and the Liberal Conscience* (New York: Rutgers University Press, 1978); Peter Brock, *Twentieth-Century Pacifism* (Toronto: Van Nostrand Reinhold, 1970); and Mark Moss, *Manliness and Militarism: Educating Young Boys in Ontario for War* (Don Mills, ON: Oxford University Press, 2001), 142. Moss adds the "failure to take stock of both the realities of the world situation and the Canadian attachment to Britain" to the weaknesses of pre-war pacifism.

9 J.M. Bliss, "The Methodist Church and World War I," *Canadian Historical Review* 49, 3 (September 1968): 214.

10 Veronica Strong-Boag, introduction to *In Times Like These*, by Nellie L. McClung (1915; repr., Toronto: University of Toronto Press, 1972), ii.

11 McClung, *In Times Like These*, 11.

12 Ibid., 26.

13 Pacifism was also important to McClung and other advocates of the social gospel, because war takes away valuable resources needed to alleviate poverty and other social ills. For discussions of the social gospel movement in Canada, see Richard Allen, *The Social Passion: Religion and Social Reform in Canada, 1914-1928* (Toronto: University of Toronto Press, 1971); Carl Berger, *Science, God, and Nature in Victorian Canada* (Toronto: University of Toronto Press, 1983); Ramsay Cook, *The Regenerators: Social Criticism in Late-Victorian English Canada* (Toronto: University of Toronto Press, 1985); and Brian John Fraser, *The Social Uplifters: Presbyterian Progressives and the Social Gospel in Canada, 1875-1915* (Waterloo: Wilfrid Laurier University Press, 1988).

14 Nellie L. McClung, *The Next of Kin: Those Who Wait and Wonder* (Toronto: T. Allen, 1917), 45. Flora Macdonald Denison is another prominent example of one in whom a maternal feminist and pacifist viewpoint shifted to a pro-war stance. See Deborah Gorham, "Vera Brittain, Flora Macdonald Denison and the Great War: The Failure of Non-violence," in *Women and Peace: Theoretical, Historical, and Practical Perspectives*, ed. Ruth Roach Pierson (London: Croom Helm, 1987), 137-48.

15 David A. Martin discusses this pattern of behaviour, which he sees as most frequent in Nonconformist and liberal denominations, in *Pacifism: An Historical and Sociological Study* (New York: Schocken Books, 1966).

16 Thomas Socknat, *Witness against War: Pacifism in Canada, 1900-1945* (Toronto: University of Toronto Press, 1987), 45-48. Ross Harkness, *J.E. Atkinson of the Star* (Toronto: University of Toronto Press, 1963). In Ralph Connor's popular wartime novel *The Major*, the protagonist, Larry Gwynne, undergoes a similar shift. Connor, *The Major* (Toronto: McClelland, Goodchild and Stewart, 1917), see especially 167, 360, 370.

17 Moss, *Manliness and Militarism*, 141.

18 Toyomasa Fusé, "Religion, War and the Institutional Dilemma: A Sociological Interpretation," *Journal of Peace Research* 5, 2 (1968): 196. See also J. Milton Yinger, *The Scientific Study of Religion* (New York: Macmillan, 1970).

19 Although, according to St. Augustine, a defensive war is always just, an offensive one must satisfy three criteria to be seen in a comparable light: the cause in which it is fought must be just, it must follow a declaration of war by a recognized sovereign, and it must arise from "right intention," that is, the good aimed at should manifestly outweigh the evil involved. Martin, *Pacifism*, 18. See also John Howard Yoder, *When War Is Unjust: Being Honest in Just-War Thinking* (Minneapolis: Augsburg, 1984); Oliver O'Donovan, *The Just War Revisited* (Cambridge: Cambridge University Press, 2003); Paul F. Robinson, *The Just War in Comparative Perspective* (Aldershot, UK: Ashgate, 2003); and Peter S. Temes, *The Just War: An American Reflection on the Morality of War in Our Time* (Chicago: Ivan R. Dee, 2003).

20 Fusé, "Religion, War and the Institutional Dilemma," 198. Fusé, ibid., 199, also remarks that "the most accurate index of the extent of pacifism in a given time and place is the number of conscientious objectors," a questionable claim. For instance, especially in its reconstruction work, the Society of Friends in Canada was probably a greater voice for pacifism than would seem to be suggested by the prevalence of conscientious objection within the sect.

21 Martin, *Pacifism*, 3.

22 Joe Mihevc adds an interesting element to the discussion in suggesting that, in Canada, differing motivations lay behind the support for the war as evinced by the established

Anglican Church and the Nonconformist Methodist Church. Mihevc connects the support of the former to the intrinsic conservatism of Anglicanism and that of the latter to Methodism's "militant nationalism and social reformism." Mihevc, "The Politicization of the Mennonite Peace Witness in the Twentieth Century" (PhD diss., St. Michael's College, Toronto School of Theology, 1989), 23.

23 Martin, *Pacifism*, 24.

24 Millman, *Managing Domestic Dissent*, 18.

25 Martin, *Pacifism*, 136. For the connection between religious dissent and other forms of dissidence in Great Britain during the eighteenth and nineteenth centuries, see also A.J.P. Taylor, *The Trouble Makers: Dissent over Foreign Policy, 1792-1939* (London: Panther Books, 1969).

26 "Spectator," "From Week to Week: Spectator's Discussion of Topics of Interest to Churchmen," *Canadian Churchman*, 3 October 1918, 683.

27 Reverend James Thayer Addison, "Christianity and Non-resistance," *Canadian Churchman*, 6 April 1916, 215.

28 Reverend C.D. Baldwin, "Conscientious Objectors," *Christian Guardian*, 12 December 1917, 20-21.

29 Jonathan Vance's *Death So Noble: Memory, Meaning, and the First World War* (Vancouver: UBC Press, 1997) discusses this vision of the war as a holy crusade and the soldiers as Christ figures, sacrificing their lives for the rest of Allied, especially Canadian, society. This perception seems to have been in part a development of the ideal of "muscular Christianity" that was popular before the war. See, for instance, David Alderson, *Mansex Fine: Religion, Manliness and Imperialism in Nineteenth-Century British Culture* (Manchester: Manchester University Press, 1998); and Donald E. Hall, *Muscular Christianity: Embodying the Victorian Age* (Cambridge: Cambridge University Press, 1994).

30 Reverend Henry Cody, "The Offering of Young Canada," *Canadian Churchman*, 27 July 1916, 473.

31 Marjorie Pickthall, "Marching Men," in *Complete Poems of Marjorie Pickthall* (Toronto: McClelland and Stewart, 1927), 194.

32 *London Free Press*, 7 March 1916, 3.

33 For interesting discussions of conscientious objection as a political phenomenon, see Margaret Levi, *Consent, Dissent, and Patriotism* (Cambridge: Cambridge University Press, 1997); Charles C. Moskos and John Whiteclay Chambers III, eds., *The New Conscientious Objection: From Sacred to Secular Resistance* (New York: Oxford University Press, 1993); and Gisela Ruebsaat, *The First Freedom: Freedom of Conscience and Religion in Canada* (Victoria, BC: Conscience Canada, 1991).

34 For instance, see Felicity Goodall, ed., *A Question of Conscience: Conscientious Objection in Two World Wars* (Thrupp, UK: Sutton, 1997); John W. Graham, *Conscription and Conscience: A History, 1916-1919* (1922; repr., New York: A.M. Kelley, 1971); Julian Bell, ed., *We Did Not Fight, 1914-1918: Experiences of War Resisters* (London: Cobden-Sanderson, 1935); and Corder Catchpool, *On Two Fronts: Letters of a Conscientious Objector* (1940; repr., New York: Garland, 1972).

35 J.P.M. Millar, "A Socialist in Wartime," in Bell, *We Did Not Fight*, 133.

36 Court martial of #3057735 Joseph Leonard Adams, 9, LAC, Ministry of the Overseas Military Forces of Canada Records (MFC Records), RG150, ser. 8, file 55-A-41, reel T-8691. Adam's attestation paper lists his religion as "Christian."

37 Quoted in E.R. Evans, *Test Case for Canada '3314545': The Experiences of a Christadelphian Conscientious Objector in World War I, 1914-1918* (Hamilton, ON: privately published, 1972), 40.

38 Ibid., 98-99.

39 Quoted in "Appeals Allowed Are One in Four," *Manitoba Free Press,* 5 December 1917, 5.

40 This statement perhaps needs some qualification. I mean loyalty to a family's ethical and spiritual beliefs. Although exemption from military service was permitted on the grounds of being a family's sole financial support, most tribunal judges were reluctant to allow it.

41 Christopher Joseph Capozzola, "Uncle Sam Wants You: Political Obligations in World War I America" (PhD diss., Columbia University, 2002), 20.

42 "Spectator," "Comments on Matters of Interest from Week to Week," *Canadian Churchman,* 21 September 1916, 600.

43 Quoted in J. Castell Hopkins, ed., *The Canadian Annual Review of Public Affairs 1916* (Toronto: Canadian Review, 1917).

44 Mrs. A. Hendron to Robert Borden, 30 November 1917, LAC, Robert Borden Papers, MG26, H1(a), vol. 86, 4432.

45 Mark G. McGowan, *The Waning of the Green: Catholics, the Irish, and Identity in Toronto, 1887-1922* (Montreal and Kingston: McGill-Queen's University Press, 1999), 250.

46 Torin R.T. Finney, *Unsung Hero of the Great War: The Life and Witness of Ben Salmon* (Mahwah, NJ: Paulist Press, 1989), viii. Gordon C. Zahn's *War, Conscience and Dissent* (New York: Hawthorne Books, 1967) offers a useful treatment of conscientious objection in the United States, with a focus on Catholic objection, especially during and after the Second World War.

47 Finney, *Unsung Hero,* x, arguing that this reliance on individual conscience is perfectly acceptable, cites Pope John Paul II lauding the "maturity" of COs. The countervailing argument is that a Catholic is not at liberty to choose which aspects of doctrine he will accept. Salmon's term "practical Catholic" does not seem to have a place in Catholic doctrine and is probably a play on "practising Catholic." I am indebted to Angela Hickling and Lou Pouwels of Holy Trinity Catholic Secondary School in Bowmanville, Ontario, for their help in understanding the position and doctrine of the Catholic Church in this matter.

48 Sidney Webb, "Conscience and the Conscientious Objector," *North Atlantic Review* 205 (March 1917): 413. Webb, ibid. 208, also praises the Society of Friends for the "remarkable self-discipline which they have taught themselves to apply to their own consciences." Beatrice Webb's views apparently accorded with those of her husband. She sent a letter to her nephew Stephen Hobhouse, while he was imprisoned as a conscientious objector, "urging me not to continue to be guilty of the sin of rebellion against a Government that was defending my liberties and way of life." Stephen Hobhouse, *The Autobiography of Stephen Hobhouse: Reformer, Pacifist, Christian* (Boston: Beacon Press, 1951), 173.

49 Reverend C.D. Baldwin, "Conscientious Objectors," *Christian Guardian,* 12 December 1917, 20.

50 Members of the clergy were excepted from the MSA.

51 "First Annual Report of the Army and Navy Board, 1916," 8, United Church of Canada Archives (UCCA), Victoria University, University of Toronto, Toronto, Methodist Church (Canada) Army and Navy Board, accession 78.100C, box 2, file 15.

52 Ibid., iv.

53 "Spectator," "Comments on Matters of Interest from Week to Week," *Canadian Churchman,* 6 July 1916, 424. Desmond Morton gives more accurate figures of denominational enlistment in the CEF. He found that Anglicans made up 30.9 percent, Catholics 22.9 percent, Methodists 13.6 percent, and Presbyterians 21.1 percent of recruits. By comparison, the 1911 census stated that 32.3 percent of Canada's population was Roman Catholic, 15.48 percent was Presbyterian, 14.98 was Methodist, and 14.47 percent was Anglican. "Table 1:

Ratio Per Cent of Specified Denomination to Total Population by Census Year," *Fifth Census of Canada, 1911* (Ottawa: C.H. Parmelee, 1913). Mark McGowan has included a valuable table titled "Voluntary Enlistment in the Canadian Expeditionary Force by Religious Denomination, to 1 June 1917," in *The Waning of the Green*, 257. Army lore claimed that those unaffiliated with any particular church or sect were recorded as Anglicans on their attestation papers. Desmond Morton, *When Your Number's Up: The Canadian Soldier in the First World War* (Toronto: Random House, 1993), 279.

54 The board requested a survey of the troops according to denomination from the Militia Department but was refused. It then appealed to individual circuits of the church for figures. Less than half of these were returned, but they showed 38,201. The board estimated that this would mean enlistment of 65,000 and of 85,000 by the end of the war. "First Annual Report of the Army and Navy Board, 1916," iv.

55 Quoted in Kenneth McNaught, *A Prophet in Politics: A Biography of J.S. Woodsworth* (Toronto: University of Toronto Press, 1959), 82.

56 Alice Chown's autobiography *The Stairway* (1921; repr., Toronto: University of Toronto Press, 1989), with its strong Christian pacifist tone, was published a few years after the war.

57 Charles Bishop, "The Minister and the War," *Christian Guardian*, 10 May 1916, 23. See also Bishop's letters to the *Christian Guardian*: "Conscription and the Conscientious Objector," 19 July 1916, 26; "Unmitigated Prussianism," 24 October 1917, 21; and "Pacifism and Prussianism," 12 December 1917, 2.

58 A.W. Keeton, letter to the editor, "The Higher Law: A Cecil Champions Liberty of Conscience," *Christian Guardian*, 6 March 1918, 13-14.

59 Rev. F. Prior to Minister of Militia and Defence, 8 June 1918, LAC, Department of National Defence Records, RG24, vol. 5953, HQ 1064-67-3.

60 The other men tried at the Niagara Camp at this time were John Garfield Phillips, a Pentecostal, and Alfred Thomas Grimsley and Albert Edward Scott, both, according to the newspaper, unaffiliated with any organized church. (His attestation paper gives Scott as a Methodist.) The sixth man is not named. "General Court Martial Held," *Toronto Globe*, 17 July 1918, 3.

61 Ibid.; service record for #3040250 Harold George Calma, LAC, CEFS Records, RG150 accession 92/93, box 1395-34; and service record for #3040251 Wilson David Calma, box 1395-35.

62 Editorial, "Baptists and the War," *Canadian Baptist*, 21 June 1917, 1.

63 Reverend W.H. Porter, letter to the editor, "Conscientious Objection to Fighting," *Canadian Baptist*, 29 March 1917, 4. See also Porter, "Conscience and the War," *Canadian Baptist*, 26 July 1917, 3.

64 Edward John Stobo Jr., "Should a Christian Go to War?" *Canadian Baptist*, 13 June 1918, 7.

65 Service record for #3310831 George VanLoon, LAC, CEFS Records, RG150 accession 92/93, box 9906-34; and service record for #2129542 Nicholas Shuttleworth, box 8890-9.

66 The Social Gospel was an early 20th century Protestant Christian movement which placed its emphasis on the application of Christian principles to society's problems. Adherents to Social Gospel movements believed in social progressivism, were optimistic about the morality and future of humanity, and sought to harmonize Christian ethics with political action.

67 Allen, *The Social Passion*, 61; Socknat, *Witness against War*, 69.

68 "The Church, the War and Patriotism," Report Adopted by General Conference at Hamilton, 1918, UCCA, D639, R4, M43. William Magney sees the Methodists' leftist stance as a "rhetorical pose, resting upon a conviction that the day of the millennium had come

and that the kingdom of Christ was not emerging." Magney, "The Methodist Church and the Conscription Crisis of 1917" (Paper for Dr. D.G. Creighton, University of Toronto, 1968), ii.

69 Bliss, "The Methodist Church," 233.

70 Court martial of #3057735 Joseph Adams, 3, LAC, MFC Records, RG150, ser. 8, file 55-A-41, reel T-8691. On his attestation paper, Adams describes his religious affiliation as simply "Christian."

71 Court martial of #3037082 Oswald Peacock, 5, LAC, MFC Records, RG150, ser. 8, file 55-A-41, reel T-8691.

72 Court martial of #3059035 Vernal Running, 6, LAC, MFC Records, RG150, ser. 8, file 55-A-41, reel T-8691.

73 Ibid. 7. Vernal's older brother, Alden Robertson Running, was married and worked as a bookkeeper in Winnipeg. When he volunteered for the CEF on 15 February 1915, he had already performed eight months' militia service and had reached the rank of staff-sergeant. On his attestation paper, Alden Running gave his religion as Presbyterian, although "Methodist" is also written and crossed out. Service record for #421019 A.R. Running, LAC, CEFS Records, RG150, accession 1992-93/166, box 8545-7.

74 Court martial of #3037082 Oswald Peacock, 12, LAC, MFC Records, RG150, ser. 8, file 55-A-41, reel T-8691.

75 For a study of the Canadian Patriotic Fund, see Desmond Morton, *Fight or Pay: Soldier's Families in the Great War* (Vancouver: UBC Press, 2004).

76 For interviews with families of conscientious objectors in Britain, see Goodall, "Those at Home," in *A Question of Conscience,* Chapter 6.

77 The CEF files for the COs listed in Table 1 of the appendix show that they refused to take army pay. I used this refusal as one determining factor when it was unclear whether a man was an objector. In Evans, *Test Case for Canada,* 103, John Evans discusses his own refusal to accept money from the army.

78 Many, possibly most, members of the NCF in Britain objected to military service on pol-itical *and* religious grounds. Thomas C. Kennedy, *The Hound of Conscience: A History of the No-Conscription Fellowship, 1914-1919* (Fayetteville: University of Arkansas Press, 1981), 165. The separation of political and religious objection, as I mentioned in the Introduc-tion, is rather artificial.

79 Susan Mayse, *Ideas,* CBC Radio, 1989, LAC, accession R1190-62-3-E. See also Mayse, *Ginger: The Life of Albert Goodwin* (Madeira Park, BC: Harbour, 1990); Mark Leier, "Plots, Shots, and Liberal Thoughts: Conspiracy Theory and the Death of Ginger Goodwin," *Labour/Le Travail* 39 (Spring 1997): 215-24; and Roger Stonebanks, *Fighting for Dignity: The Ginger Goodwin Story* (St. John's: Canadian Committee on Labour History, 2004).

80 By absence, I mean both his untimely death and his decision to resist conscription by silent evasion rather than with a more public statement.

Chapter 5: Holier than Thou

1 J.L. Granatstein and J.M. Hitsman, *Broken Promises: A History of Conscription in Canada* (Toronto: Copp, Clark, Pitman, 1985), 66; A.M. Wilms, "Conscription 1917: A Brief for the Defence," *Canadian Historical Review* 37 (December 1956): 343.

2 Mrs. Wyse, "Fetch Him Out," *London Free Press,* 14 February 1916, 4.

3 Canada, *House of Commons Debates* (22 January 1917), 367.

4 William Lacey Amy is better known for his post-war, critically panned *Blue Pete* novels about life on the frontier of the Canadian West. Keith Walden, in "Blue Pete and Canadian Nationalism: Vision and Experience in the Western Novels of William Lacey Amy," *Journal*

of Canadian Studies 24, 2 (Summer 1989): 39, argues that the novels are highly unrealistic partly because Amy simply imported the American frontier formula to Canada: "Blue Pete, like the typical American western hero, worked outside the law using violence as a surgical tool to impose order." Amy's anti-pacifist tirades during the war, also advocating violence as the proper solution to problems, help to colour and expand this argument.

5 William Lacey Amy, "Asquithian Warfare" *Saturday Night,* 9 June 1917, 4.
6 William Lacey Amy, "The Conscientious Objectors," *Saturday Night,* 15 September 1917, 2. Jack Johnson was a famous boxer of the time, the first black Heavyweight Champion of the World.
7 Quoted in "Tribunal Floored Religious One," *Toronto Daily Star,* 12 November 1917, 2.
8 Lacey Amy, "The Conscientious Objectors," 4.
9 *Punch,* 9 May 1917, 297.
10 *London Daily Mail,* 10 April 1916, 6.
11 Bart Kennedy, "The Conscientious Objector," *British Citizen and Empire Worker,* 8 April 1917, 8.
12 Ibid.
13 John Tosh, "Domesticity and Manliness in the Victorian Middle Class," in *Manful Assertions: Masculinities in Britain since 1800,* ed. Michael Roper and John Tosh (New York: Routledge, Chapman and Hall, 1991) 117-35.
14 Norma Clark, "Strenuous Idleness: Thomas Carlyle and the Man of Letters as a Hero," in Roper and Tosh, *Manful Assertions,* 126-40.
15 J.A. Mangan and James Walvin, *Manliness and Morality: Middle-Class Masculinity in Britain and America, 1800-1940* (Manchester: Manchester University Press, 1987), 21. Mark Moss, *Manliness and Militarism: Educating Young Boys in Ontario for War* (Don Mills, ON: Oxford University Press, 2001).
16 Moss, *Manliness and Militarism,* 14; W.L. Morton, "Victorian Canada," in *The Shield of Achilles: Aspects of Canada in the Victorian Age,* ed. W.L. Morton (Toronto: McClelland and Stewart, 1968), 311-33.
17 Jonathan Rutherford, *Forever England: Reflections on Race, Masculinity and Empire* (London: Lawrence and Wishart, 1997), 14. Moss, *Manliness and Militarism,* also promotes the influence of imperialism in this shift.
18 Quoted in Roper and Tosh, eds., *Manful Assertions.* The father of Canadian CO Robert Thomas Wilson saw the same connection between manliness and military service. He appeared at his son's tribunal in a markedly non-supportive role, informing the judges, "After he was drafted I advised him to be a man and put on the khaki. If I were a young man I'd go myself. I'd be no CO." Quoted in "Wouldn't Wear Khaki," *Toronto Daily Star,* 20 March 1918, 19.
19 See also her references to how American COs Bruno Grunzig and William Jasmagy made efforts to present their response as properly masculine. Frances Early, *A World without War: How US Feminists and Pacifists Resisted World War I* (Syracuse, NY: Syracuse University Press, 1997), 104, 114.
20 Gerald Shenk, "Work or Fight: Selective Service and Manhood in the Progressive Era" (PhD diss., University of California at San Diego, 1992).
21 "To Be a Christian Is a Man's Job," *Canadian Baptist,* 11 July 1918, 7.
22 "Conscientious Objector's Creed," *Saturday Night,* 29 December 1917, 2.
23 Edward John Stobo Jr., "Should a Christian Go to War?" *Canadian Baptist,* 13 June 1918, 7.
24 Lacey Amy, "The Conscientious Objectors," 2.
25 "Exemption Boards Having Busy Time," *Manitoba Free Press,* 14 November 1917, 6.

26 An interesting hint of a connection is made by Jacob Guenter in *Men of Steele* (Saskatoon: privately published, 1981), the history of an Old Colony Russian Mennonite group in Saskatchewan. Guenter records that when tensions over conscription and the school question led some Mennonites to search for a new haven after the war, they contacted Paraguay, Mexico, Argentina, and, intriguingly, Quebec. Unfortunately, I have found no solid record of cooperation between nationalist anti-conscriptionists in Quebec and pacifist anti-conscriptionists in the rest of the country.

27 Editorial, "Conscientious Objectors," *Manitoba Free Press*, 29 January 1918, 9. The sensational tone of this quotation indicates that it probably came from propaganda rather than a real letter.

28 Warden Provincial Gaol re: Treatment of Conscientious Objectors, July 1918, Library and Archives Canada (LAC), Ottawa, Department of Justice Records, RG13, A2, vol. 225, file 1582/18. The men had been sentenced to two years less a day, the usual sentence for objectors at the time. Near the end of the war, some men were sentenced to life imprisonment, which was generally commuted to ten years. Rivers did not name the men he wrote about, but the Christadelphian was probably Walter Alexander Crawford, a twenty-nine-year-old farmer from Onoway, Alberta, who served time in Alberta. James Wagner was probably the Seventh-day Adventist. The Bible Student may have been twenty-three-year-old farmer Roy Kerrison.

29 Ibid. The deputy minister of justice replied that he had no instructions about treatment of COs and "presumably the ordinary regulations of the prison would apply." Dept. of Justice, reply Warden Provincial Gaol re: Treatment of Conscientious Objectors, July 1918, LAC, Department of Justice Records, RG13, A2, vol. 225, file 1582/18.

30 Not all wardens were so antagonistic to objectors. Ernest John Swalm remembers his prison governor fondly: "Mr. Bush was a very fine Baptist with a rare sense of humour. He extended to the conscientious objectors all the consideration possible within the legal and ethical boundaries of his responsibility." Swalm, *My Beloved Brethren: Personal Memoirs and Recollections of the Canadian Brethren in Christ Church* (Nappanee, IN: Evangel Press, 1969), 29.

31 Early, *A World without War*, 97.

32 The other members were the progressive judge Julian W. Mack and Harlan Fiske Stone, dean of the faculty of the Columbia Law School.

33 Walter Guest Kellogg, *The Conscientious Objector* (New York: Boni and Liveright, 1919), 38.

34 Ibid., 41.

35 Ibid.

36 See Robert Craig Brown, ed., *Minorities, Schools and Politics* (Toronto: University of Toronto Press, 1969); Lovell Clark, *The Manitoba Schools Question: Majority Rule or Minority Rights?* (Toronto: Copp Clark, 1968); Adolf Ens, *Subjects or Citizens? The Mennonite Experience in Canada, 1870-1925* (Ottawa: University of Ottawa Press, 1994); Donald B. Kraybill, *Ethnic Education: The Impact of Mennonite Schooling* (San Francisco: R & E Research Associates, 1977); and D.A. Schmeiser, *Civil Liberties in Canada* (New York: Oxford University Press, 1964).

37 See, for example, Fred Lichti, *A History of the East Zorra (Amish) Mennonite Church, 1837-1977* (Tavistock, ON: East Zorra Mennonite Church, 1977); William Neufield, *From Faith to Faith: The History of the Manitoba Mennonite Brethren Church* (Winnipeg: Kindred Press, 1989); Leonard Doell, *The Bergthaler Mennonite Church of Saskatchewan, 1892-1975* (Winnipeg: CMBC Publications, 1987); and Leo Driedger, *Mennonites in Winnipeg* (Winnipeg: Kindred Press, 1990).

38 Guenter, *Men of Steele*; William Janzen, *Limits on Liberty: The Experience of Mennonite, Hutterite, and Doukhobor Communities in Canada* (Toronto: University of Toronto Press, 1990), 3.

39 G.K. Chesterton, "The Conscience Argument," *Saturday Night*, 21 July 1917, 3. Reprinted from *The Illustrated London News*, 2 June 1917.

40 Ibid.

41 Harriett Rashnell, "The Conscientious Objector," *Manitoba Free Press*, 30 October 1917, 9.

42 "The Temptation of Peace," *Canadian Baptist*, 11 January 1917, 2.

43 Chesterson, "The Conscience Argument," 3.

44 McLandbrugh Wilson, "The Pacifist," *London Free Press*, 30 March 1916, 4.

45 Editorial, "The Conscientious Objector," *Maclean's*, January 1918. 45.

46 Editorial, "Military Service," *Manitoba Free Press*, 17 February, 1918, 4.

47 When asked by his exemption tribunal what he would do if he saw a German soldier attempting to rape his sister, Strachey famously replied that he would "insert his body between them." In Miranda Seymour's opinion, "It was a measure of the Government's desperation that they reckoned it worth their time and money to force such an unsoldierly man into uniform"; she added that he received exemption "mainly on the grounds of looking like a bearded stick insect." Seymour, *Ottoline Morrell: Life on the Grand Scale* (London: Hodder and Stoughton, 1992), 253. Although some objectors might have fit this effete stereotype, it is, of course, not true for all. Many, including, for example, Quaker socialist Alfred Barratt Brown, saw their stance as one of manly struggle. See Thomas C. Kennedy, "Public Opinion and the Conscientious Objector, 1915-1919," *Journal of British Studies* 12, 2 (May 1973): 105-19.

48 Like those in Canada, objectors in other countries were seen as mentally deficient due to their stubbornness and the strangeness of their views. In the United States, they were subjected to psychological examination, and several were interned for the duration of the war or worse. Kellogg, *The Conscientious Objector*, 30; Newton D. Baker to Woodrow Wilson, 1 October 1917, Papers of Woodrow Wilson, vol. 44, 288, cited in Christopher Joseph Capozzola, "Uncle Sam Wants You: Political Obligations in World War I America" (PhD diss., Columbia University, 2002), 113. COs in Germany underwent similar experiences. See Peter Brock, "Confinement of Conscientious Objectors as Psychological Patients in World War I Germany," *Peace and Change* 23 (July 1988): 247-64.

49 Lacey Amy, "The Conscientious Objectors," 2.

50 Sidney Webb, "Conscience and the Conscientious Objector," *North Atlantic Review* 205 (March 1917): 415.

51 Editorial, "A New Class of Objectors," *Toronto Globe*, 25 June 1918, 6.

52 Kellogg, *The Conscientious Objector*, 42-43.

53 Ibid., 52-53.

54 "Quietus on International Bible Students," *Saturday Night*, 23 January 1918, 1.

55 Agnes C. Laut, "The Slacker," *Maclean's*, March 1918, 47.

56 Allan Sullivan, "Porteous, V.C.: The Story of a Man Who Went to the Front through Fear," *Maclean's*, January 1916, 20.

57 Ralph Connor, *The Major* (Toronto: McClelland, Goodchild & Stewart, 1917), 167, 170.

58 Ibid., 370.

59 Lucy Maud Montgomery, *Rilla of Ingleside* (Toronto: McClelland and Stewart, 1920), 85 (emphasis in original).

60 Ibid.

61 Ibid., 124.

62 Thomas Socknat, *Witness against War: Pacifism in Canada, 1900-1945* (Toronto: University of Toronto Press, 1987), 44-45.
63 Francis Marion Beynon, *Aleta Dey* (1919; repr., London: Virago, 1988). 171.
64 Ibid., 241.
65 Alice Chown, *The Stairway* (1921; repr., Toronto: University of Toronto Press, 1988). Chown was a cousin of general superintendent of the Methodist Church and prominent war supporter S.D. Chown.
66 This form of pacifist protest has a long history. The term "conscientious objector" generally applies to both those who object to being conscripted for military service and those who object to paying taxes that go towards spending on war and the military. See Constance Braithwaite, *Conscientious Objection to Various Compulsions under British Law* (York, UK: W. Sessions, 1995).
67 Philip Child, *God's Sparrows* (Toronto: McClelland and Stewart, 1937), 19 (emphasis in original). Child was himself a veteran of the Great War.
68 Ibid., 109.
69 Ibid., 168.
70 Ibid., 303.
71 "Downeaster," "Conscientious Objectors," *Canadian Churchman*, 10 August 1916, 508.
72 Webb, "Conscience and the Conscientious Objector," 141.
73 Harriet Rashnell, "The Conscientious Objector," *Manitoba Free Press*, 30 October 1917, 9.
74 Edwin Wyle, "Conscientious Objectors," *Toronto Globe*, 28 September 1918, 6.
75 Quoted in "Put Conscies on Mine Sweepers Says Teddy," *Toronto Daily Star*, 27 November 1917, 1, 14. Apparently, the "blue end of the rim" is heaven.
76 Margaret D. Gibson, letter to the editor, "Two Suggestions," *Canadian Churchman*, 20 July 1916, 458. The editor's remark appears with the letter. Gibson's other suggestion had to do with stricter control over education in Ireland.
77 Editorial, "Conscience and Combatant Service," *Manitoba Free Press*, 3 April 1918, 11.
78 Quoted in E.R. Evans, *Test Case for Canada '3314545': The Experiences of a Christadelphian Conscientious Objector in World War I, 1914-1918* (Hamilton, ON: privately published, 1972), 49; see also 39, 58, 99.
79 "10 Years for Not Donning Uniform," *Toronto Globe*, 14 November 1918, 8.
80 W.R. Smythe, letter to the editor, "The Case of Arthur Hill," *Toronto Globe*, 19 November 1918, 6.
81 Editorial, "Notes and Comments," *Toronto Globe*, 15 November 1918, 6.
82 V.A. Clark, letter to the editor, "The Case of Arthur Hill," *Toronto Globe*, 26 November 1918, 6.
83 S.J. Rutherford, letter to the editor, "The Case of Arthur Hill," *Toronto Globe*, 28 November 1918, 6. Although he did not dispute Smythe's comment that Hill's father was president of the glass company, Rutherford's signature seems to complicate the issue somewhat. Frances Early shows that a similar representation of bravery was used to defend an American conscientious objector Howard Moore. Early, *A World without War*, 119.
84 T.H. Lister, letter to the editor, "Defaulters and Objectors," *Toronto Globe*, 5 December 1918, 6.
85 Although, technically, they were not deserters, men who avoided registering or who registered but defaulted when called up for military service were often labelled as such in the press as the word "deserter" had more negative connotations than "defaulter."
86 "Spectator," "From Week to Week," *Canadian Churchman*, 22 August 1918, 358.

87 Editorial, "The Shirkers' Triumph," *Toronto Globe,* 7 February 1919, 6. At least some objectors in the United States felt themselves in a similar situation. Norman Thomas complained that "it was these men who did not so much as try to avoid the draft who were most vehemently denounced as cowards and slackers." Thomas, *The Conscientious Objector in America* (New York: B.W. Huebsch, 1923), 174.

88 Editorial, "A Failure of Justice," *Toronto Globe,* 20 February 1919, 4.

89 "Treatment of Desertion, Defaulters, Conscientious Objectors Etc.," circular letter from E.L. Newcombe, 5 February 1919, LAC, Department of Justice Records, RG13, ser. A-2, vol. 2162, file 1919-2453.

Conclusion

1 E.L. Newcombe to Major McFarland, 27 January 1919, Library and Archives Canada (LAC), Ottawa, Department of Justice Records, RG13, ser. A-2, vol. 2162, file 1919-2453.

2 "Treatment of Desertion, Defaulters, Conscientious Objectors Etc.," Circular letter from E.L. Newcombe, 5 February 1919, LAC, Department of Justice Records, RG13, ser. A-2, vol. 2162, file 1919-2453.

3 Service record for #3033956 Alan Renshaw, LAC, Canadian Expeditionary Force Service Records (CEFS Records), RG150 accession 92/93, box 8198-9; service record for #3235270 David Earl Carrick, box 1517-51; service record for #3107843 Sydney B. Curry, box 2236-4; service record for #3037082 Oswald Peacock, box 7678-16; and service record for #3035989 Frederick Egger, box 2851-17. Tunkers, Mennonites, and Quakers who were granted leaves of absence received honourable discharges at the end of the war; most other COs received discharges on grounds of misconduct or were transferred to civilian prisons. See also E. Morris Sider, *The Brethren in Christ in Canada: Two Hundred Years of Tradition and Change* (Nappanee, IN: Evangel Press, 1988), 229.

4 Canada, *House of Commons Debates* (24 March 1919), 781, 782-84. Lemieux's speech assumes a certain significance, given that his own son was killed in action during the war.

5 The numbers break down as follows: of those in federal penitentiaries, twelve were in Kingston, three in Manitoba, six in Saskatchewan, five in Alberta, and eight in British Columbia; of those in provincial jails, four were in New Brunswick, one in Saskatchewan, and one in Quebec. "Number of Conscientious Objectors Now in Jail," 2 May 1919, LAC, RG13, ser. A-2, vol. 236, file 1919-1203. In this file Harold Robertson, who was jailed in Saskatchewan, is the only CO mentioned by name. In the US, by comparison, "almost all objectors were released by December 1920, but the last WWI conscientious objector was not freed until Franklin Roosevelt took office in 1933." Mulford Q. Sibley and Philip E. Jacob, *Conscription of Conscience: The American State and the Conscientious Objector, 1940-1947* (Ithaca, NY: Cornell University Press, 1952), 16.

6 I do not mean to imply that the historic peace churches responded in a completely unified way to the exigencies of the Second World War, simply that they did so with much more unity and organization than had been the case in the First World War. The histories of the peace churches discuss the difficulties and disagreements that were part of this effort at a unified response to the Second World War and conscription. See Guy Hershberger, *The Mennonite Church in the Second World War* (Scottdale, PA: Mennonite Publishing House, 1951); T.D. Regehr, *Mennonites in Canada, 1939-1970: A People Transformed* (Toronto: University of Toronto Press, 1996); Arthur Garratt Dorland, *The Quakers in Canada: A History* (Toronto: Ryerson Press, 1968); and Sider, *The Brethren in Christ.*

7 C. Henry Smith, *The Story of the Mennonites* (Newton, KS: Mennonite Publication Office, 1964), 286. Smith sees a correlation between the strong emphasis on democracy in the US and the high levels of abuse suffered by Mennonites in that country.

8 Joe Mihevc, "The Politicization of the Mennonite Peace Witness in the Twentieth Century" (PhD diss., St. Michael's College, Toronto School of Theology, 1989), 62. Mihevc also asserts that Canadian Mennonites had more support in Parliament than did their American counterparts in Congress.

9 Leo Driedger and Donald B. Kraybill, *Mennonite Peacemaking: From Quietism to Activism* (Scottdale, PA: Herald Press, 1964); M.J. Heisey, *Peace and Persistence: Tracing the Brethren in Christ Peace Witness through Three Generations* (Kent, OH: Kent State University Press, 2003), 3. See also Carlton O. Wittlinger, *Quest for Piety and Obedience: The Story of the Brethren in Christ* (Nappanee, IN: Evangel Press, 1978).

10 Those who objected during the Second World War left more biographies and memoirs. See, for instance, William Janzen and Frances Greaser, *Sam Martin Went to Prison: The Story of Conscientious Objection and Canadian Military Service* (Winnipeg: Kindred Press, 1990); Lawrence Klipperstein, ed., *That There Be Peace: Mennonites in Canada and World War II* (Winnipeg: Manitoba CO Reunion Committee, 1979); Peter Lorenz Neufeld, *Mennonites at War, a Double-Edged Sword: Canadian Mennonites in World War Two* (Deloraine, MB: DTS, 1997); David P. Reimer, *Experiences of Mennonites in Canada during World War II* (Altona, MB: D.A. Friesen, n.d. [1946?]); and John Aron Toews, ed., *Alternative Service in Canada during World War II* (Winnipeg: Publication Committee, Canadian Conference of the MBC, 1959).

11 Devi Prasad and Tony Smythe, eds., *Conscription, a World Survey: Compulsory Military Service and Resistance to It* (London: War Resisters International, 1968). The section on Canada deals almost exclusively with the Second World War.

12 They were permitted to leave at least partly because Lenin, who had begun his New Economic Policy in 1921, needed capital. The Soviet Union thus allowed some Mennonites to leave, with their way paid by the CPR, which was later reimbursed by the Mennonites. See David Rempel, *A Mennonite Family in Tsarist Russia and the Soviet Union: 1789-1923* (Toronto: University of Toronto Press, 2003).

13 E.K. Francis, *In Search of Utopia* (Altona, MB: D.W. Friesen and Sons, 1955), 203.

14 Canada, *House of Commons Debates* (25 November 1941), 383. For the aid work of Canadian Mennonites during the famine in the USSR and the emigration of the Russlanders to this country, see especially Frank H. Epp, *Mennonite Exodus: The Rescue and Resettlement of the Russian Mennonites since the Communist Revolution* (Altona, MB: D.W. Friesen and Sons, 1962); and John B. Toews, *With Courage to Spare: The Life of B.B. Janz (1877-1964)* (Fresno, CA: Board of Christian Literature of the General Conference of the Mennonite Brethren Churches of North America, 1978). Conditions in Soviet Russia during the famine of the 1920s are described by John B. Toews in *Czars, Soviets and Mennonites* (Newton, KS: Faith and Life Press, 1982).

15 Toews, *Alternative Service in Canada*, 20, suggests that the fact that King had "lived among the Ontario Mennonites in his younger days" prompted him to favour the immigration project.

16 See Thomas Berger, "Jehovah's Witnesses: Church, State and Religious Dissent," in *Fragile Freedoms: Human Rights and Dissent in Canada* (Toronto and Vancouver: Clark, Irwin, 1982), 163-89; M. James Penton, *Jehovah's Witnesses in Canada: Champions of Freedom of Speech and Worship* (Toronto: Macmillan of Canada, 1976), 129-55; William Kaplan, *State and Salvation: The Jehovah's Witnesses and Their Fight for Civil Rights* (Toronto: University of Toronto Press, 1989), 191-223.

17 Penton, *Jehovah's Witnesses in Canada*, 165.

18 John M. Dyck, *Faith under Test: Alternative Service during World War II in the US and Canada* (Ste. Anne, MB: Gospel, 1997).

19 Reverend Douglas Rudd, correspondence with the author, September 2003. First World War objector J. Elmor Morrison was a member of the Pentecostal Assemblies of Canada. A twenty-one-year-old farmer from Ontario, he served time in Kingston Penitentiary after his conscientious objection was not recognized. See service record for #3138859 John Elmer [Elmor] Morrison, LAC, CEFS Records, RG150 accession 93/94, box 6409-24.

20 E.J. Swalm, *My Beloved Brethren: Personal Memoirs and Recollections of the Canadian Brethren in Christ Church* (Nappanee, IN: Evangel Press, 1938). Reprint 1966.

21 The committee members are named in John Botten, *The Captive Conscience: An Historical Perspective of the Christadelphian Stand against Military Service* (Birmingham, UK: Christadelphian Military Service Committee, 2002). My thanks to E.R. Evans for information about Fred and William Welshman's relationship; service record for #3132187 William Welshman, LAC, CEFS Records, RG150 accession 93/94, box 10229-54.

22 Botten, *The Captive Conscience*, 90.

23 Paul Wilson, "A Question of Conscience: Pacifism in Victoria, 1938-1945" (PhD diss., La Trobe University, 1984), cited in Peter Brock and Malcolm Saunders, "Pacifists as Conscientious Objectors in Australia," in *Challenge to Mars: Essays on Pacifism from 1918-1945*, ed. Peter Brock and Thomas Socknat (Toronto: University of Toronto Press, 1999), 287. The situation was not identical in the two countries. Canada had a much better transportation infrastructure than Australia, which had no transcontinental railway.

24 Claude Klassen, quoted in Dyck, *Faith under Test*, 183.

25 See Stephen Hobhouse, *The Autobiography of Stephen Hobhouse: Reformer, Pacifist, Christian* (Boston: Beacon Press, 1951); Margaret Hobhouse, *I Appeal unto Caesar* (London: George Allen and Unwin, [1918?]); and Fenner Brockway, *Towards Tomorrow* (London: Hart-Davis, MacGibbon, 1977). Making a statement by applying as a CO when other grounds for exemption were available went beyond these two examples. See also Arthur Marwick, *Clifford Allen: The Open Conspirator* (London: Oliver and Boyd, 1964; Thomas C. Kennedy, *The Hound of Conscience: A History of the No-Conscription Fellowship, 1914-1919* (Fayetteville: University of Arkansas Press, 1981); and Corder Catchpool, *On Two Fronts: Letters of a Conscientious Objector* (1940; repr., New York: Garland, 1972).

26 See, for comparison, Desmond Morton, *When Your Number's Up*, which provides figures for the CEF as a whole. Farmers, hunters, fishermen, and lumbermen made up 22.4 percent of the armed forces, industrial occupations 36.4 percent. Morton gives 125,387 white-collar workers and 123,060 farmers. Morton, *When Your Number's Up: The Canadian Soldier in the First World War* (Toronto: Random House, 1993), Appendix, 278-79.

27 Adrian Stephen, "The Tribunals," in *We Did Not Fight, 1914-1918: Experiences of War Resisters*, ed. Julian Bell, 377-92 (London: Cobden-Sanderson, 1935), 384.

28 In December 1918, the Military District of Montreal estimated that it had encountered no more than twelve COs during the war, the majority of them being IBSA members. "Report on the Administration of the Military Service Act in Military District No. 4," Montreal, 16 December 1918, Department of National Defence, Directorate of History and Heritage, Ottawa, RG24, vol. 4498, MD4 file 60-1-1. Catholics were also numerous in the Maritimes.

29 "Table 1: Religions of the People by Provinces for 1911 and Totals for 1901 and 1911," *Fifth Census of Canada, 1911* (Ottawa: C.H. Parmelee, 1913), 2-3.

30 It was the largest of all the Ontario churches; well over half the Methodist Church membership lived in Ontario. J. Castell Hopkins, ed., *The Canadian Annual Review of Public Affairs, 1918* (Toronto: Canadian Review, 1919), 72; and "Table 1: Religions of the People by Provinces," *Fifth Census of Canada, 1911*.

31 See Leonard Doell, *The Bergthaler Mennonite Church of Saskatchewan, 1892-1975* (Winnipeg: CMBC Publications, 1987), 64; Jacob Guenter, *Men of Steele* (Saskatoon: privately published, 1981), 14-15; Francis, *In Search of Utopia*, 178-86; and William Janzen, *Limits on Liberty: The Experience of Mennonite, Hutterite, and Doukhobor Communities in Canada* (Toronto: University of Toronto Press, 1990), 78.

32 Editorial, "The Conscientious Objector," *Maclean's,* 14 January 1918, 45.

33 Ibid.

34 Editorial, "Military Service," *Canadian Baptist,* 11 February 1918, 4.

35 Christopher Joseph Capozzola, "Uncle Sam Wants You: Political Obligations in World War I America" (PhD diss., Columbia University, 2002), 12.

36 Editorial, "This World War and – You!" *Toronto Globe,* 24 June 1916, 6.

37 Capozzola, "Uncle Sam Wants You," 1 (emphasis in original).

38 Ibid., 123.

39 Thomas Socknat, *Witness against War: Pacifism in Canada, 1900-1945* (Toronto: University of Toronto Press, 1987), 11.

Bibliography

Primary Sources

Archives
Archives of the Pentecostal Assemblies of Canada, Mississauga, ON
Canadian Baptist Archives, McMaster University, Hamilton, ON
Canadian Expeditionary Force Service Records
Courts Martial of the First World War Records
Department of the Interior Records
Department of Justice Records
Department of Militia and Defence Records
Department of National Defence, Directorate of History and Heritage, Ottawa
Department of National Defence Records
Library and Archives Canada, Ottawa
Mennonite Archives, Conrad Grebel College, University of Waterloo, Waterloo, ON
Methodist Church (Canada) Army and Navy Board
Military Problems Committee
Ministry of the Overseas Military Forces of Canada Records
Ontario Historical Society, Papers and Records
Queen's University Archives, Kingston, ON
Robert Borden Papers
Samuel Coffman Papers
Society of Friends Archives, Pickering College, Newmarket, ON
T.A. Crerar Papers
United Church of Canada Archives, Victoria University, University of Toronto

Newspapers and Magazines
British Citizen and Empire Worker (London)
Calgary Eye-Opener
Canadian Churchman (Toronto)
Canadian Friend (Newmarket, ON)
Christian Guardian (Toronto)
Halifax Chronicle
Hamilton Free Press
La Presse (Montreal)
Le Devoir (Montreal)
London Daily Mail
London Free Press
Maclean's (Toronto)
Manitoba Free Press
Mennonite (Hillsboro, KS)

Montreal Star
Ottawa Citizen
Punch (London)
Regina Post
Saturday Night (Toronto)
Scottdale (PA) Gospel Herald
Toronto Daily Star
Toronto Globe
Vancouver Sun
Watch Tower
Winnipeg Tribune

Printed Material

Anon. *Une page d'histoire: prenez, lisez et jugez d'après des faits irréfutables, tous les députés libéraux de la province de Québec ont* [sic] *le 5 juillet 1917, voté le principe de la conscription: Farceurs, hableurs et comédiens: La lettre de Laurier.* Quebec City, [1917?].

Bell, Julian, ed. *We Did Not Fight, 1914-1918: Experiences of War Resisters.* London: Cobden-Sanderson, 1935.

Beynon, Francis Marion. *Aleta Dey.* 1919. Reprint, London: Virago, 1988.

Borden, Robert. *Canada at War: A Speech Delivered by Rt. Hon. Sir Robert Laird Borden in the House of Commons Introducing the Military Service Bill.* [Galt, ON?] [1917?].

–. *Robert Laird Borden: His Memoirs.* 2 vols. Toronto: Macmillan, 1938.

Bourassa, Henri. *Conscription.* Montreal: Le Devoir, 1917.

Brock, Peter, ed. *Liberty and Conscience: A Documentary History of the Experience of Conscientious Objectors in America through the Civil War.* New York: Oxford University Press, 2002.

–. *"These Strange Criminals": An Anthology of Prison Memoirs by Conscientious Objectors from the Great War to the Cold War.* Toronto: University of Toronto Press, 2004.

Brockway, Fenner. *Towards Tomorrow.* London: Hart-Davis, MacGibbon, 1977.

Canada. *House of Commons Debates,* 1914-19.

–. *Unpublished Sessional Papers,* 1914-19.

Canadian Christadelphian Standing Committee. *A summary of the work of the Canadian Christadelphian Standing Committee, 1917, 1918, 1919: shewing the Christadelphian Church's experience under The Canadian Military Service Act 1917, during the Great War with Germany and the success of the committee's efforts in obtaining recognition by the government of Canada for the Christadelphian body to be entitled to claim exemption from all forms of military and naval service for its bonafide members: with an appendix consisting of copies of the Christadelphian constitution and articles of faith, also the official ecclesial rolls of membership, and other evidences the committee filed at Ottawa.* Toronto: Christadelphian Standing Committee, 1919.

Catchpool, Corder. *On Two Fronts: Letters of a Conscientious Objector.* 1940. Reprint, New York: Garland, 1972.

Charlebois, Joseph. *La conscription: Tristes dessins et légends triste.* Montréal: Éditions de Devoir, 1917.

Chesterton, G.K. "The Conscience Argument," *Saturday Night,* 21 July 1917, 3. Reprinted from *The Illustrated London News,* 2 June 1917.

Child, Philip. *God's Sparrows.* Toronto: McClelland and Stewart, 1937.

Chown, Alice. *The Stairway.* 1921. Reprint, Toronto: University of Toronto Press, 1988.

"A Citizen." *For All We Have and Are.* N.p.: Imperial Press, [19?].

Collinson, John Henry. *The Recruiting League of Hamilton.* Hamilton: N.p., [1918?].

Connor, Ralph. *The Major.* Toronto: McClelland, Goodchild and Stewart, 1917.

Crawley, Edward. *The Plymouth Brethren (So-Called): Who They Are – Their Mode of Worship Etc., Explained in a Letter to His Friends and Relatives.* Ottawa: Joseph Loveday, 1871.

Evans, E.R. *Test Case for Canada '3314545': The Experiences of a Christadelphian Conscientious Objector in World War I, 1914-1918.* Hamilton, ON: privately published, 1972.

Fifth Census of Canada, 1911. Ottawa: C.H. Parmelee, 1913.

Goodall, Felicity, ed. *A Question of Conscience: Conscientious Objection in Two World Wars.* Thrupp, UK: Sutton, 1997.

Hobhouse, Margaret. *I Appeal unto Caesar.* London: George Allen and Unwin, [1918?].

Hobhouse, Stephen. *The Autobiography of Stephen Hobhouse: Reformer, Pacifist, Christian.* Boston: Beacon Press, 1951.

Hopkins, J. Castell, ed. *The Canadian Annual Review of Public Affairs.* Toronto: Canadian Review, 1915-19.

Kellogg, Walter Guest. *The Conscientious Objector.* New York: Boni and Liveright, 1919.

Liberal Party of Canada. *Two Dark Blots of Shame: The Conservative Franchise Act of 1885 and the War-Time Elections Act of 1917.* [Ottawa?]: Liberal Party of Canada, [1918?].

MacLennan, Hugh. *Two Solitudes.* Toronto: Collins, 1945.

McClung, Nellie L. *The Next of Kin: Those Who Wait and Wonder.* Toronto: T. Allen, 1917.

–. *In Times Like These.* 1915. Reprint, Toronto: University of Toronto Press, 1972.

Merritt, William H. *Canada and National Service.* Toronto: Macmillan, 1917.

Military Service Council. *For the Defence of Canada.* Ottawa: Military Service Council, 1917.

Montgomery, Lucy Maud. *Rilla of Ingleside.* Toronto: McClelland and Stewart, 1920.

Morris, Philip H. *The Canadian Patriotic Fund: A Record of Its Activities from 1914 to 1919.* [Ottawa?]: Executive Secretary of the Canadian Patriotic Fund, [1920?].

Pickthall, Marjorie. *Complete Poems of Marjorie Pickthall.* Toronto: McClelland and Stewart, 1927.

Read, Daphne, ed. *The Great War and Canadian Society: An Oral History.* Toronto: New Hogtown Press, 1978.

Russell, C.T. *The New Creation.* Brooklyn, NY: International Bible Students Association, 1904.

Schlissel, Lillian, ed. *Conscience in America: A Documentary History of Conscientious Objection in America, 1757-1967.* New York: Dutton, 1968.

Sixth Census of Canada, 1921. Ottawa: F.A. Acland, King's Printer, 1924-29.

Swalm, E.J. *My Beloved Brethren: Personal Memoirs and Recollections of the Canadian Brethren in Christ Church.* Nappanee, IN: Evangel Press, 1969.

–. *Nonresistance under Test: A Compilation of Experiences of Conscientious Objectors as Encountered in Two World Wars.* Nappanee, IN: E.V. Publishing House, 1949.

Thomas, Norman. *The Conscientious Objector in America.* New York: B.W. Huebsch, 1923.

Wade, Edward Harper. *Autocracy and Democracy.* [Montreal?], [1917?].

Webb, Sidney. "Conscience and the Conscientious Objector." *North Atlantic Review* 205 (March 1917): 402-20.

Weir, William A. *A Summary Report of the Canadian Christadelphian Standing Committee, 1920-1945.* N.p., [1945?].

Secondary Sources

Alderson, David. *Mansex Fine: Religion, Manliness and Imperialism in Nineteenth-Century British Culture*. Manchester: Manchester University Press, 1998.

Allen, Richard. *The Social Passion: Religion and Social Reform in Canada, 1914-1928*. Toronto: University of Toronto Press, 1971.

Armstrong, Elizabeth H. *The Crisis of Quebec, 1914-1918*. New York: Columbia University Press, 1937.

Avery, Donald. *Dangerous Foreigners: European Immigrant Workers and Labour Radicalism in Canada, 1896-1932*. Toronto: McClelland and Stewart, 1979.

Barons, Kirk. "Mennonites and Non-resistance: The Canadian Experience (World War I)." Research paper, Carleton University, Ottawa, 1974.

Barrett, John. *Falling In: Australia and 'Boy Conscription,' 1911-1915*. Sydney: Hale and Iremonger, 1979.

Beck, J. Murray. *Pendulum of Power: Canada's Federal Elections*. Scarborough, ON: Prentice-Hall, 1968.

Berger, Carl. *Science, God, and Nature in Victorian Canada*. Toronto: University of Toronto Press, 1983.

Berger, Thomas. *Fragile Freedoms: Human Rights and Dissent in Canada*. Toronto and Vancouver: Clark, Irwin, 1982.

Bliss, J.M. "The Methodist Church and World War I." *Canadian Historical Review* 49, 3 (September 1968): 213-33.

Botten, John. *The Captive Conscience: An Historical Perspective of the Christadelphian Stand against Military Service*. Birmingham, UK: Christadelphian Military Service Committee, 2002.

Bouvier, Patrick. *Déserters et insoumis: Les Canadiens-français et la justice militaire (1914-1918)*. Outremont, QC: Athéna Éditions, 2003.

Braithwaite, Constance. *Conscientious Objection to Various Compulsions under British Law*. York, UK: W. Sessions, 1995.

Brinton, Howard. *Friends for 300 Years: The History and Beliefs of the Society of Friends since George Fox Started the Quaker Movement*. Wallingford, PA: Pendle Hill, 1965.

Brock, Peter. "Confinement of Conscientious Objectors as Psychological Patients in World War I Germany." *Peace and Change* 23 (July 1988): 247-64.

–. *Pioneers of the Peaceable Kingdom*. Princeton: Princeton University Press, 1968.

–. *The Quaker Peace Testimony, 1660-1914*. York, UK: Sessions Book Trust, 1990.

–. *Twentieth-Century Pacifism*. New York: Van Nostrand Reinhold, 1970.

Brock, Peter, and Malcolm Saunders. "Pacifists as Conscientious Objectors in Australia." In *Challenge to Mars: Essays on Pacifism from 1918-1945*, ed. Peter Brock and Thomas Socknat, 272-91. Toronto: University of Toronto Press, 1999.

Brown, Robert Craig, ed. *Minorities, Schools and Politics*. Toronto: University of Toronto Press, 1969.

Brown, Robert Craig, and Ramsay Cook. *Canada, 1896-1921: A Nation Transformed*. Toronto: McClelland and Stewart, 1974.

Capozzola, Christopher Joseph. "Uncle Sam Wants You: Political Obligations in World War I America." PhD diss., Columbia University, 2002.

Carmichael, Don, Tom Pocklington, and Greg Pyrcz. *Democracy, Rights, and Well-Being in Canada*. Toronto: Harcourt Brace Canada, 2000.

Childress, James F. *Moral Responsibility in Conflicts: Essays on Nonviolence, War, and Conscience*. Baton Rouge: Louisiana State University Press, 1982.

Cooke, Miriam, and Angela Woollacott. *Gendering War Talk*. Princeton, NJ: Princeton University Press, 1993.

Corbett, Gail H. *Barnardo Children in Canada*. Peterborough, ON: Woodland, 1981.

Crerar, Duff. *Padres in No Man's Land: Canadian Chaplains in the Great War*. Montreal Kingston: McGill-Queen's University Press, 1995.

Doell, Leonard. *The Bergthaler Mennonite Church of Saskatchewan, 1892-1975*. Winnipeg: CMBC Publications, 1987.

Dorland, Arthur Garratt. *The Quakers in Canada: A History*. Toronto: Ryerson Press, 1968.

Driedger, Leo. *Mennonite Identity in Conflict*. Lewiston, NY: Edwin Mellen Press, 1988.

–. *Mennonites in Winnipeg*. Winnipeg: Kindred Press, 1990.

Driedger, Leo, and Donald B. Kraybill. *Mennonite Peacemaking: From Quietism to Activism*. Scottdale, PA: Herald Press, 1994.

Duffy, John. *Fights of Our Lives: Elections, Leadership, and the Making of Canada*. Toronto: Harper Collins, 2002.

Durnbaugh, Donald F. "The Brethren and Non-resistance." In *The Pacifist Impulse in Historical Perspective*, ed. Harvey L. Dyck, 125-44. Toronto: University of Toronto Press, 1996.

Dyck, John M. *Faith under Test: Alternative Service during World War II in the US and Canada*. Ste. Anne, MB: Gospel, 1997.

Early, Frances. *A World without War: How US Feminists and Pacifists Resisted World War I*. Syracuse, NY: Syracuse University Press, 1997.

Ens, Adolph. *Subjects or Citizens? The Mennonite Experience in Canada, 1870-1925*. Ottawa: University of Ottawa Press, 1994.

Epp, Frank H. *Mennonite Exodus: The Rescue and Resettlement of the Russian Mennonites since the Communist Revolution*. Altona, MB: D.W. Friesen and Sons, 1962.

–. *Mennonites in Canada, 1786-1920: The History of a Separate People*. Toronto: Macmillan, 1974.

Evans, E.R. *"Ye Are Strangers and Sojourners with Me": A Study of the Christadelphian Teaching Concerning a Christian's Relationship to the State*. Hamilton, ON: privately published, 1990.

Fell, Brian John. "A Question of Conscience: British and Canadian Socialist Quakers and Their Parliamentary Allies in the First World War." Master's thesis, University of Manitoba, 1972.

Filteau, Gerard. *Le Québec, le Canada et la guerre, 1914-1918*. Montreal: Éditions de l'Aurore, 1977.

Finn, James, ed., *A Conflict of Loyalties: The Case for Selective Conscientious Objection*. New York: Pegasus, 1969.

Finney, Torin R.T. *Unsung Hero of the Great War: The Life and Witness of Ben Salmon*. Mahwah, NJ: Paulist Press, 1989.

Flynn, George Q. *Conscription and Democracy: The Draft in France, Great Britain, and the United States*. Westport, CT: Greenwood Press, 2002.

Francis, E.K. *In Search of Utopia*. Altona, MB: D.W. Friesen and Sons, 1955.

Fraser, Brian John. *The Social Uplifters: Presbyterian Progressives and the Social Gospel in Canada, 1875-1915*. Waterloo: Wilfrid Laurier University Press, 1988.

Fusé, Toyomasa. "Religion, War and the Institutional Dilemma: A Sociological Interpretation." *Journal of Peace Research* 5, 2 (1968): 196-210.

Gingerich, Orland. *The Amish of Canada*. Waterloo, ON: Conrad Press, 1972.

Gorham, Deborah. "Vera Brittain, Flora Macdonald Denison and the Great War: The Failure of Non-violence." In *Women and Peace: Theoretical, Historical, and Practical Perspectives,* ed. Ruth Roach Pierson, 137-48. London: Croom Helm, 1987.

Graham, John W. *Conscription and Conscience: A History, 1916-1919.* 1922; Reprint; New York: Garland Publishing, 1971.

Granatstein, J.L., and J.M. Hitsman. *Broken Promises: A History of Conscription in Canada.* Toronto: Copp, Clark, Pitman, 1985.

Gravel, Jean-Yves. *Le Québec et la guerre, 1914-1918.* Montreal: Éditions du Boréal Exprès, 1974.

Guenter, Jacob. *Men of Steele.* Saskatoon: privately published, 1981.

Guion, Davis Roger. "Conscientious Cooperators: The Seventh-Day Adventists and Military Service, 1860-1945." PhD diss., George Washington University, 1970.

Hall, Donald E. *Muscular Christianity: Embodying the Victorian Age.* Cambridge: Cambridge University Press, 1994.

Harkness, Ross. *J.E. Atkinson of the Star.* Toronto: University of Toronto Press, 1963.

Hart, John Edward. "William Irvine and Radical Politics in Canada." PhD diss., University of Guelph, 1972.

Hartzler, J.S. *Mennonites in the World War, or, Nonresistance under Test.* Scottdale, PA: Mennonite Publishing House, 1922.

Heisey, M.J. *Peace and Persistence: Tracing the Brethren in Christ Peace Witness through Three Generations.* Kent, OH: Kent State University Press, 2003.

Hershberger, Guy. *The Mennonite Church in the Second World War.* Scottdale, PA: Mennonite Publishing House, 1951.

Higonnet, Margaret, Jane Jenson, Sonya Michel, and Margaret Collins Weitz, eds. *Behind the Lines: Gender and the Two World Wars.* New Haven: Yale University Press, 1987.

Hillerbrand, Hans. "The Anabaptist View of the State." *Mennonite Quarterly Review* 32 (April 1958): 83-110.

Homan, Gerlof D. *American Mennonites and the Great War, 1914-1918.* Waterloo, ON: Herald Press, 1994.

Hopkins, J. Castell. *The Province of Ontario and the War.* Toronto: Warwick Bros. and Rutter, 1919.

Horst, Samuel. *Mennonites in the Confederacy: A Study in Civil War Pacifism.* Scottdale, PA: Herald Press, 1967.

Hostetler, John A., and Gertrude Enders Huntington. *The Hutterites in North America.* New York: Holt, Rinehart and Winston, 1967.

Howard, Michael Eliot. *War and the Liberal Conscience.* New York: Rutgers University Press, 1978.

Huxman, Susan Schultz. "Mennonite Rhetoric in World War One: Lobbying the Government for Freedom of Conscience." *Mennonite Quarterly Review* 67 (July 1993): 283-303.

Hyatt, A.M.J. "Sir Arthur Currie and Conscription: A Soldier's View." *Canadian Historical Review* 13 (September 1969): 285-96.

Iacobelli, Teresa. "Arbitrary Justice? A Comparative Analysis of Death Sentences Passed and Death Sentences Commuted during the First World War." Master's thesis, Wilfrid Laurier University, 2003.

Ignatieff, Michael. *The Rights Revolution.* Toronto: Anansi, 2000.

Janzen, William. *Limits on Liberty: The Experience of Mennonite, Hutterite, and Doukhobor Communities in Canada.* Toronto: University of Toronto Press, 1990.

Janzen, William, and Frances Greaser. *Sam Martin Went to Prison: The Story of Conscientious Objection and Canadian Military Service.* Winnipeg: Kindred Press, 1990.

Jolliffe, Kyle. *Seeking the Blessed Community: A History of Canadian Young Friends, 1875-1996.* Guelph, ON: Ampersand Printing, 1997.

Jordan, Mary Veronica. *Survival: Labour's Trials and Tribulations in Canada.* Toronto: McDonald House, 1975.

Juhnke, James C. *Vision, Doctrine, War: Mennonite Identity and Organization in America, 1890-1930.* Scottdale, PA: Herald Press, 1989.

Kaplan, William. *State and Salvation: The Jehovah's Witnesses and Their Fight for Civil Rights.* Toronto: University of Toronto Press, 1989.

Kennedy, Thomas C. *British Quakerism, 1860-1920: The Transformation of a Religious Community.* New York: Oxford University Press, 2001.

–. *The Hound of Conscience: A History of the No-Conscription Fellowship, 1914-1919.* Fayetteville: University of Arkansas Press, 1981.

–. "Public Opinion and the Conscientious Objector, 1915-1919." *Journal of British Studies* 12, 2 (May 1973): 105-19.

Keshen, Jeffrey. *Propaganda and Censorship during Canada's Great War.* Edmonton: University of Alberta Press, 1996.

Klipperstein, Lawrence, ed. *That There Be Peace: Mennonites in Canada and World War II.* Winnipeg: Manitoba CO Reunion Committee, 1979.

Kreider, Robert. "Environmental Influences Affecting the Decisions of Mennonite Boys of Draft Age." *Mennonite Quarterly Review* 16 (October 1942): 247-59, 275.

LaPierre, Laurier L. *Wilfrid Laurier and the Romance of Canada.* Toronto: Stoddart, 1996.

Legault, Roch, and Jean Lamarre, eds. *La Première Guerre Mondiale et le Canada: Contributions sociomilitaires Québécoises.* Montreal: Meridien, 1999.

Leier, Mark. "Plots, Shots, and Liberal Thoughts: Conspiracy Theory and the Death of Ginger Goodwin." *Labour/Le Travail* 39 (Spring 1997): 215-24.

Levi, Margaret. *Consent, Dissent, and Patriotism.* Cambridge: Cambridge University Press, 1997.

Lichti, Fred. *A History of the East Zorra (Amish) Mennonite Church, 1837-1977.* Tavistock, ON: East Zorra Mennonite Church, 1977.

Madison, Gary Brent. *Is There a Canadian Philosophy? Reflections on the Canadian Identity.* Ottawa: University of Ottawa Press, 2000.

Magney, William. "The Methodist Church and the Conscription Crisis of 1917." Paper for Dr. D.G. Creighton, University of Toronto, 1968.

Mangan, J.A., and James Walvin, eds. *Manliness and Morality: Middle-Class Masculinity in Britain and America, 1800-1940.* Manchester: Manchester University Press, 1987.

Martin, David A. *Pacifism: An Historical and Sociological Study.* New York: Schocken Books, 1966.

Martin, Donald. *Old Order Mennonites of Ontario: Gelassenheit, Discipleship, Brotherhood.* Kitchener, ON: Pandora Press, 2003.

Marwick, Arthur. *Clifford Allen: The Open Conspirator.* London: Oliver and Boyd, 1964.

Mayse, Susan. *Ginger: The Life of Albert Goodwin.* Madeira Park, BC: Harbour, 1990.

McCormack, A. Ross. *Reformers, Rebels, and Revolutionaries: The Western Canadian Radical Movement, 1899-1919.* Toronto: University of Toronto Press, 1977.

McGowan, Mark G. *The Waning of the Green: Catholics, the Irish, and Identity in Toronto, 1887-1922.* Montreal and Kingston: McGill-Queen's University Press, 1999.

McLaren, John. "The Doukhobor Belief in Individual Faith and Conscience and the Demands of the Secular State." In *Religious Conscience, the State and the Law*, ed. John McLaren and Harold Coward, 117-35. Albany: State University of New York Press, 1999.

McNaught, Kenneth. *A Prophet in Politics: A Biography of J.S. Woodsworth.* Toronto: University of Toronto Press, 1959.

Mihevc, Joe. "The Politicization of the Mennonite Peace Witness in the Twentieth Century." PhD diss., St. Michael's College, Toronto School of Theology, 1989.

Miller, Carman. *Canada's Little War.* Toronto: Lorimer, 2003.

–. *Painting the Map Red: Canada and the South African War, 1899-1902.* Ottawa: Canadian War Museum, 1998.

Miller, Thomas. *Canadian Pentecostals: A History of the Pentecostal Assemblies of Canada.* Mississauga, ON: Full Gospel Publishing House, 1994.

Millman, Brock. *Managing Domestic Dissent in First World War Britain.* London: Frank Cass, 2000.

Mills, Allen George. *Fool for Christ: The Political Thought of J.S. Woodsworth.* Toronto: University of Toronto Press, 1991.

Monteith, J. Ernest. *The Lord Is My Shepherd: A History of the Seventh-day Adventist Church in Canada.* Oshawa, ON: Canadian Union Conference of the Seventh-Day Adventist Church, 1983.

Morton, Desmond. *Fight or Pay: Soldier's Families in the Great War.* Vancouver: UBC Press, 2004.

–. *Marching to Armageddon: Canadians and the Great War, 1914-1919.* Toronto: Lester and Orpen Dennys, 1989.

–. "Polling the Soldier Vote: The Overseas Campaign in the Canadian General Election of 1917." *Journal of Canadian Studies* 31 (1975): 39-58.

–. "The Supreme Penalty: Canadian Deaths by Firing Squad in the First World War." *Queen's Quarterly* 79, 3 (Winter 1972): 345-52.

–. *When Your Number's Up: The Canadian Soldier in the First World War.* Toronto: Random House, 1993.

Moskos, Charles C., and John Whiteclay Chambers III, eds. *The New Conscientious Objection: From Sacred to Secular Resistance.* New York: Oxford University Press, 1993.

Moss, Mark. *Manliness and Militarism: Educating Young Boys in Ontario for War.* Don Mills, ON: Oxford University Press, 2001.

Neufeld, Peter Lorenz. *Mennonites at War, a Double-Edged Sword: Canadian Mennonites in World War Two.* Deloraine, MB: DTS, 1997.

Neufield, William. *From Faith to Faith: The History of the Manitoba Mennonite Brethren Church.* Winnipeg: Kindred Press, 1989.

Nevitte, Neil, and Allan Kornberg, eds. *Minorities and the Canadian State.* Oakville, ON: Mosaic Press, 1985.

Nicholson, G.W.L. *Canadian Expeditionary Force, 1914-1919.* Ottawa: Queen's Printer, 1964.

Noone, Michael F., Jr., ed. *Selective Conscientious Objection: Accommodating Conscience and Security.* Boulder: Westview Press, 1989.

O'Donovan, Oliver. *The Just War Revisited.* Cambridge: Cambridge University Press, 2003.

Oliver, Bobbie. *Peacemongers: Conscientious Objection to Military Service in Australia, 1911-1945.* Perth: Freemantle Arts Centre Press, 1997.

Penton, M. James. *Jehovah's Witnesses in Canada: Champions of Freedom of Speech and Worship.* Toronto: Macmillan of Canada, 1976.

Peterson, H.C., and Gilbert Fite. *Opponents of War, 1917-1918.* Seattle: University of Washington Press, 1971.

Phillips, Paul Arthur. *No Power Greater: A Century of Labour in British Columbia.* Vancouver: Federation of Labour and Boag Foundation, 1977.

Prasad, Devi, and Tony Smythe, eds. *Conscription, a World Survey: Compulsory Military Service and Resistance to It.* London: War Resisters International, 1968.

Provencher, Jean. *Québec sous la Loi des Mesures de Guerre, 1918.* Trois Rivières: Éditions du Boréal Exprès, 1971.

Rae, John. *Conscience and Politics: The British Government and the Conscientious Objector to Military Service, 1916-1919.* London: Oxford University Press, 1970.

Regehr, T.D. *Mennonites in Canada, 1939-1970: A People Transformed.* Toronto: University of Toronto Press, 1996.

Reid, Brian A. *Our Little Army in the Field: The Canadians in South Africa, 1899-1902.* St. Catharines, ON: Vanwell, 1996.

Reimer, David P. *Experience of Mennonites in Canada during World War II.* Altona, MB: D.A. Friesen, [1946?].

Rempel, David. *A Mennonite Family in Tsarist Russia and the Soviet Union: 1789-1923.* Toronto: University of Toronto Press, 2003.

Roberts, Barbara. *"Why Do Women Do Nothing to End the War?" Canadian Feminist-Pacifists and the Great War.* Ottawa: Canadian Research Institute for the Advancement of Women, 1985.

–. "Women against War, 1914-1918: Francis Beynon and Laura Hughes." In *Up and Doing: Canadian Women and Peace,* ed. Janice Williamson and Deborah Gorham, 48-65. Toronto: Women's Press, 1989.

Robertson, Barbara. *Wilfrid Laurier, the Great Conciliator.* Toronto: Oxford University Press, 1971.

Robertson, John S. *In His Name: A History of Assemblies of Christians Who Have Gathered in the Name of the Lord Jesus Christ for the Past Hundred Years in the City of Toronto, Ontario.* Toronto: Committee of "Food for the Flock," 1960.

Robinson, Paul F. *The Just War in Comparative Perspective.* Aldershot, UK: Ashgate, 2003.

Roper, Michael, and John Tosh, eds. *Manful Assertions: Masculinities in Britain since 1800.* London: Routledge, 1991.

Ruebsaat, Gisela. *The First Freedom: Freedom of Conscience and Religion in Canada.* Victoria, BC: Conscience Canada, 1991.

Rutherford, Jonathan. *Forever England: Reflections on Race, Masculinity and Empire.* London: Lawrence and Wishart, 1997.

Sanger, S.F., and D. Hays. *The Olive Branch of Peace and Good Will to Men: Anti-war History of the Brethren and Mennonites, the Peace People of the South, during the Civil War, 1861-1875.* Elgin, IL: Brethren, 1907.

Schlabach, Theron, ed. "An Account, by Jakob Waldner: Diary of a Conscientious Objector in World War I." Trans. Ilse Reist and Elizabeth Bender. *Mennonite Quarterly Review* 48 (January 1974): 73-111.

Schmeiser, D.A. *Civil Liberties in Canada.* New York: Oxford University Press, 1964.

Seymour, Miranda. *Ottoline Morrell: Life on the Grand Scale.* London: Hodder and Stoughton, 1992.

Sharpe, Chris. "Enlistment in the Canadian Expeditionary Force, 1914-1918: A Regional Analysis." *Journal of Canadian Studies* 18, 4 (Winter 1983-84): 15-29.

Shenk, Gerald. "Work or Fight: Selective Service and Manhood in the Progressive Era." PhD diss., University of California at San Diego, 1992.

Sibley, Mulford Q., and Philip E. Jacob. *Conscription of Conscience: The American State and the Conscientious Objector, 1940-1947.* Ithaca, NY: Cornell University Press, 1952.

Sider, E. Morris. *The Brethren in Christ in Canada: Two Hundred Years of Tradition and Change.* Nappanee, IN: Evangel Press, 1988.

–. "History of the Brethren in Christ Church in Canada." Master's thesis, University of Western Ontario, 1955.

Smith, C. Henry. *The Story of the Mennonites.* Newton, KS: Mennonite Publication Office, 1964.

Smith, Hugh. "Conscience, Law and the State: Australia's Approach to Conscientious Objection since 1901," *Australian Journal of Politics and History* 35, 1 (April 1989): 13-28.

–. *Conscientious Objection to Particular Wars: The Australian Approach.* Canberra: Strategic and Defence Studies Centre, Australian National University, 1986.

Socknat, Thomas. "Canada's Liberal Pacifists and the Great War." *Journal of Canadian Studies* 18, 4 (1983-84): 30-44.

–. *Witness against War: Pacifism in Canada, 1900-1945.* Toronto: University of Toronto Press, 1987.

Southgate, Jane. "An Examination of the Position of the Mennonites in Ontario under the Jurisdiction of the Military Service Act, 1917." Master's cognate paper, Wilfrid Laurier University, 1976.

Stewart, Roderick. *Wilfrid Laurier: A Pledge for Canada.* Montreal: XYZ Publishing, 2002.

Stonebanks, Roger. *Fighting for Dignity: The Ginger Goodwin Story.* St. John's: Canadian Committee on Labour History, 2004.

Taylor, A.J.P. *The Trouble Makers: Dissent over Foreign Policy, 1792-1939.* London: Panther Books, 1969.

Teichroew, Allan. "World War One and Mennonite Migrations to Canada to Avoid the Draft." *Mennonite Quarterly Review* 45 (July 1971): 219-49.

Temes, Peter S. *The Just War: An American Reflection on the Morality of War in Our Time.* Chicago: Ivan R. Dee, 2003.

Thomas, Norman. *The Conscientious Objector in America.* New York: Huebsch, 1923.

Thompson, John Herd. *The Harvests of War: The Prairie West, 1914-1928.* Toronto: McClelland and Stewart, 1978.

Toews, John Aron, ed. *Alternative Service in Canada during World War II.* Winnipeg: Publication Committee, Canadian Conference of the MBC, 1959.

Toews, John B. *Czars, Soviets and Mennonites.* Newton, KS: Faith and Life Press, 1982.

–. *With Courage to Spare: The Life of B.B. Janz (1877-1964).* Fresno, CA: Board of Christian Literature of the General Conference of the Mennonite Brethren Churches of North America, 1978.

Tran, Luan-Vu N. *Human Rights and Federalism: A Comparative Study on Freedom, Democracy, and Cultural Diversity.* Boston: Kluwer Law International, 2000.

Wade, Mason. *The French Canadians, 1760-1967.* 2 vols. Toronto: Macmillan, 1968.

Wagner, Gillian. *Barnardo.* London: Weidenfeld and Nicholson, 1979.

Walden, Keith. "Blue Pete and Canadian Nationalism: Vision and Experience in the Western Novels of William Lacey Amy." *Journal of Canadian Studies* 24, 2 (Summer 1989): 39-51.

Weber, John S. "History of S.F. Coffman, 1872-1954." PhD diss., University of Waterloo, 1975.

Westfall, William. *Two Worlds: The Protestant Culture of Nineteenth-Century Ontario.* Montreal and Kingston: McGill-Queen's University Press, 1989.

Wilkinson, Alan. *The Church of England and the First World War.* London: Camelot Press, 1978.

Wilms, A.M. "Conscription 1917: A Brief for the Defence." *Canadian Historical Review* 37 (December 1956): 338-51.

Wittlinger, Carlton O. *Quest for Piety and Obedience: The Story of the Brethren in Christ.* Nappanee, IN: Evangel Press, 1978.

Vance, Jonathan. *Death So Noble: Memory, Meaning and the First World War.* Vancouver: UBC Press, 1997.

Vellacott, Jo. *Bertrand Russell and the Pacifists in the First World War.* London: St. Martin's Press, 1981.

Yinger, J. Milton. *The Scientific Study of Religion.* New York: Macmillan, 1970.

Yoder, John Howard. *When War Is Unjust: Being Honest in Just-War Thinking.* Minneapolis: Augsburg, 1984.

Young, Nigel James. "The Nation State and War Resistance." PhD diss., University of California Berkeley, 1976.

Zahn, Gordon C. *War, Conscience and Dissent.* New York: Hawthorne Books, 1967.

Zeiger, Susan. "She Didn't Raise Her Boy to Be a Slacker: Motherhood, Conscription, and the Culture of the First World War." *Feminist Studies* 22, 1 (Spring 1996): 7-39.

Index

Church of Christ, 78-79
citizenship: change in relationship to
  state in WWI, 7; conscientious objection as exercise in liberal individuality,
  6, 142, 163-64. *See also* voting rights
"citizen-soldiers," 21, 25
Clark, J. Murray, 22
Clark, V.A., 145-46
class: Britain, effect on CO treatment,
  8, 158-59; Canada, most CO's from
  working class, 158
Clegg, Robert Litler, 89-90, 94, 96, 157
Coatsworth, Judge, 36
Cody, Henry (Rev.), 105
Cody, Joseph Cameron, 50
Coffman, S.F., 54, 56, 58, 59-60, 61, 62, 63,
  65
Commonwealth Defence Act, 30
Connor, Ralph, 138
conscientious objection: definition, 3, 5,
  16-17; exemption based on membership in specific church, not personal
  beliefs, 4, 28, 78, 86, 97; exemptions, as
  difficult to obtain, 42, 63; as exercise
  in liberal individuality, 6, 142, 163-64;
  lack of organized movement, 155, 157;
  more common in sects, than churches,
  102; multiple grounds for exemption,
  17; recognition in other countries, 3-4;
  recognized in Military Service Act
  (1917), 3, 21, 28; religious reasons for, 4;
  seen as lesser sacrifice by churches than
  enlistment, 104; as threat to authority
  of state, 142. *See also* conscientious objectors (COs), Britain; conscientious
  objectors (COs), Canada; conscription;
  exemption tribunals; Military Service
  Act (MSA)(Canada, 1917); non-
  combatant service; pacifism
conscientious objectors (COs), Britain:
  alternative service as option, 99; and
  class system, 8; critiqued as pretentious
  intellectuals, 8-9, 11, 134; critiqued as
  unmasculine, 8-9; publicity regarding,
  9, 10, 12; treatment of, 9, 158-59. *See also*
  No-Conscription Fellowship (NCF)
conscientious objectors (COs), Canada:
  absence of desire for martyrdom, 156;
  absolutists, 4, 50, 91, 116-17, 128, 135, 155;

alternative service option in WWII, 153-
  54; compared with deserters, 146-47;
  court-martial statements of defence,
  116, 117; critiqued as anti-democratic,
  121, 133; critiqued as anti-social, 131-32;
  critiqued as boorish, 134-35, 148; critiqued as cowardly, 8, 23, 34, 115, 121,
  124, 127, 134, 148; critiqued as degenerate
  physical type, 123-24, 125; critiqued as
  egotistical, 131, 132-33; critiqued as
  hypocritical, 127-28; critiqued as illogical, 132, 133, 134, 142; critiqued as
  immature, 126, 127; critiqued as neurotic, 122-23; critiqued as physically degenerate, 123; critiqued as pretentious
  intellectuals, 122, 123, 124, 133; critiqued
  as selfish, 8, 23, 34, 115, 121, 127, 133, 143-
  44, 158; critiqued as slackers, 11, 122; critiqued as stubborn, 8-9, 132, 133, 134,
  139, 148, 158; critiqued as stupid, 8-9,
  130, 134-35; critiqued as unmasculine,
  8-9, 124, 125, 127, 134, 148; critiqued as
  unpatriotic, 126, 128-29, 148; critiqued
  for lack of religious virtue, 126-27; dif-
  ferentiation among, in public mind,
  135-37; disenfranchised by Wartime
  Elections Act (1917), 8, 32, 33, 112; diversity, as factor in lack of organized
  movement, 155; ethnicity, 7-8, 136;
  farmers, disproportionate numbers of,
  158; importance of church support to,
  14; isolation of, 33, 92-93, 106; loss of
  income during imprisonment, 118;
  military records, lack of, 14-15, 16, 115;
  names of, 157-58, 166-90; as non-
  conforming to group loyalty, 126, 131-32,
  133; not seen as significant threat, 120-21;
  peace church members, majority from
  Ontario, 158, 159, 160; profile, compared
  with British COs, 148, 158; public antipathy towards, 99, 120-44, 160; publicity
  regarding, 15-17, 134; release from prison,
  147-48, 150, 157; religious, considered
  differently than secular objectors, 12,
  120; religious, unaffiliated, 117-18; religious differences, and lack of acceptance
  among, 156; religious fundamentalism
  as common factor, 159; religious sects
  unrecognized by government for

recognition issues under Military Service Act, 65-66; delegation to Ottawa offering alternative service, 152-53; disenfranchised by Wartime Elections Act (1917), 32, 33; emigration of some groups after WWI, due to CO experience, 43, 131, 160; enlistment in military service, at cost of church membership, 47; evolution of cooperation with other peace churches, 58-59; exemption from military service by order-in-council, 10, 21, 31, 43, 45, 46, 66-67; history of non-resistance and nonconformity, 44; immigration from Russia, after abolition of exemption from military service, 44-45; immigration from US, as reaction against conscription, 44, 69-70; immigration from USSR, on specific conditions, 152; immigration to Canada, due to tolerance of religious pacifism, 164; immigration to Canada under promise of military exemption, 18, 66; lack of publicity regarding conscientious objection, 13; leadership as unassuming, lacking spokespersons, 12, 57; low enlistment of members for military service, 47; in Maritime provinces, 159-60; membership statistics (1911), 48; non-resistance teachings of, 47, 54-57; obedience to authority of state as religious tenet, 43, 78; as pacifist sect, 102; public acceptance of, 137; public hostility against, 68, 69-70; refusal to participate in national registration, 27; shift from *non-resistance* to *peace* after WWI, 151; support for British during American Revolution, 44; as suspected pro-German sympathizers, 130, 136, 148, 160; viewed as requiring education in citizenship, 130-31; wartime contributions, 60-61, 71. *See also* Amish

Mennonites in Canada, 1976-1920: The History of a Separate People (Epp), 5

Methodist Church: COs, members of, 113-14; Free Methodist Branch, support for pacifism, 113, 114; on "Mennonite menace," 62; ministers as recruiting officers, 111-12; objection to CO stance,

104-5, 110-14; shift away from pacifism, 104, 112, 160; support for conscription, 25, 111, 115, 160

Mewburn, S.C., 90, 91

Mihevc, Joe, 151

Military Service Act (MSA) (Canada, 1917): amendments for exemption of additional churches, 12; conscientious objection exemption, as narrowly defined, 29; conscription, introduction of, 3, 27; CO status, approval for organized pacifist religious denominations, 12-13, 28, 31, 35, 40, 43, 135-36, 159, 162, 164; CO status granted to specific groups, not individuals, 11-12, 13-14; enforced by Department of Justice, Military Service Branch, 15, 35; evolution of definition of exempted groups, 31; exemptions categories, 20-21, 29, 63; farmers, exemption on basis of occupation, 28, 63-64, 118, 156; option of non-combatant service, 66; terms, as isolating COs of various religious and political beliefs, 77; viewed as democratic measure, 23

Military Service Board (New Zealand), 30

Military Service Branch, Dept. of Justice (Canada), 15, 35

Military Service Council (Canada): arguments for conscription, 22, 23; on decision to restrict exemption to religious organizations, 29; enforcement of Military Service Act, 15, 35; and selection of judges for exemption tribunals, 36

Military Voters Act (Canada, 1917), 32

Militia Act (Canada, 1793), 45, 63, 74

Militia Act (Canada, 1868), 20, 21, 27

Millennial Dawnites. *See* International Bible Students Association (Jehovah's Witnesses)

Millman, Brock, 51, 99, 102-3

Mitchell, Sydney, 80

Montgomery, Lucy Maud, 138

Moore, S.J., 34

Moral Responsibility in Conflicts: Essays on Nonviolence, War, and Conscience (Childress), 6

Morton, Desmond, 32, 35

Moskos, Charles, 6

Quakers (Society of Friends): avoided association with COs of questionable motives, 155-56; Britain, as leaders of pacifist movement, 12, 49-50, 51, 52; Canada, lack of anti-conscription leadership, 52-54; Canada, small membership in WWI, 13; COs, imprisonment of, 50-51; as different from historic peace churches, 44; exemption from military service, 10, 18, 21, 31, 43, 45, 78; farmers, exemption from military service, 64; as "integrational pacifists," 48; low rate of members enlisting for military service, 47-48; membership statistics (1911), 48; non-combatant work, 48, 104, 150, 152-53; non-resistance as central religious tenet, 48; public approval of, 135, 136, 137, 148; small number in Maritime provinces, 159; suspension of member enrolment during WWI in Canada and US, 52; volunteers for Friends Ambulance Unit (FAU), 48
Quakers in Canada: A History (Dorland), 5
Quebec: anti-conscription movement, 62-63, 119, 159; significant numbers of Catholic COs, 109. *See also* French Canadians
Le Québec et la guerre, 1914-1918 (Gravel), 5

Rae, John, 8, 9, 29-30
Ramseden, Horace G., 36
Reformers, Rebels, and Revolutionaries (McCormack), 5
"Religion, War and the Institutional Dilemma" (Fusé), 101
religious organizations. *See* Brethren in Christ (Tunkers); Christadelphians; Doukhobors; historic peace churches; Hutterites; International Bible Students Association (Jehovah's Witnesses), Plymouth Brethren; Mennonites; Methodist Church; Presbyterian Church; Quakers (Society of Friends); Roman Catholic Church
Rempel, Abraham, 47
Richards, H.M.J., 82

Rilla of Ingleside (Montgomery), 138-39
Rivers, J.S., 129
Roberts, Barbara, 6
Roberts, Hugh, 38, 40
Rogers, Albert S., 51-52
Rogers, David Pearson, 48
Rogers, J. Ellsworth, 48
Roman Catholic Church: Canada, military service recruitment numbers, 111; COs, lack of support for, 109, 110; Quebec, significant numbers of COs, 109; support for war, 109
Roosevelt, Theodore, 143
Ross, H.J., 75
Rowntree, Arnold, 52
Rudd, Douglas, 154
Running, Vernal, 94, 117-18, 156-57
Russell, Bertrand, 12
Russell, Charles Taze, 72, 136
Russellites. *See* International Bible Students Association (Jehovah's Witnesses)
"Russlanders," 152
Rutherford, Joseph Franklin, 74, 136
Rutherford, S.J., 146
Ruttan, Brig.-Gen., 91

Salmon, Ben, 109-10
Saunders, Malcolm, 13
Schleitheim Confession (1527), 54-55
Scott, F.S., 70
Second World War. *See* World War II
Selective Service Act (US, 1917), 30, 126
Seventh-day Adventists: acceptance of non-combatant service, 81, 161; beliefs, 81; as "conscientious cooperators," 82, 155; exemption from military service, 10, 18, 31
Shenk, Gerald, 126
Shields, Thomas T., 32
Shuttleworth, Nicholas S., 94, 115
Sider, E. Morris, 5
Simpson, G.J. (Sgt.), 91
"The Slacker" (*Maclean's*), 137
Smith, Allen F., 85
Smith, C.H., 151
Smith, Hugh, 30-31
Smythe, Tony, 152